Comedy

A CRITICAL INTRODUCTION

To Atara,
with immense love
and profound admiration
for her keen intellect and humane wisdom.

Comedy

A CRITICAL INTRODUCTION

Eli Rozik

sussex
ACADEMIC
PRESS
Brighton • Portland • Toronto

2 4 6 8 10 9 7 5 3 1

First published 2011 in Great Britain by
SUSSEX ACADEMIC PRESS
PO Box 139
Eastbourne BN23 9BP

and in the United States of America by
SUSSEX ACADEMIC PRESS
920 NE 58th Ave Suite 300
Portland, Oregon 97213–3786

and in Canada by
SUSSEX ACADEMIC PRESS (CANADA)
90 Arnold Avenue, Thornhill, Ontario L4J 1B5

British Library Cataloguing in Publication Data
A CIP catalogue record for this book is available from the British Library.

Library of Congress Cataloging-in-Publication Data
Rozik, Eli.
Comedy : a critical introduction / Eli Rozik.
p. cm.
Includes bibliographical references and index.
ISBN 978-1-84519-477-2 (h/b : alk. paper) —
ISBN 978-1-84519-478-9 (p/b : alk. paper)
1. Comedy—History and criticism—Theory, etc. I. Title.
PN1922.R69 2011
808.2'523—dc23

2011019190

Typeset and designed by Sussex Academic Press, Brighton & Eastbourne.
Printed by TJ International, Padstow, Cornwall.
This book is printed on acid-free paper.

Contents

Contents

Contents

Preface and
Acknowledgments

This book offers an introduction to a theory of 'comedy' in any language or medium. While focusing on the analysis of this genre in theatre, which is my own main field of research, it considers its conclusions to be valid for all the media capable of describing comic fictional worlds, including, for example, opera, painting/drawing, animation, puppet theatre and cinema.

A critique of all theories of comedy is presented from Aristotle to the present day. 'Critique' is understood here as either rejecting or accepting theses on the grounds of evidence. Indeed, in contrast to most theories of comedy, which are deductive in nature, this study adopts an inductive approach, whose generalizations are supported by a broad-based reading and analysis of extant play-scripts and by experience and analysis of performance-texts. Furthermore, it applies findings regarding both the nature of the theatre medium and the nature of fictional thinking and creativity, for which I refer the readers to my previous books *Generating Theatre Meaning — A Theory and Methodology of Performance Analysis* (2008), and *Fictional Thinking — A Poetics and Rhetoric of Fictional Creativity in Theatre* (2009), both published by Sussex Academic Press.

I have taken into consideration major contributions to a general theory of comedy and to a sound methodology for the analysis of comedies, which are presented as faithfully as possible, even if criticized. Ample quotation is provided to enable readers to grasp ideas in their original terminology and own logic — thus allowing an independent opinion. Each presentation is accompanied by critical comments, which attempt both to introduce the problems involved and suggest possible solutions.

The text reflects the format of a university course, and has been purposefully designed not only to address undergraduate and postgraduate students, university teachers, scholars of theatre studies, and theatre practitioners, but also all those with a deep interest in fictional creativity and theatre art.

The theoretical chapters are amply illustrated by references to comedies and/or pertinent analyses of such comedies, written over the course of 2,500 years of theatre recorded history, and which should be seen as a minimal reading list for the keen student of theatre.

I am profoundly grateful to my wife Atara for her fervent and loving support and to Naomi Paz for her careful and enlightening English editing of this book.

Introduction

In the last hundred years the notion of 'comedy' has attracted substantial theoretical attention, probably due to the increased popularity of satiric drama in democratic regimes and the creation of grotesque drama, with their broad use of laughter-eliciting devices for addressing deadly serious matters. It is sensible to assume, therefore, that for the same reasons comedy has climbed to the top of the hierarchy of genres, together with tragedy, and that, therefore, the determination of its nature has became extremely problematic. Indeed, the current application of 'comedy' ranges from the unbridled nature of farce to the romantic atmosphere of Shakespearean comedy; from humorous narratives to satiric and even grotesque ones; and from literary fiction to cinema; not to mention obvious misapplications of this generic term. Currently, the problem lies in that, when reading theoretical works on comedy, it is not always clear as to which kind of comedy they relate and take as their paradigmatic model. The only sensible conclusion is, therefore, that what is usually termed 'comedy' applies to a heterogeneous set of loosely-related works whose only common denominator is their use of laughter-eliciting devices, albeit reflecting different moods and aiming at different effects. This fundamental heterogeneity indicates the need for subtler generic distinctions and a richer terminology.

Basic observations

Let us begin with several fundamental observations: First, according to Northrop Frye's distinction, comedy belongs in the class of works of art by means of which authors express themselves not through a 'thematic mode' or, rather, a discursive verbal description (pp. 52–67 & 367), e.g., poetry; but through a 'fictional mode', i.e., through the mediation of a world of characters and their actions (pp. 33–52 & 365), e.g., theatre, comics and cinematic comedy. In other words, the fictional mode is the expression of a single psyche through a multiple world of characters and their actions. Under the assumption that a fictional world, like a poem, is a self-referential description of the author's psychical state of affairs, it follows that such a world reflects the multi-personification of a single psyche, which is spontaneously partitioned and represented by different characters. These principles also apply to the spectators who adopt a description of a fictional world as an expression of themselves. I believe that Frye's distinction reflects a valuable insight, despite 'thematic' being employed in such an unusual and unjustified sense: fictional worlds too are thematic in nature. I would prefer: 'fictional' vs. 'non-fictional'.

In contrast to Frye, who defines 'fictional' as a basic mode of representation and expression of the psyche, Bruce Wilshire defines it 'in a generic sense to refer to all works of fine art in respect to their being embodied by beings which have a reality distinct from whatever actual things *or* inactual things are depicted by them' (p. 28). Similarly, Patrice Pavis defines 'fiction' as a '[t]ype of discourse that refers to people and things that exist only in the imagination of their author, then in that of the reader/spectator' (p. 149). Both Wilshire and Pavis stress the imaginative nature of fictional worlds, which, assumedly, reveal a mode of existence ontologically different from that attributed to the real world. In principle, these definitions complement that of Frye, while focusing on one of its implied aspects.

However, although basically true, Wilshire's and Pavis' definitions are deficient in a crucial respect. They imply that narratives such as those of Isaac (Old Testament), Jesus (New Testament), and Macbeth (Holinshed), who are perceived as historical personae in the Bible and Holinshed, have nothing to do with fictionality. Nonetheless, these narratives should be included on the grounds of 'fictionalization', meaning that these worlds reflect their being processed through the principles that characterize the fictional mode of thinking (Rozik, 2009). It is this processing that transmutes the narrations of historical events and people, at least partially, into fictional ones. Similar considerations apply to mythical characters such as Oedipus, Clytemnestra and Medea, and to pagan gods such as Aphrodite, Artemis and Dionysus, who were believed to enjoy real existence either in the remote past of the nation or in a different existential sphere.

Moreover, the said definitions fail to account for the sense of "reality" that such personae command even in the minds of receivers who do not believe in their existence at all. In principle, fictionalized narratives neither contrast the historical authenticity of personalities, nor peoples' beliefs. They rather tend to buttress beliefs due to finding an echo of truth in the receivers' minds, which are too conditioned by the principles of fictional thinking. In other words, the worlds of these personae/gods, as depicted in the Bible, mythology, ancient chronicles and the arts, totally or partially reflect the workings of the fictional mode of thinking.

Such a complex view of 'fictionality' considerably broadens the set of fictional narratives to encompass all those that are processed by the rules of fictional thinking, while excluding factual descriptions of real people and events such as documentary reports and historical studies in the modernist sense. Hence, 'fictional' applies here to the whole gamut of wholly or partly imagined characters and their actions (including their circumstances of time and place), their temporary and final successes or failures, and the meanings of their worlds, which represent and express the psyches of the authors and potentially also those of the receivers.

It is widely accepted that human psyches spontaneously create fictional worlds that express their innermost thoughts and feelings, e.g., in dreaming, daydreaming and children's imaginative play. There is also a vast body of theoretical literature that connects mythology to this spontaneous creativity, and conceives of it as a primeval form of thinking (Rozik, 2002: 293–313). In this sense, each fictional world embodies a thought, which bestows form on the amorphous stirrings of the psyche. The question is, therefore: How does a fictional world generate meaning? or, in other words, what are the rules that explain the formulation of each fictional thought by means of a particular fictional world?

Second, because of their imperceptible nature, (non-existing) fictional worlds created by the human imagination cannot be communicated without descriptions capable of evoking them in the minds of receivers; i.e., they are dependent on a language or other medium, albeit not on a specific one. Whereas the common denominator of literature is the use of the medium of language in its ability to describe and evoke such macro-images through the evocative power of words, the common denominator of other fictional arts, such as theatre, opera, puppet theatre, comic strips and cinema, which are iconic media, is the use of images imprinted on matter (see CHAPTER 13). Whereas the rules that generate fictional worlds belong in the domains of poetics, aesthetics and rhetoric, the rules that characterize different media belong in the domain of semiotics (Rozik, 2009).

In principle, medium and fictional world are mutually independent, in the sense that the same fictional world can be described by different media; and the same medium can describe different fictional worlds. It follows that each comedy is an integrated macro-unit composed of a describing text, generated by a language or an iconic medium, and a described fictional world. The possible translation of a comic fictional world from medium to medium, including language, which poses no problem, corroborates this mutual independence, which in turn supports the claim that the notion of 'comedy' applies to the nature of the fictional world — regardless of the medium that describes and communicates it; i.e., a given comedic fictional world in different media can be analyzed by the very same methodology. Although each medium makes a distinct contribution to the overall experience of the receiver, this is assumedly of minor importance and does not contradict the above principle of mutual independence. In this sense, for any fictional art, its fictional world is not only a legitimate object of analysis, but also essentially supplements the analysis of its medium (Rozik, 2009). The introductory text below is devoted to the analysis of comedy as a fictional genre in any possible medium.

The origin of comedy — historical evidence

Aristotle, who was the scholar closest to the possible birth of Attic comedy, albeit living about two centuries later, notes that '[t]he claim to [the invention of] Comedy is put forward by the Megarians, — not only by those of Greece proper, who allege that it originated under their democracy, but also by the Megarians of Sicily, for the poet Epicharmus, who is much earlier than Chionides and Magnes, belonged to that country' (*Poetics*: III, 3).

The existence of comedy prior to the advent of Attic comedy is corroborated by remarks made by Aristophanes in various plays; e.g., the speech of the coryphaeus in the *parabasis* of *Clouds* asserts the superiority of his comedies over what he terms 'vulgar comedy', and comments that the Athenian public was getting tired of the latter's coarse means:

> And see [my comedy] how modest she is. To begin with, she comes before you not decorated with the broad, red-tipped thing of stitched leather (the phallus), to raise a laugh among the children; then, there is no jeering at the Bald-head, no high-kicking Kordax [a comic dance]; and the old man who speaks his lines shall not beat the bystander with his stick to conceal the badness of his jokes. My Comedy does not rush upon the scene with torches in her hands, screaming 'Iou! Iou!'; she comes with full trust in herself and her verses. (quoted by Cornford: 178)

In Aristophanes' view, these vulgar laughter devices characterize Megarian comedy. In his prologue to *Wasps*, the slave Xanthias promises laughter, which 'shall not be laughter thieved from Megara' (*ibid.*). Ecphantides, another poet of Old Comedy, says that he is 'ashamed to make his play like a product of Megara'; and Eupolis, a contemporary of Aristophanes, speaks of 'a joke as being brutal and dull, like a joke from Megara, that would only draw a laugh from a child' (*ibid.*: 179).

In his attempt to trace the precursors of *commedia dell'arte*, Allardyce Nicoll endorses the possible existence of farce since the beginning of the sixth century BCE, in the Dorian region, particularly in Megara, almost two hundred years before the advent of Old Comedy, i.e., before Aristophanes' playwrighting and his contemporaries (p. 19). On the grounds of archeological evidence, vase paintings in particular, Nicoll tries to demonstrate that the tradition of farce goes from Dorian mime (ca. sixth century BCE), through the Roman Phlyakes (beginning ca. 350 BCE), the Fabula Atellana (beginning ca. first century BCE) and the Roman mimes (Roman Empire–Middle Ages), to the *commedia dell'arte* (sixteenth–eighteenth centuries) (pp. 20–134). Indeed, there is much in common to all these styles, as reflected in the physical traits of the actors, stock-type characters, costumes and often masks. It is noteworthy that, in linking these comic styles, Nicoll is nonetheless very cautious about the nature of the evidence.

What about the possible existence of comedy before Megarian comedy? Aristotle claims that "Comedy has had no history, because it was not at first treated seriously. It was late before the Archon granted a comic chorus to a poet; the performers were till then voluntary. Comedy had already taken definite shape when comic poets, distinctively so called, are heard of. Who furnished it with masks, or prologues, or increased the number of actors, — these and other similar details remain unknown. As for the plot, it came originally from Sicily" (*Poetics*: V, 2–3; cf. Halliwell: 36). The possible origin of comedy prior to Megarian comedy thus seems to be uncertain.

It should be noted that none of these quotations refer to the creation of the medium of theatre, but only to that of the comic fictional world (Rozik, 2002: 49–68).

The origin of comedy — ritual theory

In contrast to the historical evidence for the origin of comedy, in *The Origin of Attic Comedy*, published in 1914, Francis Macdonald Cornford suggests a theory of the ritual origin of Greek comedy, which parallels and complements Gilbert Murray's theory of the ritual origin of Greek tragedy. As the title of the book states, his theory relates not to the origin of comedy in general, but to the advent of Attic Old Comedy, and particularly to that of Aristophanes' play-scripts.

The main thesis of both Murray and Cornford, members of the Cambridge School of Anthropology, is that both tragedy and comedy developed from fertility rituals, Dionysiac in nature. This thesis has been adopted by many scholars, even in the present day, despite the lack of empiric support (Rozik, 2002: 29–68).

In order to substantiate this thesis, Cornford presupposes the existence of a fertility ritual, even prior to Megarian comedy, which he terms the ritual of the Year Spirit; and, in his view, the structure of Aristophanes' comedies retains the traces of this ritual. He suggests the following structural components of Old Comedy, which in their temporal order, are: (a) *prologue*, (b) *parodos*, (c) *agon*, (d) sacrifice, (e) feast, (f) resurrection, (g) marriage, and (h) *komos*. In various sections of the book, Cornford explains these components in the terms of either the typical features of the synchronic performances of Aristophanes' comedies; e.g., (a) the prologue 'is the exposition' (p. 2), (b) the *parodos* 'is the entrance of the chorus' (*ibid.*) and (h) the *komos* marks the exit of the chorus (p. 8); or in the terms of the alleged ritual of the Year Spirit: (c) The *agon* is 'a fierce "contest" between the representatives of two parties or principles, which are in effect the hero and villain of the whole piece' (*ibid.*). 'The Agonist is the hero, who is attacked, put on his defense, and [eventually] comes off victorious. The Antagonist is the villain, who is in the stronger position at first, but is [finally] worsted and beaten from the field' (p. 71). The hero and the villain are often identified as the old and the new year or Winter and Summer respectively. (d) The sacrifice: 'the God himself, in human or animal form, . . . [who] is the victim. . . . is dismembered' (p. 99). (e) The feast: in which 'the pieces of his body are either devoured raw in a savage omophagy [the eating of raw flesh], or cooked and eaten in a sacramental feast. . . . In all these cases . . . the essential purpose is that of the phallic rites, which aim at spreading the benign influence as widely as possible, so that all members of the community may have their share' (*ibid.*). (f) The resurrection of the god: 'The *Agon* is the beginning of the sacrifice in its primitive dramatic form — the conflict between the good and evil principles, Summer and Winter, Life and Death. The good spirit is slain, dismembered, cooked and eaten in the communal feast, and yet brought back to life' (p. 103). And (g) The marriage of the 'victor of the *agon*' (p. 70): 'The pair often represent, under a more or less transparent disguise, the two great agents of vegetable fertility, the Earth-mother and the Heaven-father, whose rain falls in the life-giving stream into the womb of Earth' (p. 19). Moreover, '[i]n other instances, the spirit of fertility may be Dionysus himself' (*ibid.*). In the *komos* (h), '[t]he plays regularly end with a procession in which the chorus marches out of the orchestra, conducting the chief character in triumph and singing a song technically known as the "*exodos*"' (p. 8).

Cornford attempts to integrate in his theory Aristotle's statement that '[comedy] originated with the authors [. . .] of the phallic songs, which are still in use in many of our cities' (*Poetics*: IV, 12). He correctly presupposes the Dionysiac nature of these songs, which are sung in ceremonies in honor of the god. This ceremony, which is described by Aristophanes in *Acharnians* in the guise of the rite performed by Dikaiopolis at the Country [Rural] Dionysia, reflects a definite structure. In bare outline, it features three parts: '(1) The procession of the worshippers of Phales moves on its way, carrying the emblem of the God on a pole and the instruments of sacrifice. (2) It pauses at some fixed place for the sacrifice, accompanied by a prayer to Dionysus. (3) the procession moves on again singing the Phallic song' (Cornford: 103). However, the comic or comedic nature of this rite does not follow from this description.

Cornford also tries to accommodate Aristotle's dictum that comedy originated in Megarian comedy. He thus assumes that comedy 'appears to have existed for centuries on the humble level of popular farce' (p. 180). He thus argues that comedy only indirectly derives from ritual, while presupposing an intermediate phase in the guise of a folk-play: 'Attic Comedy, as we know it from Aristophanes, is constructed in the framework of what was already a drama, a folk play; and that behind this folk play lay a still earlier phase, in which its action was dramatically presented in religious ritual' (p. 4). In other words, in contrast to Murray's direct descent of tragedy from ritual, Cornford introduces the intermediate phase of a folk play, with sufficient evidence for its existence.

In addition, Cornford attempts a synthesis between his theory, Murray's theory of ritual origin of tragedy, and the Aristotelian principle of *hamartia*, 'hubris' in particular:

> Professor Murray has pointed out the affinity between the recurrent life-story of the Year Spirit, the theme of our supposed ritual, and that deep-rooted doctrine of *Hubris*. . . . He says: 'The life of the Year-Daemon, as it seems to be reflected in Tragedy, is generally a story of Pride and Punishment. Each year arrives, waxes great, commits the sin

of Hubris, and then is slain. The death is deserved; but the slaying is a sin: hence comes the next Year as Avenger, or as the Wronged One re-risen: . . . Our supposed ritual, accordingly, as a representation of the cycle of seasonal life, of the annual conflict of Summer and Winter, provides [also] the essential structure of the tragic plot, the fundamental conception of the tragic reversal or peripeteia. (Cornford: 207–8)

Already in 1927 Arthur W. Pickard-Cambridge, who offers the most authoritative criticism of the School of Cambridge, refuted Cornford's convoluted theory of ritual origin on three accounts: (a) lack of any evidence for the existence of the alleged ritual of the Year Spirit; (b) inconsistency in the application of type-events and their suggested order; and c) lack of explanatory power in regard to both ritual and Old Comedy. *Inter alia*, he comments:

The question, whether there is any reason to suppose that this complex ritual [of the Year Spirit] ever really existed, is one which Mr. Cornford practically does not touch. It need only be said that it would require very strong evidence indeed to prove that one and the same rite included the birth of a wonder-child, his Agon, death and resurrection, a sacred marriage in which he took part. . . . we certainly do not find these elements combined in any ancient Greek ritual about which we have information. But does the supposed ritual actually explain the plays? (Pickard-Cambridge: 330)

He goes on to say that 'there is no evidence at all that a god was ever slain in any ritual with which comedy can be connected; and the idea that the *Agon* arose from a ritual in which an Eniautos-Daimon or Good Principle underwent a simulated death must be pronounced wholly unproved' (Pickard-Cambridge: 348). Furthermore,

Mr. Cornford states that there can be little doubt that "the protagonist in comedy must originally have been the spirit of fertility himself, Phales or Dionysus' [Cornford: 20], and that it must have been he who originally led the final *komos* as male partner in a marriage. The evidence for these does not appear. The fact that some Athenian actors wore the phallus certainly does not prove it. There is no trace of Phales as a character in any kind of procession or drama in ancient Greece, though he is invoked in song, or represented by the phallus carried aloft; and Dionysus did not wear the phallus in art or drama. . . . It is important to note that evidence for connecting a *ieros gamos* [a ritual wedding] with a phallic procession in any actual ancient Greek ritual is non-existent. (*ibid.*: 334–5)

In regard to 'marriage', for example, Pickard-Cambridge claims that 'there is no trace of any kind of *gamos* or indecency in the conclusion of the *Clouds* or the *Frogs*, and there is actually no feast in either, though in the *Frogs*, Pluto invites Dionysus and Aeschylus to a meal before their journey' (p. 332). After reviewing all Aristophanes' comedies, Pickard-Cambridge concludes 'that in several plays there is no marriage at all; that in several there is simply gross indecency in the presence of one, or more often two, courtesans; and that these courtesans are there as common accompaniments of the feast, not representing the female partner in a ritual marriage' (p. 334). He also claims that there is no evidence of the role of Dionysus, or for that matter of any Year Spirit, in comedy prior to Old Comedy, whether folk-play or developed form.

Indeed, Cornford's methodology is somewhat surprising. He actually reverses the logic of demonstration, initially by contending that Aristophanes' comedies reflect the traces of a Dionysiac ritual; then by attempting to determine the structural components of these comedies, subsequently by attributing them to the hypothetical ritual of the Year Spirit; and, finally by seeking to demonstrate that the traces of this ritual are found in Aristophanes' comedies. This is a circular demonstration: he ascribes the traits he allegedly "discovered" in Aristophanes' comedies to both the invented ritual of the Year Spirit and to Aristophanes' comedies. Moreover, these traces cannot be seen as components of a structure, in being no more than a series of type-events in a predetermined order that assumedly recurs in Aristophanes' play-scripts, from which they were allegedly abstracted. Ironically, as suggested by Pickard-Cambridge, most of these type-events are not found in these play-scripts either. Consequently, Cornford's model is abstracted from neither ritual nor dramatic data, but is clearly imposed on both, while failing to explain either of them. Oddly enough, in suggesting these sequences of events as parts of a structure, Cornford does not relate them to the spectator in the terms of a possible comic or comedic experience. In the terms of Pickard-Cambridge's critique, Cornford's theory attests to a faulty reading of Aristophanes' comedies. Corrigan correctly comments:

There is really very little plot to most of Aristophanes' plays (certainly not in the sense that there is a plot in the comedies of Shakespeare, Molière, Congreve, or Shaw), only a series of episodes which serve as the occasions for his wit and satiric thrusts. His plays move from moment to moment and have a sense of spontaneity rather than structure. (p. 359)

Despite severe criticism on scientific and poetical grounds, the theory of ritual origin of comedy, like that of tragedy, is still adopted by many a scholar. What is the secret of its appeal? Ronald Vince's reply is illuminating:

> However inaccurate as a record of the historical origins of the theatre, the ritual theory appeals on a metaphorical level to unconscious patterns and longings in our own psyches and we find drama considered in its terms a richer and more satisfying experience than it might otherwise be. (p. 16)

'Comedy' as a theoretical term

The term 'comedy' has been applied and still applies to a wide range of fictional worlds, which explains both its extremely abstract sense and its possible misapplication.

It is widely assumed that Aristotle wrote an additional tractate on comedy, similar to that on tragedy, but which has been lost. This assumption is probably based on Aristotle's remark 'and of Comedy, we will speak hereafter' (*Poetics*: VI, 1; cf. Umberto Eco's *The Name of the Rose*). Diverse attempts have been made to reconstruct the main tenets of this allegedly lost work on the grounds of the *Poetics* and the *Tractatus Coislinianus* (cf. Cooper and Janko). However, as we shall see below, due to Aristotle's assumption that there are common principles that generate both tragedy and comedy, and to his specific remarks on comedy whenever these genres differ, it is indeed possible that a special tractate on comedy would have been redundant.

Nonetheless, any attempt to reconstruct Aristotle's theory of comedy, i.e., to make explicit what is implied in the *Poetics*, in addition to the interpretation of what is explicitly stated, is commendable. This study assumes that Aristotle's remarks on comedy in the *Poetics* constitute the very first attempt to create a theory of comedy; and that his insights and presuppositions regarding both tragedy and comedy are of utmost importance to any theory of fictional genres. Therefore, the model of comedy suggested here is basically rooted in the Aristotelian tradition, although further developed along its own presuppositions, and enriched by later theories of fictional creativity.

Regrettably, there is a basic inconsistency in the *Poetics*: Aristotle takes for granted that, in its essential guise, just as a final catastrophe characterizes tragedy, a happy ending or, rather, an ending that gratifies the spectators' expectations characterizes comedy. This view is implied in two of his remarks: first, '[such a structure] is shocking without being tragic, for no disaster follows' (*Poetics*: XIV, 7), which implies that tragedies should essentially end in catastrophe. And second, tragedies that eventually gratify the spectators' expectations are closer in nature to comedy: '[t]he pleasure . . . thence derived is not the true tragic pleasure. It is proper rather of Comedy, where those who, in the piece, are the deadliest enemies — like Orestes and Aegisthus — quit the stage as friends at the close, and no one slays or is slain' (*ibid.*: XIII, 8). Aristotle labels this kind of fictional world 'second rank tragedy'. This observation probably explains the later introduction of 'tragicomedy' as a theoretical term. Unfortunately, he does not distinguish between tragic and comic reconciliation.

Nonetheless, this quotation from the *Poetics* implies that despite the affinity of second rank tragedy to comedy, its ending is of secondary importance, and that in labeling fictional worlds as tragedies he prefers the criterion of their shared serious/sublime mood. By contrasting implication, comedies too share their specific lighthearted mood. Moreover, Aristotle does not distinguish between comic fiction and comic drama, and employs 'comedy' even for Homer's *Margites*, which was a comic epos (*Poetics*: IV, 9). This too indicates that for him the mood is of capital importance and that, on this level, the difference between fiction and drama is marginal (see CHAPTER 13).

It should be borne in mind that Aristotle only relates to Old Comedy and to its possible predecessors, the Megarian comedies (*Poetics*: III, 3). He also conjectures that comedy originated in the Phallic songs, which are invective in nature (*Poetics*: IV, 12), and which do not fit the nature of comedy in general, but only that of Aristophanes' play-scripts. To see Old and New Comedy under the same label is thus problematic because, as we shall see below, they evince different moods (see CHAPTERS 7 & 8). Aristotle already distinguishes between dramatizing the 'ludicrous' and 'personal satire' (*ibid.*: IV, 9; cf. Nicoll: 37).

The anonymous *Tractatus Coislinianus* from the tenth century CE, although its contents are possibly from the first century BCE, is often 'supposed to be based on the lost part of Aristotle's treatise [the *Poetics*]' (Cornford: 35; cf. Stott: 20) or at least as representing Aristotle's view on comedy. This is doubtful, however, because of the nature of its departures from the *Poetics*, which are: (a) It suggests a description of comedy's catharsis, modeled on Aristotle's definition of tragedy: 'through pleasure and laughter effecting the purgation of the like emotions. It has laughter for its mother' (Cooper: 224). This is quite absurd, as Elder Olson comments: 'Why anyone should want to get rid of pleasure, or be pleased by getting rid of pleasure, or how he could get rid of pleasure and still have it, [it] fails to say' (p. 45). (b) The *Tracatatus* claims that 'the comic plot is the structure binding together the ludicrous incidents' (Cooper: 226). This contention presupposes that comedy does not reflect a structure in the Aristotelian sense (see CHAPTER 5). And (c) Basically, albeit not contradicting the possible existence of a special treatise on comedy, the *Tracatatus* lacks the empirical spirit that characterizes Aristotle's *Poetics*.

Nonetheless, the *Tractatus* presents several thought-provoking remarks: (a) it mentions three typical characters of comedy: (1) the 'buffoonish', (2) the 'ironical' [eiron] and the 'impostor' [alazon] (Cooper: 226), most probably based on Aristotle's *Nicomachean Ethics* (IV, vii, 1 — viii. 12). It should be noted that the *Nicomachean Ethics* addresses these characters in the context of discussing the value of the golden mean, in which he mentions, among other deviant characters, the 'boaster' (*alazon*), the 'self-depreciator' (*eiron*), the buffoon (*bomolochos*) and the boor (*agroikos*) — with the latter not being mentioned in the *Tractatus* — without any clear-cut distinction between life and comedy. Other deviant characters may be seen as deserving comic treatment as well. (b) The *Tractatus* correctly distinguishes between 'comedy' and 'abuse' (invective), what I term 'satire' in the present study (Cooper: 225; cf. *Poetics*: IX, 4). And (c) the *Tractatus* rightly notes that '[t]he joker will make game of faults in the soul and the body' (*ibid.*). As we shall see below, despite schematic presentation, such remarks offer substantial contributions to a theory of comedy.

In the Spanish Golden Age playwrights used to label their play-scripts 'comedies', probably due to their combining tragic and comic characters, and featuring endings that satisfied the spontaneous expectations of the audiences. The paradox is that a play-script, such as Calderón de la Barca's *Life is a Dream*, which deals with predestination, one of the most serious themes in world dramaturgy, was categorized as 'comedy' despite its highly serious nature. It was actually labeled '*comedia famosa*' (famous comedy), probably reflecting the intention to distinguish it from comedy proper on modal grounds. Such a dramatic work deserves, rather, the label 'tragedy' even according to the *Poetics*.

Lope de Vega published his short theoretical work *El Arte Nuevo de Hacer Comedias* (*The New Art of Making Comedies*; my trans.) in 1609.

This work, which was written at the peak of his success, is satiric in nature. It derides the learned critics for condemning his playwriting, although being unable to write even a single play. It is in this sense that the use of 'making' (*hacer*) comedies, rather than 'writing' them, should be understood as the self-deprecation of an eiron. In this treatise, he repeatedly declares his intentional disregard of Aristotle's rules, while his preference for a mixture of serious and humorous moods (17; p. 65) contradicts what is implied in the *Poetics* and explicitly condemned by Horace (p. 82). His other recommendations are practical in nature and are in full accord, as is his dramatic practice, with the spirit of Aristotle's theory. Even Lope's permission to disregard the unity of time (Lope, 1965: 18; p. 65) contrasts not the *Poetics*, but the three unities suggested by its sixteenth-century Italian interpreters, Robortello and Castelvetro in particular (Clark: 49). In fact, their interpretations reflect a misreading of the *Poetics*, which only discerns tragedy's tendency to restrict the enacted action to the final stages of a narrative, but without discarding its possible longer duration (*Poetics*: V, 4). Furthermore, Lope refers neither to a humorous mood nor to laughter, in line with his own tendency to create fictional worlds that may or may not feature comic elements. I suggest again, therefore, that his use of 'comedy' for such worlds is basically ungrounded. Lope justifies his alleged deviations from the *Poetics* by declaring that he seeks the applause of the crowd, 'for, since the crowd pays for the comedies, it is fitting to talk foolishly to it to satisfy its taste' (5; p. 64). In contrast to the *Poetics* essentialist approach to drama, this comment reflects a hedonistic approach, while ironically echoing Aristotle's derogatory remark on the taste of his contemporary audience (*Poetics*: XIII, 7).

In *Three Discourses on the Dramatic Poem* (1660) Pierre Corneille follows Aristotle in perceiving most of the traits of comedy as shared with tragedy, and adding but a few differentiating remarks whenever he perceives divergence. In his view, the specific differences of comedy are: (a) whereas tragedy features an 'illustrious, extraordinary and serious' theme, comedy features an 'ordinary and enjoyable' one (p. 177; my trans.); and (b) whereas in tragedy the unity of action consists in the 'unity of danger' for the hero, in comedy it consists in the 'unity of intrigue or obstacle' (p. 240; my trans.). Like Lope, he does not address the comic mood at all; and endorses a hedonist approach to both tragedy and comedy (p. 174). In general, the influence of Spanish drama on Corneille is conspicuous, and reflected not only in theoretical matters but also in his 'translations' of Spanish play-scripts to the conventions of French theatre such as *Le Cid* (from Guillen de Castro's *Las Mocedades del Cid*) and *Le Menteur* (from Juan Ruiz de Alarcón's *La Verdad Sospechosa*).

Corneille is widely perceived as a representative of French classicism. He indeed endorses its fundamental endeavor to emulate the achievements of classical Greek drama. In this sense, only apparently in contrast to Lope, he declares adherence to the rules of the *Poetics*. He also accepts the three unities suggested by its Italian interpreters. He even sees them in terms of Aristotle's the 'necessary', and as more compelling than any other rule. However, while apparently accepting these unities with no qualification, he also advises how to circumvent them: (a) the unity of time, by never mentioning time altogether, and leaving the audience to imagine the duration as they wish (p. 252); and (b) the unity of place, by mentioning only the name of the city in which the action takes place, while ignoring specific locations; e.g., Paris and Rome (p. 258). Corneille's advices, which also concern comedy, require a reconsideration of classicist poetics.

Possibly under the influence of Spanish drama, Shakespeare's practice too evinces an improper extension of the term 'comedy'; e.g., *The Merchant of Venice* (cf. Olson: 86–7). Nonetheless, some of his comedies do deserve the label of 'comedy' such as *Twelfth Night* and *A Midsummer Night's Dream*. The reasons for labeling them as such lie in their emphasis on the theme of love, their happy endings, and the inclusion of comic characters and action and, most important, in their comic, light-hearted mood (see CHAPTER 7).

It is not at all clear why Chekhov insisted on viewing his play-scripts in terms of 'comedy'. This might be explained by perceiving his own plays as not fitting the sublime style of tragedy, and probably even more so by his reluctance to accept Stanislavsky's melodramatic interpretations. Although some scenes in his play can be performed in the spirit of comedy, reflecting a singular interpretation, his major play-scripts are definitely not comic in mood and do feature endings, meant to frustrate the spontaneous expectations of the audience (cf. Weitz: 166).

In the last two centuries there has been a substantial increase of theoretical interest in comedy, epitomized by the major contributions of William Hazlitt (1819), Henry Bergson, French: 1900, English trans. 1956; Sigmund Freud, German, 1905, English trans. 1960; Allardyce Nicoll, 1931; K. M. Lea, 1934; Enid Welsford, 1935; Susanne Langer, 1953; Wolfgang Kayser, German, 1957, English trans. 1963; Northrop Frye, 1957; Mikhail Bakhtin, Russian, 1965, English trans. 1968; Eric Bentley, 1964; Elder Olson, 1968; Erich Segal, 2001; Andrew Stott, 2005; and Eric Weitz, 2009. This increase is probably due to the growing prominence of satiric and grotesque drama. Naturally, interest has also focused on their precursors.

There is indeed a parallel tradition — that of satire, probably stemming from the phallic songs and Aristophanes' play-scripts. There is also a tendency to attribute satiric elements to Molière's play-scripts, although only some of them undoubtedly justify this claim. This genre, however, should be distinguished from comedy on modal grounds (see CHAPTER 8). Friedrich Dürrenmatt's *The Visit* and Hal Ashby's film *Being There* are modern examples of satire. Similar considerations apply to grotesque drama, which in its current form is a unique modernist breed. The twentieth century developed these two genres, which employ laughter-eliciting devices, without conveying a comic mood. They aim instead at producing different effects on audiences. Furthermore, a relatively new non-dramatic genre called stand-up comedy, which can be either comic or satiric, should also be taken into account (see CHAPTER 8).

A basic assumption of this study is that there has been an uninterrupted tradition of comedy that is neither satiric nor grotesque but humoristic in nature, and which combines a comic mood, possible comic laughter, and endings that satisfy the spontaneous expectations of the audience. This tradition probably originated in Megarian comedy, continued in New Comedy (Menander), Roman comedy (Plautus and Terence), *commedia dell'arte*, Molière, Goldoni, and developed into cinematic and TV comedy. My thesis is that only fictional worlds in this tradition deserve the term 'comedy'.

Methodological considerations

In the theory of theatre there is a tendency to use 'drama' for serious fictional worlds that cannot be classified in the usual generic terms of 'comedy', 'tragedy', 'farce' and 'melodrama'. Aristotle remarks that men can be represented 'either as better than in real life, or as worse, or as they are', which he views as 'true to life', and that whereas 'Comedy aims at representing men as worse, Tragedy [aims] as better than in actual life' (*Poetics*: II, 1 & 4). These observations leave naturalistic fictional worlds without a generic term, possibly explaining the use of 'drama' for those that are 'true to life'. The distinction between melodrama and farce cannot help in either case because of their emphasis on aiming at either tears or laughter. Similar considerations apply to the term 'dramatic', usually employed for extreme real events or situations, probably because of the connotations of intensity typical of dramatic events and situations.

In contrast, as used by Aristotle, 'drama' conveys a different sense: '[Tragedy and comedy] both imitate persons *acting and doing*. Hence, some say, the name of "drama" is given to such poems, *as representing action*. For the same reason the Dorians claim the invention both of Tragedy and Comedy, . . . They add also that the Dorian word for "doing" is *'dran'* (*Poetics*: III, 2–3; my italics). These remarks imply that 'drama' is used not for the nature of the fictional world, but for the mode of representation that characterizes the medium of theatre, which is shared by tragedy and comedy. It is in this sense that 'drama' is employed in this study.

There is also a tendency to perceive comedy as totally opposing tragedy, in the sense that every feature of the latter should have the opposite counterpart in the former. But this is not the case. In addition to medium, these genres have far more elements in common than differences; e.g., as we shall see below, the structures of action are shared by all genres. It is the comic mood that is the specific difference of comedy. In this study, the comic mood is perceived not only as opposing the serious mood, but also as presupposing it; i.e., as an inversion of the serious mood.

A basic distinction is often made between 'comic' and 'comedic'. Here, 'comic' denotes whatever promotes the comic mood, and 'comedic' relates to the nature of the entire fictional world, which promotes the comic mood and reflects a fictional structure that is akin to this mood. Nonetheless, the comic mood is not necessarily connected to a comedic fictional structure; e.g., stand-up comedy.

There are several subdivisions of 'comedy': in the narrow sense, the best known and theoretically probably the most productive is that between comedy of character and comedy of situation (sitcom). Whereas the former focuses on character as the main resource of the comic mood, including laughter, the latter focuses on situations that are comic without the characters being necessarily comic. This distinction is adopted here, and it is applicable even on the level of a single scene.

As shown below, this study leads to a set of distinctions that criss-cross the entire set of what is regularly termed 'comedy'. There is nothing wrong in such a multiple categorization. It is in the nature of rational thinking to aim at configurations of traits, resulting from the application of several distinctions, which characterize different genres despite the non-essential similarities. I shall suggest, for example, that the use of laughter-eliciting devices does not always justify the label 'comedy', and that additional distinctions should apply. I aim at distinguishing between 'comedy', which is humorous in nature, and other related genres that employ laughter means in order to produce different moods and effects on audiences. Consequently, the following chapters deal first with comedy in this narrow sense, in order to subsequently distinguish it from tangential genres such as satiric and grotesque drama.

A fundamental distinction is assumed between play-script and performance-text. Whereas the former is an incomplete notation of a possible performance, the latter is the actual text of theatre. In principle, the analysis of comedy should be carried out on the level of performance, which realizes all its potentialities, unless such a primary source is unavailable.

I assume here that theatre is not the only possible medium of comedy, and suggest a set of media that are capable of generating comedies, including cinema, animation and puppet theatre. While stressing their shared abilities, substantial differences between them are taken into account. Albeit focusing on dramatic comedy, this study acknowledges the existence of literary comedy, while attempting a common explanation for both.

It is also suggested that the contribution of the spectator to the generation of comedic meaning is no less important than the performance-text itself.

There is a question in regard to whether comedies written in different cultures and times can be seen as belonging in the same genre. In this respect I accept Weitz's remark: 'what allows us to understand and appreciate comic texts from other times and other places is owed at least in part to the fact that some patterns can still be seen to betray their roots in past practices' (p. 39).

I abstain here from etymological considerations, in that they are usually misleading. A new word or new sense of an existing word may be coined on a feeble analogy or metonymy, which has occurred spontaneously to somebody, without necessarily reflecting an attempt to determine the essence of an object (cf. Segal: 1–9).

Structure of the book

Chapter 1 suggests that the comic mood opposes the serious mood, and presupposes it as its standard. Mode and mood are different aspects of the modality of a fictional world and, in determining the generic nature of a fictional world, mood subordinates mode. Comedy is thus characterized by the humorous mood, regardless of mode.

Chapter 2 examines the nature of laughter, which is a preprogrammed psychical mechanism, and explores the conditions for eliciting comic laughter, which are: failure, foolishness, and anxiety. Laughter can also be triggered under different conditions and used for different purposes. Making one laugh is the aim of satire and grotesque drama too; but only in comedy is laughter humorous and purely cathartic.

Chapter 3 ponders the nature of laughter-eliciting devices, which aim at producing laughter regardless of genre. These constitute a set that is open to the inventive capacity of a playwright. Although comedy shows a clear predilection for such devices, these are also employed in satiric and grotesque fictional worlds. Comic acting and comic atmosphere are vital conditions for laughter.

Chapter 4 relates to the combination of Aristotle's and Hegel's poetics as providing the grounds for a sound theory of comedic structure of action. In principle, all genres share the structures of action, but differ in their typical moods. Structures of action and moods are mutually independent, in the sense that all combinations are possible, even in the very same fictional world, albeit from different viewpoints.

Chapter 5 offers a complex model of the structure of a fictional world, and contends that mood is an integral part of it. Comedy is characterized by the predominant humorous mood and its preference for surface structures that satisfy the spontaneous expectations of the spectator. Comedy is a genre that often combines comic laughter, which is a cathartic mechanism, and holistic catharsis.

Chapter 6 maintains that there is a fundamental correspondence between the structure of a character and the structure of a fictional action. The subordination of the former to the latter reveals that these are two forms of organization of the same fictional material: temporal vs. atemporal, which are two sides of the same coin. The implication is that in any fictional world *no character can be reduced to a single trait.*

Chapter 7 determines that there are certain kinds of drama (e.g., farce, romantic comedy and sketch comedy) that share with proper comedy the humorous mood, the eliciting of anxiety (due to the temporary lifting of inhibitions), the cathartic function of laughter, the archetypal structure of action and holistic catharsis. The differences among these sub-genres are a matter of degree in lifting inhibitions or emphasis on types of comedic characters.

Chapter 8 accepts the view that comedy shares with satire and grotesque drama the use of laughter devices. However, it suggests that their moods and the expected responses of the audience are completely different, justifying their perception as tangential genres. Stand-up comedy is not a fictional genre, but a thematic one. Although it often shares the humorous mood with comedy, it is basically a satiric genre.

Chapter 9 views *commedia dell'arte* as a crucial link in the tradition of comedy: it reflected the earlier tradition of comedy, farce in particular, and has had a significant influence on subsequent comedy and farce, their acting mode in particular. Its performances were characterized not by improvisation in the regular sense of the term, but by a form of modular creativity, probably making their scripting redundant.

Chapter 10 contends that despite basic differences, comedy and carnival have several features in common such as lighthearted mood, comic laughter, and the ultimate aim to reaffirm and buttress the prevalent values and beliefs of their synchronic culture. It is difficult to establish what is the primary and what is the derived phenomenon — with both probably originating at the very beginnings of human history.

Chapter 11 considers Sigmund Freud's significant contribution to a theory of comedy, based on his theory of joke and witticism, which turns scholarly attention to the unconscious repercussions of comedy and satiric drama — with both involving all the levels of the psyche. It explores the implications of his seminal distinction between 'innocent' and 'tendentious' jokes for a theory of fictional genres.

Chapter 12 probes the theoretical trend that attempted the vindication of comedy on the grounds of reflecting a unique vision, which is shared by all kinds of comedy, and concludes that this endeavor does not stand to reason. This was a fleeting trend that has provided no insight into the nature of comedy. Only the humorous mood and its cathartic functions amount to a set of common traits that characterize all comedies.

Chapter 13 ponders the ability of iconic media, other than theatre, to generate descriptions of comedic fictional worlds; e.g., opera, cartoon and cinema. In order to substantiate this claim, 'iconicity' is redefined in terms of 'imagistic thinking'; i.e., as being grafted upon the spontaneous ability of the human brain to create mental images, and to employ them as units of thinking.

Chapter 14 suggests that the spectator's contribution to the generation of comedic meaning is no less crucial than that of the performance-text itself. It distinguishes between the real spectator, who may be limited in various respects, and the 'implied spectator', who is fully qualified to complement the text by definition. The meaning of a comedy results from the dialogue between implied author and implied receiver.

The last section, *Conclusions*, attempts to define comedy, while not ignoring the limitations of definitions in any endeavor to understand the nature of a genre. It also puts comedy within the wider context of the preverbal and suppressed imagistic/metaphoric/symbolic mode of thinking. Comedy thus offers the opportunity to confront shameful and suppressed contents of the spectators' psyches under the safe conditions of a socio-cultural permit.

Comic Mood

1

In comedy, in contrast to real life, not everything is in the eyes of the beholder. Since the writing and performing of a comedy is an intentional act, a set of objective features, meant to trigger a comic effect, must be found in it. Within this frame of mind there is a general agreement that what characterizes comedy is its comic mood. The aim of this chapter is to determine the nature of this mood. Furthermore, because laughter-eliciting devices are employed not only in comedy but also in satiric and grotesque drama, the use of such devices cannot constitute the specific difference of comedy. Therefore, 'comic' is used here in the sense of 'lighthearted' or, rather, 'humorous' mood, under the assumption that in other genres laughter is subordinated to different moods and effects.

In his definition of 'tragedy', Aristotle defines the tragic action as '*spodaious*', which conveys the senses of both 'lofty' and 'serious' (*Poetics*: VI, 2) and, by the same token, blurs the distinction between these two terms. I suggest that this single term '*spodaious*' refers to different aspects of the fictional world: 'mode' and 'mood' respectively.

(A) *The notion of 'mode'* relates to the quality of behavior that characterizes a character. The lofty mode concerns traits such as superior intelligence, enhanced awareness, superb eloquence, courage and readiness for self-sacrifice on the altar of communal values. In contrast, the lowly mode relates to traits such as inferior intelligence, lack of awareness, poor eloquence, cowardice and selfishness.

Aristotle contends that there are three basic kinds of characterization: 'as better than in real life, or as worse, or as they are' (*ibid.*: II, 1). While 'Comedy aims at representing men as worse, Tragedy [does so] as better than in actual life' (*ibid.*: II, 4). Assumedly, these observations relate to the level of mode. It follows that 'as they are' implies that for both tragedy and comedy, the typical mode of the spectator is the standard, which he also characterizes as 'true to life' (*ibid.*: II, 1), and which characterizes naturalist drama. Both tragedy and comedy presuppose this standard, and equally depart from it. These departures condition the spectators' attitudes of either admiration or contempt for characters and their actions, and their consequent spontaneous expectations.

(B) The notion of 'mood' (or 'tone') applies to the serious or light-hearted nature, which characterizes a fictional world and particularly a character, and which conditions the spectators' attitudes to them. Whereas the typical mood of traditional tragedy is serious, i.e., severe, intolerant and even merciless; the typical mood of comedy is light-hearted i.e., benevolent, tolerant and even merciful. The comic mood is characterized by creating an atmosphere of permissiveness, in which anything can be expected and even accepted. In particular, this atmos-phere is induced mainly by ludicrous characters, which presuppose both seriousness as the standard, and any departure from it; as in Olson's view regarding the ridiculous: "the 'serious' is here the standard, and prior in definition: just as the good is prior in definition to, and the standard by which we judge, the bad' (p. 13). Moreover, '[t]he ridiculous is then the contrary of this [the serious], in some characteristic on which its whole value depends, so that the idea of its value is completely destroyed' (p. 14). The comic mood thus reflects an inversion of the serious mood of tragedy and melodrama.

Frye's approach to mode and mood

Frye suggests five basic 'modes' defined in terms of power of action: 'Fictions [. . .] may be classified, not morally, but by the hero's power of action, which may be greater than ours, less, or roughly the same' (p. 33). While offering a correct criticism of those interpretations of the *Poetics* given on exclusively moral grounds, Frye's classification preserves the spectators' mode as the standard. On the grounds of the Aristotelian triadic distinction between modes (*Poetics*: II, 1), and secondary aspects, Frye proposes five basic narrative modes: (a) *myth* (of divine beings), (b) *romance* (of heroes), (c) *high mimetic* (of kings), (d) *low mimetic* (of regular people) and (e) *ironic* (of lesser people) (pp. 33–4). In (a), (b) and (c) the characters are more powerful than the typical spectator, in (d) they meet the spectator's standard; and in (e) they are less powerful. Frye also correlates these modes with fictional genres, e.g., the high mimetic and above with tragedy (lofty mode), the low mimetic with naturalist drama, and the ironic (lowly mode) with comedy and farce.

Indeed, there is a theoretical and practical tradition that correlates social status with mode: lofty for nobility and above, and lowly for commoners and below. In this tradition, tragedy is characterized by the lofty behavior of fictional or fictionalized kings, heroes and gods, and comedy by the lowly behavior of low-class people; while bourgeois drama is drawn to the naturalistic style. Classical comedy epitomizes this tradition. In contrast, just as in later tragedy there is no necessary correlation between lofty mode and high social status (e.g., Federico García Lorca's *Yerma*), in later comedy too there is no necessary correlation between lowly mode and low social status (e.g., Sir Toby Belch in Shakespeare's *Twelfth Night*).

Whereas the combination of low social status and serious mood does not contrast the spectators' spontaneous models of coherence, the combination of high social or existential status and humorous mode, does. Through their 'comic treatment', such a combination is currently perceived as generating a grotesque mood; e.g., the ludicrous death of Bérenger the king in Ionesco's *Exit the King*.

Olson claims that '[w]e do not take seriously anything which we regard as unimportant to the well-being of anyone, nor anything which happens to people for whom we feel no important concern' (p. 162). However, there is nothing to prevent concern for low-status characters and lack of concern for high-status ones.

Furthermore, while Frye links power of action to existential or social status, the distribution of power among characters does not necessarily overlap these categories. Even in the course of a single fictional world: a reversal of power of action often characterizes relations between characters such as Othello and Iago in Shakespeare's *Othello* or Julia and Jean in August Strindberg's *Miss Julia*. Similar considerations apply to the obstructing and obstructed characters in comedy; e.g., Harpagon and his children in Molière's *The Miser*: the former not only obstructs the happiness of his children, but also the latter obstruct his own happiness. Although power of action can be perceived as an aspect of mode, its relation to social or existential status is variable.

Freud's approach and its implications

In his *Jokes and their Relation to the Unconscious*, Freud suggests a seminal distinction between innocent and tendentious jokes (1989: 106–39). Whereas the aim of an innocent joke lies in the telling itself, in promoting the comic mood and the listener's laughter, that of a tendentious joke reflects a purpose beyond such as aggressiveness or sexual exposure (see CHAPTER 11). Although he makes this distinction in an attempt to understand the effects of jokes and witticisms, it is to the point here: on such grounds, the humorous mood typical of comedy can be characterized as 'innocent', in not having any purpose beyond that of its possible cathartic effect (see CHAPTER 2). In contrast, tendentiousness suits the nature of satiric drama (see CHAPTER 8).

Mode and mood relations

The lofty and even sublime mode is traditionally combined with the serious mood, possibly explaining their being coupled under the single category of '*spodaious*' in Aristotle's definition of 'tragedy' (*Poetics*: VI, 2). However, this linkage is not one of necessity. The correct scholarly tendency is to expand the use of 'tragedy' to include modernist fictional worlds that, while promoting a serious mood, avoid the sublime mode, albeit its mode being higher than usual; e.g., Georg Büchner's *Woyzeck* and Orson Welles film *Citizen Kane*. The lower mode probably reflects a realistic tendency.

Similar considerations apply to comedy: the lowly mode is traditionally combined with the comic mood; e.g., in his definition of comedy Aristotle asserts 'Comedy is ... an imitation of characters of *a lower type*, — not, however, in the full sense of the word bad, the *Ludicrous* being merely a subdivision of the ugly. It consists in some defect or ugliness which is not painful or destructive' (*ibid.*: V, 1; my italics). He thus suggests that comedy should combine lowly characterization, which is a specific kind of mode, with a comic equivalent of the tragic *hamartia*, the 'ludicrous', which reflects a comic mood. However, this linkage too is not one of necessity. The correct scholarly tendency is indeed to expand the use of 'comedy' to include later fictional worlds that, while promoting a comic mood, avoid the lowly mode — with the latter still remaining lower than usual; e.g., Shakespearean and cinematic comedies.

Nonetheless, these changes do not affect the fundamental correspondences between lofty mode and serious mood, and between lowly mode and comic mood. I suggest that these correspondences should be seen as the standard on the grounds of which departures are perceived. Furthermore, these correspondences reflect the dominant function of mood.

Menander's *The Arbitration*

In this fragmentary play-script, Charisios' wife Pamphile has given birth to a baby after only five months of marriage. She had been raped at a festival and kept the incident secret. The marriage of this would-be loving couple thus faces collapse. He drowns his sorrows in wine and women; and she, in order to safeguard the baby's future, deserts him leaving his father's ring on the baby's cradle. Habrotonon, the harp-girl (a high-class servant), disentangles the knot: she feigns being the raped girl and, wearing the baby's father's ring (after it has been recognized by the servant Onesimos as belonging to his master), she brings the baby to Charisios. He admits to having raped her and being the child's father. She then reveals that, unknowingly, he had actually raped the maiden whom he eventually wedded, which brings about the final reconciliation of the unhappy couple.

In this narrative, two people become entangled because of a blunder. As a consequence, husband and wife, who are expected to care for one another, engage in needless animosity. The peripeteia is brought about by Habrotonon, who disentangles the situation, while probably gratifying the spectators' archetypal expectations for the happiness of these relatively positive characters, and possibly producing catharsis. I note that in contrast to Aristophanes' play-scripts (Old Comedy), there is no satiric intent but only the lighthearted mood that characterizes New Comedy.

Euripides' *Ion* and New Comedy

In contrast to B.M.W. Knox, who perceives Euripides' *Ion* as the first European comedy (1979), Segal sees this play-script only as a significant step *toward* New Comedy (pp. 126–33). Indeed this narrative too features a rape, an abandoned baby, a matrimonial problem, an anagnorisis and a happy end; a theme which is not only shared by Menander's *The Arbitration*, but is also a recurrent theme in several of his comedies.

Princess Creusa is violated by Apollo. She becomes pregnant and, when the baby is born, she abandons him where she was raped. She is then given to Xuthus in matrimony. Xuthus is the grandson of Zeus, and because of the lack of an heir, despite being a foreigner to Athens, he becomes the king of the polis. After many years of looking for her son, Creusa and Xuthus arrive in Delphi. She meets Ion, who is a chaste youngster in the service of Apollo's shrine. A prophetess had adopted and raised him. According to a prophesy, Xuthus recognizes him as his own son; but, while trying to find out who is the mother, Creusa attempts to murder Ion and fails, and Ion too tries to murder Creusa and fails. Eventually, Athena dispels the mystery: Creusa is the mother of Ion. Apollo himself had been ashamed to reveal the truth. Creusa prefers not to share the secret with Xuthus. The ending is thus happy, but with a critical innuendo in regard to Apollo.

I assume that Segal is aware that the predominant mood of *Ion* is serious/sublime, not to mention Euripides' proclivity to dramatize myths that expose the non-divine nature of the gods (cf. Rozik, 2009: 259–67). Nonetheless, on the grounds of the shared theme and happy ending, he wrongly concludes that this play-script was a forerunner of the new breed of comedy (p. 152). What he should have concluded, rather, is that these elements can be shared by comedy and tragedy, as Aristotle himself does, and that their specific differences lie in their respective moods.

Mixing moods

Horace's typical position is that moods should not be mixed: 'A comic subject is not susceptible of treatment in a tragic style [mood], and similarly the banquet of Thyestes cannot be fitly described in the strains of everyday life or in those that approach the tone [mood] of comedy. Let each of these styles be kept for the role properly allotted to it' (p. 82). This is in line with Horace's tendency to prescribe harmony in every respect. Indeed, both classical and classicist drama opted for purity of mood; e.g., the serious mood of Jean Racine's *Phèdre* and the comic mood of Molière's *The Trickeries of Scapin* (my translation; see CHAPTER 10). Aristotle does not even envisage the possible mixture of moods. Nonetheless, such a mixture is quite common practice, even in some of the most significant tragedies ever created; e.g., the porter scene in *Macbeth*, and the *gracioso* (Clarín) in Calderón's *Life is a Dream* (cf. Lope, 1965: 17, p. 65 & Dryden: 143), not to mention modern and postmodern drama. In fact, such a mixture is typical of comedy from its earlier specimens; e.g., in Menander's *The Arbitration*, only the existence of a cook, Karion attests to its comic element.

There are two basic kinds of mixture:

(A) The linear: the serious and comic moods are employed in linear succession, by interactive characters and 'buffoons' or, rather, 'fools' (in a generic sense) respectively, to depict the same fictional situations from contrasting viewpoints; e.g., Sganarelle in Molière's *Don Juan*. In such a case, the humorous mood does not hinder the serious mood, and may even highlight it (comic relief), and save it from becoming ridiculous due to sheer exaggeration.

Following Menander, the tradition of comedy no longer features a unity of comic mood. It is quite clear that the main action is serious in nature; e.g., the obstruction of the youngsters' love in many a comedy. The comic mood is thus promoted by special characters, such as the cook and the parasite, which actually create a mixture of moods. Nonetheless, in such a mixture, moods do not counteract each other: whereas in a predominantly tragic fictional world the comic mood produces what is called 'comic relief'; in a predominantly comic world, as shown in the following chapter, the serious mood feeds the anxiety that constitutes the raw material of both comic laughter and holistic catharsis (in contrast to Segal, who tries to find a tragic touch in most comedies; e.g., pp. 317 & 354). For such a mixture, in both comedy and tragedy, the question is: which mood is the dominant component?

(B) The juxtaposed: the laughter devices are imposed on an extremely serious theme, which contrasts the spectators' associations and sensibilities in regard to such a theme. In such a case, the comic mood aims at subverting the serious attitude of the audience — thus creating a grotesque mood; e.g., the theme of death in both Eugène Ionesco's *Exit the King* and Samuel Beckett's *Happy Days* (see CHAPTER 8 — cf. the notion of 'dark comedy' in Styan: 1968).

The grotesque mood reveals that the serious associations attached to a certain theme are vital and basic components of its distinct effect. By implication, it also reveals that not only discrepancy but also agreement on this level is a crucial factor in determining the resulting effect on the audience. That this factor is revealed only in cases of contrast should not conceal the fact that it also operates in cases of agreement; e.g., tragedy treats grave themes seriously and comedy treats less significant themes lightheartedly. Since these indicate the existence of spontaneous models of harmony on the level of mood in the spectators' minds, it is clear that the grotesque mood contrasts them.

The existence of spontaneous models of harmony in the spectators' minds seems to support Olson's view that '[i]t is not the events by themselves which are matter for gravity or levity: it is the view taken of them' (p. 35). Nonetheless, although this might be true for real life, in comedy character and situations are designed purposefully for matching or contrasting the above-mentioned models. In other words, in comedy there is something objective in the spectator's field of perception.

Shakespeare's *Romeo and Juliet* reveals that even in the very same fictional world a linear transition from a comic to a serious mood is possible. While the comic mood of the beginning, which verges on the farcical, characterizes the elderly parents of both Romeo and Juliet, this mood is subsequently replaced by the extremely serious mood that prevails toward the extremely sad ending (Rozik: 2009). This ending probably produced a sense of absurdity in the synchronic audience, which the eventual reconciliation of the families may hardly have compensated.

The comic mood opposes the serious mood, and takes it as its standard, from which it departs. Mode and mood are different aspects of the modality of a fictional world and, in determining the generic nature of a fictional world, mood subordinates mode. Comedy is thus characterized by the comic mood, regardless of mode.

Comic Laughter   2

The potential effects of the comic mood range from a feeling of contentment, through gentle smiling, and up to belly laughter. Nevertheless, the aim of producing laughter does not characterize comedy alone. As we shall see below, there are additional genres that also aim at producing it such as satiric and grotesque drama (see CHAPTER 8). The aim of this chapter is to determine the kind of laughter that characterizes the comic mood and thus comedy.

Many attempts have been made to determine the causes of laughter — with the main theories being those of Hazlitt's 'incongruity' and Bergson's 'mechanical inelasticity' — albeit none should be seen as providing a definitive answer due to not having addressed the nature of the psychical mechanism of laughter and its function in the economy of the psyche. In general, between authorial design and actual laughter there is a black box that theory is expected to explain. In this respect, I believe, the psychoanalytic school has provided valuable insights.

Hazlitt's 'incongruity'

The principle of 'incongruity' was first suggested by Arthur Schopenhauer in *The World as Will and Idea*, first published in 1818. Probably quite in parallel, in his introductory lecture to his *Lectures on the English Comic Writers* (1819) Hazlitt suggests that '[m]an is the only animal that laughs and weeps; for he is the only animal that is struck with the difference between what things are, and what they ought to be' (p. 9). Moreover, '[t]he essence of the laughable . . . is the incongruous, the disconnecting one idea from another, or the jostling of one feeling against another' (p. 12).

Hazlitt's theory poses a severe problem: not only comedy is incongruous, but tragedy too is basically so; e.g., in Sophocles, *Oedipus the King*, killing a father and marrying a mother. Aristotle even claims that 'a perfect tragedy should . . . imitate actions which excite fear and pity' (*Poetics*: XIII, 2), which he perceives as a precondition for catharsis. In his view, this is best achieved when suffering is inflicted on 'those who are near or dear to one another — if, for example, a brother kills, or intends to kill, a brother, a son his father, a mother her son, a son his mother, . . . these are the situations to be looked for by the poet' (*ibid.*: XIV, 4); namely, when characters who are supposed to care for and even love one another, inflict severe suffering or even death on one another. Such an action is highly incongruous and probably conveys a deep sense of absurdity in being perceived as contrary to human nature (Corneille: 219). Indeed, whereas harm inflicted upon enemies is rational, if inflicted upon kin it is inherently irrational and producing anxiety — thus probably adding to the anxiety that the spectators usually harbor prior to exposing themselves to a tragic fictional world. This condition is satisfied by all archetypal structures, including Aristotle's tragedies of the first and second ranks, and comedy; e.g., a father who precludes the happiness of his children in Molière's comedies.

Following Aristotle, Corrigan discards 'incongruity' as the only explanation of laughter. He correctly observes that 'a terrible act committed by a character from which we expect love (hence, an incongruous act), is the most effective way of producing a tragic effect' (p. 6). Therefore, laughter cannot be explained 'in the simple terms of incongruity' (*ibid.*; cf. Olson: 9–10). However, this does not contradict the fact that a sense of incongruity is presupposed by laughter. The difficulty lies in determining the factor that makes the difference.

Hazlitt is aware that incongruity explains not only laughing but also weeping. Indeed, in regard to incongruity, he correlates laughing and weeping (p. 9): 'We weep at what thwarts or exceeds our desires in serious matters; we laugh at what only disappoints our expectations in trifles. We shed tears from sympathy with real and necessary distress; as we burst into laughter from want of sympathy with that which is unreasonable and unnecessary' (*ibid.*). This passage implies that for Hazlitt too incongruity alone cannot be the cause of laughter. He adds, therefore, that '[t]he follies and absurdities that men commit, or the odd incidents that befall them, afford us amusement from the very rejection of these false claims upon our sympathy, and end in laughter' (*ibid.*). In other words, in his view, it is the combination of both incongruity and lack of sympathy (the additional factor) that explains laughter. The addition of the latter should be seen as an improvement on Aristotle's definition of the 'ludicrous' as a 'defect or ugliness that is not painful or destructive' (*Poetics*: V. 1).

Hazlitt adds: '[l]aughter may be defined to be the . . . convulsive and involuntary movement, occasioned by mere surprise or contrast (in the absence of any more serious emotion), before it has time to reconcile its belief to contradictory appearances' (p. 10). Furthermore, 'the ludicrous, or comic, is the unexpected loosening or relaxing this stress below its usual pitch of intensity, by such an abrupt transposition of the order of our ideas, as taking the mind unawares throws it off its guard, startles it into a lively sense of pleasure, and leaves no time nor inclination for painful reflections' (p. 12). 'Surprise' is thus an additional ingredient to Hazlitt's formula. It should be noted that Hazlitt employs 'incongruity' and 'absurdity' as synonymous terms; e.g., 'We laugh at absurdity; we laugh at deformity' (p. 13).

Théophile Gautier suggests a similar thesis in claiming that what makes us laugh is the absurd realized in concrete shape, a 'palpable absurdity' (Bergson: 177). Bergson rejects this view: 'Gautier said that the comic in its extreme form was the *logic of the absurd*. More than one theory of laughter revolves around such an idea. Every comic effect, it is said, implies contradiction in some of its aspects' (*ibid.*, my italics; cf. Sypher: 197). Nonetheless, it is difficult to accept that the spontaneous nature of laughter presupposes a previous logical operation. Olson too ponders both the theories of 'incongruity' (including 'absurdity') and rejects them on similar grounds:

> all the terms expressing purely *logical* relations — such as "incongruity," "inappropriateness," "discrepancy," "contradiction," "paradox," and the like . . . are by themselves unsatisfactory. They are ambivalent, or rather multivalent, for they may be involved as much in one emotion as another. . . . A child wearing a man's hat is an instance of incongruity, and may amuse us. But children in William Golding's *Lord of the Flies* also supply instances of the same incongruity between the childish and the adult, and horrify us. For that matter, one and the same incongruity . . . may amuse or horrify you, depending on the circumstances, and your view on the matter. Indeed, the universe is full of incongruities, and if this theory is true, we should never stop laughing. (1968: 9–10)

This logical implication does not necessarily concern Hazlitt's 'incongruity', if we assume that spontaneous laughter presupposes the existence of models of congruous behavior in the spectator's mind. Perhaps congruity should be viewed as an aesthetic category, synonymous with 'disharmony', in the spirit of Martin Esslin who mentions that 'absurd' originally meant 'out of harmony' in a musical context (p. xix). This explanation makes more sense, because it enables the linking of laughter to models of harmony and disharmony in the spectators' minds.

Bergson quite correctly detects the problem of seeing absurdity as the sole cause of laughter in Gautier's theory: 'absurdity, when met with in the comic, is not absurdity *in general*. It is an absurdity of a definite kind. It does not create the comic; rather, we might say that the comic infuses into it its own particular essence. It is not a cause but an effect — an effect of a very special kind, which reflects the special nature of its cause [the mechanical]' (Bergson: 178). Indeed, both Hazlitt and Gautier ignore the existence of tragic absurdity. Absurdity can cause laughter, but it does not follow that all absurdity is potentially comic. Nonetheless, although Bergson's criticism is basically correct, like Hazlitt's theory his own principle of 'mechanical inelasticity' alone cannot explain laughter for the very same reason: the existence of tragic inelasticity.

Bergson's 'mechanical inelasticity'

Henri Bergson advances three basic observations on laughter: (a) 'The comic does not exist outside the pale of what is strictly *human*. A landscape may be beautiful, charming and sublime, or insignificant and ugly; it will never be laughable' (p. 62). This observation is problematic because even animals, which are basically a-modal, can be ludicrous if human expressions or attitudes are detected in them. This can be solved by widening the application of 'strictly human'. (b) Laughter is usually accompanied by '*the absence of feeling*' (p. 63). This observation should be understood in the context of Aristotle's dictum that 'the *Ludicrous* [is] merely a subdivision of the ugly. It consists in some defect or ugliness which is not painful or destructive' (*Poetics*: V, 1). It is noteworthy that whereas Bergson speaks in terms of 'feeling', Aristotle restricts his remark to pain. The inclusion of *all* feelings is indeed problematic. As shown below, scholars have correctly offered examples to the contrary. And (c) laughter is a social phenomenon: 'You would hardly appreciate the comic if you felt yourself isolated from others. Laughter appears to stand in need of an echo. . . . Our laughter is always the laughter of a group' (p. 64). This observation too is problematic because people also laugh when alone, without contradicting the possible social function of laughter.

In Bergson's view, laughter is caused by '*[s]omething mechanical encrusted on the living*' (p. 84); and '*[t]he attitudes, gestures and move-*

ments of the human body are laughable in exact proportion as that body reminds us of a mere machine' (p. 79). Moreover, '[w]e laugh every time a person gives us the impression of being a thing' (p. 97). These claims presuppose that '[w]hat life and society require of each of us is a constantly alert attention that discerns the outlines of the present situation, together with a certain elasticity of mind and body to enable us to adapt ourselves in consequence. *Tension* and *elasticity* are two forces, mutually complementary, which life brings into play' (p. 72). In other words, social life requires constant alertness and adaptation to changing circumstances. 'Society will therefore be suspicious of all *inelasticity* of character' (p. 73). Laughter is thus a reaction to 'lack of elasticity' (p. 66). Bergson employs various synonyms of this term; e.g., 'rigidity' (*ibid.*), 'mechanical inelasticity' (p. 67) 'inelasticity' and 'automatism' (p. 76).

Since society expects adaptability, Bergson adds: '[t]his rigidity is the comic, and laughter is its corrective' (p. 74) or, rather, its 'penalty' (p. 73). In this sense, laughter is essentially a social device, whose aim is to foster alertness and adaptability; i.e., the optimal functioning of the individual — with the opposite being absentmindedness (cf. p. 68). 'Laughter must be . . . a *sort of social gesture*' (p. 73).

One of Bergson's examples of rigidity is when Dorine tells Orgon about the illness of his wife Elmire, and Orgon inattentively and repeatedly asks 'Et Tartuffe?' (And Tartuffe?) (I, iv), (cf. Bergson: 108). He is absorbed in his admiration of Tartuffe to such a degree that he is incapable of giving attention to his wife's health, as if operated by a spring — thus recalling the mechanism of the Jack-in-the-box. Inelasticity can also be found in the use of language; e.g., when the figurative sense of a word is taken literally (cf. *ibid.*: 135).

This theory raises several problems:

(A) Bergson reduces all cases of laughter to the single principle of 'mechanical inelasticity', which contrasts the intuition that there are additional causes for laughter. In this sense, J. L. Styan is probably correct in observing, that '[l]aughter, a recurring and therefore an evidently important ingredient [of comedy], seems to arise from a great variety of sources' (1968: 38) In this respect, lack of elasticity can be regarded as a particular kind of incongruity; i.e., it does not contradict Hazlitt's principle.

(B) Bergson ignores the fact that a lack of elasticity also characterizes tragedy; e.g., in Sophocles' *Antigone* the inflexibility of both Antigone and Creon, which explains their eventual failures and sufferings, does not trigger laughter at all.

(C) Bergson's contention that 'laughter has no greater foe than emotion' (p. 63); i.e., that laughter combines mechanical inelasticity and a lack of emotion, does not solve the problem either. In response to Bergson's claim that 'laughter is incompatible with emotion . . . it leaves *our* emotions unaffected' (p. 150; my italics), Styan correctly remarks: 'we know well enough from experience, if not from countless moments on the comic stage, that we *do* have the faculty of laughing and feeling at one and the same time' (1968: 42).

Bergson's contention echoes Aristotle's 'which is not painful'. However, the attribution of a lack of pain to a character does not mean 'lack of emotion' in the audience. Corrigan observes that 'The two key ideas in this [Aristotelian] definition [of comedy] are *the Ludicrous* and *the absence of pain*; and although it is clear from what follows that Aristotle is more concerned with their tragic contrasts — the serious and the painful — he does establish two fundamental boundaries of the comic' (Corrigan: 4–5). Indeed, both 'laughter' and 'absence of pain' are implied in the notion of 'ludicrous'. Slapstick 'remains funny only so long as it is quite clear that no real pain [for the slapped character] is involved' (*ibid.*: 7). In other words, only the spectator's intuition that a character's inelasticity does not involve pain, may explain the difference. Moreover, lack of pain does not preclude other emotions.

(D) Bergson disregards the fact that *laughter is basically not a punishment or corrective per se but healthy and pleasurable*. This is clear in comedy, as opposed to satiric laughter, and corroborated by the laughter of babies and parents' laughter at the antics of their babies. Therefore, it is sensible to suggest that, since laughter indicates a kind of imperfection or failure, it can also be employed as a corrective. It follows that laughter is fundamentally a healthy psychical phenomenon and only derivatively can it be considered a socially-corrective. It is because of being a psychical phenomenon that it can be employed as a social one. It should be stressed that this difference suits the distinction between comedy and satire. Bergson does not make such a distinction.

(E) Bergson also ignores the fact that people not only laugh *at* the object of laughter, but also *with* the agent of laughter such as the wit and the fool, who either pretend malfunction or expose the malfunction of their butt; e.g., in Molière's *L'Amour Médicin*, Clitandre, who pretends to be a doctor, in attending Sganarelle's daughter, by checking her father's pulse, declares 'Your daughter is very ill!' (cf. Bergson: 131).

Bergson's claim regarding automatism might be basically sound, and probably explains a variety of laughter phenomena. Nonetheless, his theory rather regards the set of objective phenomena that can elicit laughter, while ignoring, like Hazlitt, the nature of the psychical mechanism of laughter. Authors of comedy do possess a kind of technological knowledge of the events that may trigger laughter. To be successful, an author of comedy probably does not need more than that. It is this technological aspect that is captured by Bergson. Nevertheless, the task of a theory of laughter is to explain the psychical mechanism itself. It is the intention of the following sections to discuss its nature.

Laughter, failure and foolishness

Both Hazlitt and Bergson focus on the objective cues that trigger laughter, but ignore the psychical mechanism that actually enables such an effect. It can be safely assumed that a spectator could not react by laughter without presupposing such a mechanism. We should see a comedy as an authorial macro-act whose optional purpose is to trigger the psychical mechanism of comic laughter.

When considering laughter, my persistent personal association is that of the act of a clown in a performance by the Moscow circus, which made me laugh more than I have ever laughed in my whole life, to the verge of breathlessness. The act was very simple: the clown, with his typical white face, baggy trousers and giant shoes, tried to climb over the very low fence encircling the circus arena. In his attempts to cross it, he performed an endless series of variations, each time trying out a different idea and always ending in failure. Laughter was intensified perhaps by the clown's blank face and/or by the mere accumulation of failures. This was pure laughter, with almost no characterization or narrative in the usual sense. The characterization was just 'clown' and 'serious', and the bare narrative merely a series of attempts to cross the hurdle, the repeated failures until the last one, and the frustrated clown's exit.

The possible explanations are various. In Freud's view, 'we laugh at the clown's movements [because] they seem to us extravagant and inexpedient. We are laughing at an expenditure that is too large' (1989: 235). He claims that for this effect the spectators are the standard (*ibid.*: 236), and that 'our laughter expresses a pleasurable sense of the superiority which we feel in relation to [the clown]' (*ibid.*: 256). The answer to the question of why spectators laughed at the clown's efforts could also be sensibly explained in terms of 'mechanical inelasticity', despite the clown's constantly different attempts; and even better in terms of 'incongruity' between end and means. In other words, Freud's explanation can be reduced to the principle of 'incongruity'. In contrast, I suggest that *the key reason for this ever increasing laughter was the clown's repeated fail-*

ures and their accumulative effect, which revealed his foolishness or, rather, clumsiness — with the latter being the physical counterpart of stupidity. It should be noted that it was clear that the clown only pretended failure; i.e., the spectator laughed not at him, but with him.

In the context of the theory of action, failure is a performative category. Only an act/action of a character that reflects the definite intention to change a state of affairs, e.g., to cross the fence, and possible purposes beyond it, can be said to succeed or fail. This implies that a comic character should be defined as ludicrous not on the level of characterization, but on the level of his actions; i.e., laughter is a reaction to a 'foolish action' (Hazlitt: 9). For example, Harpagon is a miser; but a miser can also be a serious and even suffering character (e.g., Balzac's M. Grandet in *Eugénie Grandet*). In other words, stinginess is not ludicrous in itself, but only inasmuch it causes the character to fail foolishly; e.g., when Harpagon is trying to find out whether or not La Flèche has stolen anything:

> *La Flèche*: Very well! I am going.
> *Harpagon*: Wait: you are not taking anything away with you?
> *La Flèche*: What should I take from you?
> *Harpagon*: I do not know until I look. Show me your hands?
> *La Flèche*: Here they are.
> *Harpagon*: The others.
> *La Flèche*: The others?
> *Harpagon*: Yes.
> *La Flèche*: Here they are.
> *Harpagon*: (*pointing to the breeches of* La Flèche). Have you put nothing in there?
> *La Flèche*: Look for yourself! (I, iii)

Harpagon asks La Flèche to show him his hands, which he does. Then, he asks him to show the other hands, which suggests that he has more than one pair of hands and that it is a foolish request. This foolish action, in addition to his obsessive stinginess, indicates Harpagon's irrational suspicious nature.

Indeed, there is an inherent causal connection between failure and laughter. However, in regard to incongruity and mechanical inelasticity, tragic characters usually fail too; e.g., Oedipus fails in his endeavor to avoid his fate. Therefore, there must be something in a comic failure that channels the spectator to perceive it differently. It is thus sensible to suggest that in contrast to the serious failure that involves reasoning,

1 Harpagon searching La Flèche's trousers, in the Khan Theatre *The Miser*.
Photo: Gadi Dagon. Courtesy of the Jerusalem Khan Theatre.

painful consequences and responsibility, the humorous failure is characterized by foolishness and/or clumsiness, painless consequences and lack of responsibility.

Whereas foolish failure is possibly due to inelasticity or incongruity, other reasons may also be valid. In *The Trickeries of Scapin*, Scapin persuades Géronte to hide in a sack under the pretence that Zerbinette's brother is about to beat him up. Scapin then impersonates the brother, including his Gasconian accent, and repeatedly slaps the sack with a stick (III, ii). Géronte behaves neither incongruently nor mechanically, but merely foolishly.

A fool is a person who acts unwisely or imprudently, and this applies also but not only to an absent-minded person. Absent-mindedness, the chief laughable trait for Bergson, is only a particular instance of foolishness. 'Foolish failure' is neither the only factor that explains laughter, nor the only trigger of laughter, but probably offers a better explanation than those given previously.

2 Géronte in the sack, in the Khan Theatre *The Trickeries of Scapin.*
Photo: Gadi Dagon. Courtesy of the Jerusalem Khan Theatre.

There are three basic ways of producing laughter: first: by a ludicrous character that acts foolishly/clumsily; second, by exposing the propensity of a character to act foolishly/clumsily; and third, by pretending a foolish/clumsy failure. When people perceive that a foolish/clumsy act is done on purpose, it usually produces not only laughter but also astonishment and even admiration. Whereas spectators laugh *at* a ludicrous character in its typical failure, they laugh *with* the fool in his ability to expose or pretend failure.

Weitz suggests that 'a human need to take the world *playfully* lies at the heart of comedy's predilection for humour and upbeat endings. . . . [comedy] takes the world in a particular playful fashion' (p. 18; my italics; cf. his 'amusement', p. 63). This is a correct insight under three conditions: (a) that 'playful' is taken not in the sense of children's attitude to play, which, as I have suggested elsewhere, fulfils a very serious thinking function (Rozik, 2002: 270–92), but in the sense of 'humorous' and 'done for fun'; (b) that the psychical nature of 'amusement' and its mechanism are explained; and (c) that 'playful' is not attributed to all the works usually perceived under 'comedy', but is circumscribed to 'comedy' in the restricted sense of this study.

To conclude, whereas the principle of 'foolish failure' explains the role of 'automatism', 'incongruity' and 'absurdity' due to their causing particular kinds of failure, the opposite is not the case: neither incongruity/absurdity nor automatism fully explains laughter. Serious drama too deals with failure, but comic failure is foolish. Foolish failure is comic in the sense of promoting the comic mood. As we shall see below, foolish failure is not perceived as causing pain, while possibly producing both anxiety and catharsis.

Laughter, anxiety and catharsis

Neither Hazlitt's nor Bergson's approaches aim at explaining the psychical mechanism of laughter and its function in the psyche. In this respect, I believe that the psychoanalytic school has made a substantial contribution.

In Grotjahn's view, 'Freud's thesis is simple and straightforward: Laughter occurs when repressing energy is freed from its static function of keeping something forbidden under repression and away from consciousness' (p. 270). Laughter is thus explained by the simple release of accumulated tension through the lifting of a cultural inhibition. It is noteworthy that 'tension' is a euphemism for 'anxiety'. However, an inhibition is a mechanism that is meant to prevent the activation of a shameful or forbidden drive (taboo) and the anxiety involved in such a possible behavior. Assumedly, comedy addresses shameful drives, because there is probably nothing more dreadful than being ridiculous and a great deal of psychical energy is invested in preventing such an experience. An inhibition is also imposed on laughter in the wrong places; e.g., laughing at a funeral. The problem is that the confrontation with a lifted inhibition on stage most probably produces additional anxiety to the diffuse anxiety that the spectator harbors prior to experiencing a comedy; i.e., the lifting of an inhibition, which is a serious matter, cannot be cathartic in itself. This is very conspicuous when laughter is produced by an action or a repartee that contravenes a tacit prohibition; e.g., in Lenny Bruce's stand-up comedy. It follows that the psychoanalytic school fails to explain the transition from augmented anxiety to its pleasant release, which is usually termed 'catharsis'.

It can be assumed that the actions of a comic character embody the lifting of an inhibition, which is perceived as a foolish failure, and which is shameful in nature. By the same token such actions reveal the existence of such an inhibition in the spectators' psyches. However, a comic character is not meant to comply with such an inhibition. In fact, it is designed to embody what the spectators intend to preclude. The latter are thus expected to see this embodiment as unwished for themselves, while unconsciously identifying with the inhibited drive; i.e., the lifting of an inhibition by a character assumedly produces anxiety in the spectators due to their extreme caution in preventing any confrontation with inhibited drives. Only the intuition that this is done in a humorous spirit, under the circumstances of the social permit that is granted by the theatre's communal experience, is capable of discharging such an accumulated anxiety.

Consequently, it is highly plausible that comic laughter too is a cathartic mechanism, similar to Aristotle's catharsis (henceforth: 'holistic catharsis'), which presupposes and is fueled by the anxiety produced by confrontation with lifted inhibitions. In this respect; the anxiety elicited by confrontation with inhibited shameful drives is not only a precondition for holistic catharsis in either tragedy or comedy (cf. 'liberation of tensions' in Freud, 1990: 141), but also for laughter, which is a response to even a single act. I thus suggest that comic laughter, which is cathartic in nature, happens when the lifting of an inhibition, which is reflected in a foolish failure, is intuitively perceived as reflecting a sudden change from a serious to a comic mood. In other words, anxiety is produced by the prospect of a character's ludicrous failure, and laughter by the mere signaling that this is treated humorously.

Whereas comedy is built upon the spectators' all too human fear of failure, which might expose them as stupid and/or clumsy, the norms that determine what is stupid and clumsy are culturally-dependent. Therefore, the understanding of comedy presupposes knowledge of the synchronic norms of behavior.

Olson suggests that laughter 'is a relaxation, or as Aristotle would say, a *katastasis*, of *concern* due to a manifest absurdity of the grounds of concern' (p. 16; my italics; cf. p. 36). Moreover, 'this [*katastasis*] is a pleasant emotion, for concern of any kind induces *tension*; [and] the relaxation of concern involves, as Aristotle would say, the settling of the soul into its natural or normal condition, which is always pleasant' (*ibid.*: 16; my italics). This 'normal condition' is:

a pleasant, or rather a euphoric condition of freedom from desires and emotions which move men to action, and one in which we [are] inclined to take nothing seriously and to be gay about everything. The *transition* to this state [is] effected through a special kind of relaxation of concern: a *katastasis* . . . of concern through the annihilation of the concern itself — not by the substitution for desire of its contrary, aversion, nor by the replacement, say, of fear, by the contrary emotion of hope, which is also serious, but by the conversion of the grounds of concern into absolute nothing. (*ibid.*: 25; cf. Styan, 1968: 42)

Olson's thesis is basically sound. Nonetheless, its formulation raises several questions: (a) '*katastasis*' denotes the release of 'tension' or 'concern', with both being euphemisms for 'anxiety', which in turn is too a euphemism for 'fear'. Therefore, there is every reason to see 'katastasis' as a synonym of 'catharsis' — with no reason for suggesting a new term; and (b) although Olson probably had in mind 'homoeostasis, it is difficult to say what is the natural or normal condition of the soul. It is clear, nonetheless, that the process of catharsis is pleasant in itself and of social significance, especially if it is assumed that it sweeps away the excess anxiety, which is produced by merely living, especially under inhibitions of all kinds, and which hinder the normal function of the individual. It is catharsis that explains Olson's sense of freedom. This implies, in contrast to Bergson, that laughter can be employed not only as a social corrective, but fundamentally as a pleasant cathartic means, which is the hallmark of comedy.

If laughter is indeed nourished by anxiety, then it must be triggered in two steps, which can only be separated analytically: (a) the presentation of an action that increases anxiety; and (b) the total release of accumulated anxiety. In other words, there is a serious phase, the loading of additional anxiety, which is prior to laughter, and a cathartic phase; i.e., in order for something to be laughable it must be basically serious. As suggested above, the abrupt transition from the attitude to one mood to another is a necessary condition for laughter.

These qualifications, however, do not entail that there is no difference between holistic catharsis and comic laughter. Whereas the former is supposed to happen when experiencing an entire fictional world, i.e., it is holistic in nature; the latter *is a reaction to a shorter unit, even to single act, including a single speech act.* Laughter is thus essentially episodic. Benjamin Lehmann correctly observes that 'though we laugh at actions and utterances in comedy, we do not laugh at the comedy as a whole' (p. 164). Neither the entanglement nor the dénouement is related to laughter. A comedy may end in laughter, yet this is not necessarily holistic catharsis. Being cathartic on different structural levels, these principles can combine in a single comic work. Furthermore, the entanglement that is serious by definition fuels tension for both comic laughter and holistic catharsis. Nonetheless, assumedly, they may even counteract one another: a frequent release of tension through laughter may thwart the intensity and pleasure of holistic catharsis, for catharsis is a single biologically pre-programmed outlet and anxiety is not an unlimited resource.

Gustave Lanson suggests that a fictional action can be 'only a thread to link comic situations, a framework for witty scenes' (p. 389). In other words, a set of comic scenes can be produced without an overarching action that produces holistic catharsis; e.g., a sketch comedy (see CHAPTER 7). It follows that, in principle, holistic catharsis and cathartic comic laughter are different and mutually independent experiences, reflecting different principles that, assumedly, operate the very same psychical mechanism.

Laughter, pain and pity

In light of the above conclusion, it is sensible to reconsider the claim that lack of pain is a pre-condition of laughter, based on Aristotle's observation that the ludicrous 'consists in some defect or ugliness which is not painful or destructive' (*Poetics*: V, 1). It would appear that Aristotle's observation is correct; e.g., whereas a person skidding on a banana peel (a kind of clumsiness) causes laughter, provided that pain is not taken into account, the moment it is perceived that a leg has been broken, laughter usually ceases. It is possible, therefore, that the prevalent humorous mood signals that whatever happens on stage is not of painful consequence for the character — thus channeling the spectators' responses to possible laughter. Similarly, the serious mood probably signals possible harmful consequences — thus channeling their responses to possible concern and even tears. Nonetheless, it should be taken into account that under certain circumstances the spectator is expected to laugh at the suffering of a ludicrous character; e.g., George Dandin's expressions of misery and frustration in Molière's *George Dandin*.

This problem requires a clear distinction between the possible pain of a character and the attitude of the spectator to its pain. It is possible that foolish behavior involves pain, but in order to trigger laughter foolish behavior should preclude pity (cf. Hazlitt's notion of 'sympathy': p. 9). Aristotle claims that tragedy should 'excite pity and fear . . . for pity is aroused by unmerited misfortune, [and] fear by the misfortune of a man like ourselves' (*Poetics*: XIII, 1–2). It is possible, therefore, that a foolish failure is somehow perceived as a merited misfortune; e.g., George Dandin. The fact is that the moment the receiver is aware that sliding on a banana peel involves unmerited pain, 'pity' is elicited. In addition, due to his foolishness, a ludicrous character is probably neither aware of the painful consequences of his acts, nor of his own foolishness — thus precluding the spectator's pity. In other words, lack of pity too, in addition to anxiety, and under conditions of sudden transition to a humorous mood, is a factor in producing comic laughter. In contrast to Bergson, it is not a lack of emotions that characterizes comic laughter, but only a lack of pity.

To conclude, the conditions for comic laughter are: a foolish failure, additional anxiety, a lack of pity and an indication of a sudden transition to a comic mood.

Laughing and crying

There is a parallel and opposite outlet that can be triggered through short units, and is also cathartic: crying. Serious drama, melodrama in particular, may combine both kinds of cathartic outlets: holistic catharsis and episodic crying. Olson contends that '[t]he human body tends to *cathart* any excessive emotion by certain physical outlets such as laughter and weeping. Since these outlets are few, and the emotions many, an ambiguity ensues . . . Thus weeping, for instance, can betoken extreme joy as well as extreme grief' (p. 11; my italics).

In principle, a frequent release of tension through weeping too may counteract the intensity and pleasure of holistic catharsis, because anxiety is not an unlimited resource; e.g., Douglas Jerrold's *Black-Ey'd Susan* and Brian Friel's *Dancing at Lughnasa*. A fictional world may end in tears, but this is not holistic catharsis.

Holistic catharsis and either laughter or weeping are mutually independent. This is corroborated by absurdist structures, whose final accords, which contrast the archetypal expectations of the audience, are not affected by episodic laughter or crying. From the viewpoint of the opposition laughter-tears, comedy is the opposite not of tragedy but of melodrama.

Neither laughter nor crying is a necessary response to comedy or tragedy respectively. First, laughing and crying are psychical mechanisms, biologically-determined and culturally-conditioned, which are also operated in real life; second, as in real life, these mechanisms can be triggered by different causes; and third, there are comedies that do not promote laughter and tragedies that do not promote crying. *Just as the humorous mood should not be reduced solely to laughter* (Olson: 64), *the serious mood should not be reduced solely to crying.* Fundamentally, comedy satisfies by merely inducing its typical comic mood.

It follows that there are three distinct pleasurable outlets of anxiety: laughter, crying and holistic catharsis, and that their activation is the result of an author's intentional manipulation of an audience into these preprogrammed outlets of anxiety (cf. Olson: 11). It can be conjectured, therefore, that if human beings had been created with more, less or different outlets of anxiety, the generic categorization would also have been different.

Although the cathartic mechanisms of laughter and crying are not fully understood, their cathartic function is self-evident. Both the theoretical tradition and the iconic/fictional practice of millennia reflect a knowledge of these psychical mechanisms that is more technological than scientific. Such knowledge relates to how a certain feature of a fictional world can produce a particular effect on the (synchronic) receivers, without fully understanding the psychical mechanism that predisposes it. Even holistic catharsis, which is a biological mechanism that can be activated under certain conditions, is not fully understood. It follows that in order to trigger a specific response in the receiver the scientific understanding of a certain psychical mechanism is not a necessary condition. The knowledge of previous successful attempts is usually sufficient.

Although there is nothing wrong with such an intuitive technology, which is often verified *a posteriori* by scientific methods; e.g., catharsis (cf. Kreitler), attempts to find deeper explanations may prove revealing. It is the task of the spectators to detect the intended mood and react accordingly, which they usually do intuitively and proficiently. Laughter (or crying) 'in the wrong places' supports the claim that there are rules that underlie laughter (or crying) in the right places.

Cultural dependency

Laughter is culture-dependent: 'It is . . . notorious that a 'sense of humour' is an unreliable quality, and what will seem laughable to an English audience will not necessarily seem so to a Scottish' (Styan, 1968: 39). This can be explained by the fact that in different cultures spectators are subject to different inhibitions. Conversely, a certain culture may even reject laughter on themes that are too painful. Jewish people, for example, will generally denounce any attempt to be humorous about the Holocaust; e.g., Roberto Benigni's film *Life is Beautiful* (1998). Such a combination creates a grotesque mood and thus a different genre (see CHAPTER 8).

◆

Seeing laughter as a cathartic mechanism implies that there are four main factors involved in triggering it: foolish failure, anxiety, a lack of pity, and a sudden transition to a humorous mood. However, laughter is a psychical mechanism that can be triggered by different causes and used for promoting different moods in different genres. Producing laughter is the aim of satire and grotesque drama too. Comic laughter is inherent in the humorous mood, but not necessarily produced by it. Only in comedy is laughter lighthearted and purely cathartic.

Laughter-Eliciting Devices 3

Comedy is characterized by a humorous mood and optional comic laughter. The intention to produce laughter, however, is not restricted to comedy. It also characterizes other genres, such as satiric and grotesque drama, which reflect different moods (see CHAPTER 8). In each of these genres, the prevalent mood determines the particular nature of its laughter. It is sensible, therefore, to distinguish between comic and either satiric or grotesque laughter. I thus term 'laughter devices' the set of means designed to produce laughter regardless of mood, while leaving their specific natures to be elucidated subsequently, depending on the nature of the embedding genre (see CHAPTERS 7 & 8).

Laughter devices are episodic in nature. They are stock-devices, in the sense of being ready-made and recycled in different fictional worlds. The set of such devices is open, meaning that the creation of new ones depends only on the inventive talent of a playwright or director. Prior to presenting some examples, the following section discusses 'dramatic irony', which is presupposed by all such devices. Subsequently, all examples are given in English translation. However, whenever possible it is advisable to read them in the original language, because laughter often depends on it.

Dramatic irony

'Dramatic irony' denotes the authors' and spectators' advantage over the characters in understanding their own worlds (Sedgewick: 32–3; cf. Styan, 1967: 48–63). Basically, the ironic perspective in drama enjoys authorial authority, meaning that whoever adopts it understands the fictional world better than the characters themselves. A character's perspective is thus naïve from an ironic point of view. In other words, the spectator is enabled to enjoy a double perspective, that of the author and that of the character, and to see the advantage of the former (cf. Stott: 14). *It is this duality that creates the structural cognitive gap that defines 'dramatic irony'.*

An ironic perspective reflects an ethical system, which is indicated by key terms, scattered in the speeches of functional characters and/or interactive characters in functional situations; e.g., in soliloquy. These key terms are metonyms of such a cognitive/ethical system on a part/whole basis. In other words, these metonyms are capable of evoking an entire system, in being, assumedly, part of the spectators' cultural baggage. The entire system thus becomes an integral part of the description of a fictional world. It follows that a full and systematic presentation of such a system is superfluous.

I have proposed elsewhere the following elements of 'dramatic irony': (a) *'super-understanding'*, (b) *'inversion of meaning'* , (c) *'ironic contemplation'*, and (d) *'ironic pleasure'* (Rozik, 2009: 59–61). (a) 'Super-understanding' means that the privileged spectator is accorded the superior ability of both to detect the naïve and ironic perspectives and to prefer the latter: whereas the former is found inadequate, the latter is found advantageous. In contrast to Styan, irony is not only a matter of 'superior knowledge' (1967: 49), but also of superior understanding. (b) 'Inversion of meaning' means that the ironic perspective may change the meaning attributed by the naïve one, even to the extent of opposition; e.g., a motive that is positive from a naïve viewpoint can be perceived as negative from the ironic viewpoint and vice versa. (c) 'Ironic contemplation' means that, in contrast to the characters' total involvement in their own worlds, ironic superiority produces a sense of detachment: the spectators are accorded freedom in their ethical attitudes to a fictional world — with both worlds being separated by an ontological gap. And (d) 'Ironic pleasure' means that dramatic irony produces a particular kind of pleasure, which derives not from the achievement of a goal, the reaffirmation of a value system or catharsis, but from the sheer opportunity to enjoy cognitive *superiority* and *contemplative freedom*, of which human beings are existentially deprived.

Since 'dramatic irony' applies to all dramatic genres, including tragedy, the specific difference of comedy should be established. It might appear that this difference is obvious, due to the lowly mode of most characters of comedy and farce. Indeed, there is something in the low mode of ludicrous characters that is ironic in nature: assumedly, they understand less. However, paradoxically, dramatic irony is even more powerful when relating to a lofty character, especially if endowed with higher intellectual powers; e.g., in Sophocles' *Oedipus the King*, Oedipus is characterized by superior intelligence, in the context of which his mental blindness is even more conspicuous (Knox, 1966: 3–52). Existential human blindness is probably the main object of dramatic irony, and in all genres interactive characters are usually blind in one way or the other. In this sense, *dramatic irony and mode are mutually independent.*

Consequently, I suggest that the difference between serious and comic dramatic irony depends on the specific mood. In other words, dramatic irony is not a source of laughter in itself, but allows differentiation depending on the serious, humorous or any other modal treatment of a narrative. Nonetheless, in the context of the humorous mood, dramatic irony is a precondition for presenting a character as ludicrous; i.e., a necessary condition for laughter.

An ironic viewpoint is not necessarily true (cf. Stott: 14), but only held to be true by an author, and expected to be so by a synchronic audience. Therefore, it may become naïve from the viewpoint of a different culture/period. In such a case, only a creative interpretation can save a certain fictional world from being dated; i.e., enable its universality.

Therefore, an intentional ironic perspective on an alleged ironic viewpoint is also possible. Such a structure has been employed not only in literary fiction in which a narrator is a character who, despite commanding an ironic position in regard to other characters, becomes the object of irony for the reader, but also in dramatic works; e.g., the ironic perspective of Aphrodite's prologue in Euripides' *Hippolytus*, which is meant to become the object of the authorial/spectatorial perspective.

The ironical structure can be reversed at will; i.e., ironic superiority can be denied, and the spectator made the object of dramatic irony, in the sense of producing disorientation in regard to the meaning of a fictional action. Such a reversal characterizes not comedy, but serious play-scripts that reflect an absurdist structure, as in some modernist and post-modernist fictional worlds; e.g., Beckett's *Waiting for Godot* and Harold Pinter's *The Birthday Party* (see CHAPTER 8).

Verbal irony in the speeches of characters should be interpreted in relation to their degree of authority. If articulated by a functional character that represents the ironic viewpoint in the fictional world, it should be seen as an instance of dramatic irony. In contrast, if articulated by an interactive character, it is usually an object of irony.

In principle, the ultimate meaning of a fictional world is determined by the spectators, and conditions the nature of their concluding experiences and responses. *A fictional world should thus be seen as a mechanism that manipulates the audience into a preconceived perspective on a fictional world.* In western culture, the vast majority of canonic fictional worlds feature main characters that, from an ironic viewpoint, err in one way or another. Dramatic irony is, therefore, a central structural component of a fictional world, regardless of genre (see CHAPTER 5).

Foolishness presupposes dramatic irony, which is a precondition for all the following devices to potentially produce laughter.

Quid pro quo

The original sense of this Latin expression is 'something for something else'; e.g., a gift for a favor. As a theoretical term, in the theory of drama, it applies to situations in which a character erroneously takes the intended meaning of a sentence for something else. Usually, two characters mutually misunderstand one another — thus creating a kind of dialogue of the deaf, which is ludicrous in itself (cf. the notion of 'crossed conversations' in Weitz: 73–5). It is actually an exchange of failing perceptions that, if foolish, potentially produces laughter; for example, an excerpt from the dialogue between Harpagon and Valère in Molière's *The Miser*:

> *Harpagon*: Come near, and confess to the blackest deed, the most horrible crime that ever was committed.
> *Valère*: What do you wish, Sir?
> *Harpagon*: How, wretch! you do not blush for your crime.
>   . . .
> *Harpagon*: And what pretty motives can you advance, infamous thief?
>   . . .
> *Valère*: For pity's sake, do not get angry. When you have heard me, you will see that the harm is not so great as you make it.
> *Harpagon*: The harm is not so great as I make it! What! my blood, my very heart, hang-dog!
> *Valère*: Your blood, Sir, has not fallen into bad hands. I am of a rank not to do it any injury; and there is nothing in all this but what I can easily repair.
> *Harpagon*: That is what I intend, and that you should restore to me what you have robbed me of.
> *Valère*: Your honour shall be amply satisfied, Sir.
> *Harpagon*: There is no question of honour in it. But tell me, who has driven you to such a deed?

Valère: A god who carries his excuse for all he makes people do: Love.

Harpagon: Love?

Valère: Yes.

Harpagon: A pretty love, a pretty love, upon my word! The love for my gold pieces!

Valère: No, Sir, it is not your wealth that has tempted me; it is not that which has dazzled me; and I protest that I have not the slightest design upon your property, provided you leave me that which I have got.

Harpagon: No, by all the devils I shall not leave it to you. But see what insolence to wish to keep that of which he has robbed me!

Valère: Do you call that robbery?

Harpagon: If I call it a robbery? A treasure like that!

Valère: It is a treasure, that is true, and the most precious which you have got, no doubt; but it would not be losing it to leave it to me. I ask you for it on my knees, this treasure full of charms? And to do right, you should grant it to me.

Harpagon: I shall do nothing of the kind. What does it all mean?

Valère: We have pledged our faith to each other, and have sworn never to part.

Harpagon: The oath is admirable, and the promise rather funny.

Valère: Yes, we have bound ourselves to be all in all to each other for ever.

Harpagon: I shall hinder you from it, I assure you.

Valère: Nothing but death shall separate us.

Harpagon: It is being devilishly enamoured of my money.

Valère: I have told you already, Sir, that interest did not urge me to do what I have done. My heart did not act from the motives which you imagine; a nobler one inspired me with this resolution.

Harpagon: You shall see that it is from Christian charity that he covets my property! But I shall look to that; and the law will give me satisfaction for all this, you bare-faced rogue.

Valère: You shall act as you like, and I am ready to bear all the violence you please; but I implore you to believe, at least, that if harm has been done, I only am to be blamed, and that in all this, your daughter is in nowise culpable.

Harpagon: Indeed, I believe you! It would be very strange if my daughter had had a part in this crime. But I will have my property back again, and I will have you confess where you have carried it away to.

Valère: I? I have not carried it away at all. It is still in your house.

Harpagon (aside): O! My beloved cash-box! (Aloud). Then it has not gone out of my house?

Valère: No, sir.

Harpagon: Just tell me that you have not made free with it?

Valère: I make free with it! Ah! You wrong us both; and it is with a wholly pure and respectable ardour that I burn.

Harpagon (aside): Burn for my cash-box!

Valère: I would sooner die than show her any offensive thought: she is too prudent and honourable for that.

Harpagon (aside): My cash-box too honourable!

Valère: All my wishes are confined to enjoy the sight of her; and nothing criminal has profaned the passion with which her beautiful eyes have inspired me.

Harpagon (aside): The beautiful eyes of my cash-box! He speaks of her as a lover speaks of his mistress.

Valère: Mistress Claude, Sir, knows the truth of this affair; and she can testify to it.

Harpagon: What! My servant is an accomplice in the matter?

Valère: Yes, Sir; she was a witness to our engagement; and it is after having known the honourable intent of my passion, that she has assisted me in persuading your daughter to plight her troth, and receive mine.

Harpagon (aside): He? Does the fear of justice make him rave? (To Valère.) What means all this gibberish about my daughter?

. . .

Harpagon: O Heaven! Another disgrace! (V, iii)

This dialogue takes place after Harpagon's safe (*cassette*) has been stolen. Whereas Valère wishes to appease Harpagon regarding his daughter Élise, and to ask for her hand, Harpagon is only concerned about his money. Therefore, when Valère speaks in terms of 'satisfying his honor', 'love', 'treasure' and 'never to part', Harpagon, although astonished by these expressions, relates them to his safe throughout the dialogue. Not only does Harpagon fail to understand Valère, but the latter too fails to understand Harpagon. He understands, for example, Harpagon's literal 'blood' as a metaphor for his daughter. Even when the meanings of their words become quite explicit, misunderstanding still prevails. Harpagon keeps failing until eventually Valère makes explicit his request for Élise's hand.

This double quid pro quo is enabled by Molière's skillful handling of ambiguous words; for example, 'treasure' can be interpreted literally, as Harpagon does for his safe, or metaphorically, as Valère does for his beloved Élise.

The quid pro quo is a laughter device that presupposes dramatic irony, i.e., a spectator who can perceive the foolishness of the misunderstandings, which are meant to produce laughter. Although this excerpt presents two persistent failures in understanding one another, there is a substantial difference: whereas Valère is not a ludicrous character, Harpagon is. Lovers in comedy are basically naïve and beautiful. Whereas Valère's failures reflect his deep love for Élise, which is a healthy disposition, Harpagon's failures reflect an obsession with money, which is a mental deformation that results in foolish behavior. In other words, a quid pro quo is ludicrous only if it is foolish (cf. the similar quid pro quo between Euclio and Lyconides in Plautus' *The Pot of Gold*: pp. 38–39).

Trickery and disguise

Comedy is characterized by much use of base means such as trickery, deception, secrecy and eavesdropping; e.g., in Molière's *The Trickeries of Scapin*, when Scapin slaps Géronte, the father of his master Leandre, his trickery breaches the inhibition of attacking a father, which is circumvented by attributing it to a servant (III, ii; cf. CHAPTER 10). As the lifting of an inhibition produces anxiety, this is released by the ludicrous nature of the scene, which explains its high potential to produce laughter.

In this scene, Scapin most probably employed a slapstick, which is a kind flexible wooden bat made of several blades and used by a clown to simulate blows because of the loud noise that it makes ('slapstick' is more usually employed as a term for a physical and rough kind of humor (cf. Stott: 92–3)).

Trickery, however, can also be found in serious drama, e.g., the play within the play in Shakespeare's tragedy *Hamlet*, and particularly in melodrama, e.g., Eugène Scribe's *A Glass of Water*. I suggest, therefore, that the distinction between ludicrous and serious trickery too is conditioned by the specific mood of a fictional world. Trickery implies concealing true motives and often, in order to avoid exposure, characters must fabricate explanations that are ludicrous in themselves (Weitz: 79–82).

Disguise can be used as a particular form of trickery, albeit not being ridiculous in itself, e.g., in disguising as her brother Federigo, Beatrice is dead serious in Goldoni's *The Servant of two Masters* (cf. *ibid.*: 82). In general, mistaken identities do not necessarily produce laughter, unless resulting in foolish behavior (cf. *ibid.*: 76–9); e.g., the exchange of identities between Dionysus and Xantias, which are always to the detriment of the god, in Aristophanes' *Frogs* (pp. 175–81).

Compulsive repetition

Repetition per se is not ludicrous, unless manifested in repeated foolish failures; e.g., in *The Trickeries of Scapin*, when Scapin tells Géronte that his son has been taken prisoner and is under the threat of being taken to Alger, the father's repeated reaction is 'Que diable allait-il faire dans cette galère?' (What the hell was he doing in that galley? — II, vii; my trans.) Géronte's failure lies in that the reason for being in the galley is totally irrelevant to the situation. His compulsive behavior is manifested in repeating the very same foolish reaction, which is the main condition for laughter. Furthermore, it has cumulative effects, meaning that it increases laughter the more it is repeated.

Foul language

Comedy and farce profit from the inhibition of expressions such as foul or indecent language and obscene gestures referring to tabooed themes. While the lifting of inhibitions in comedy is restricted to mild expressions, farce excels in violent transgressions, which become sources of comic laughter through the sudden insight that they reflect a humorous mood. This is highly conspicuous in words that refer explicitly to sexual organs and relations. In such a case, the spectator laughs *with* the intentional transgressor

This tendency is also characteristic of metaphoric descriptions that feature highly ignoble terms; e.g., the metaphoric description of women in terms of soup, and adultery in terms of someone dipping his fingers in one's soup, in Molière's The School for Wives:

> *Alain*: A woman is in fact the broth of a man; and when a man
> sees other men . . . trying to dip their fingers into his soup he soon
> shows extreme anger (II, iii; my translation).

This obscene and ludicrous metaphor, which is put in the mouth of a servant, would be unconceivable in serious drama.

Sexual innuendos

Molière wrote his plays in a cultural period whose decorum imposed taboos not only on sexual relations prior to marriage, but also on openly speaking about sex. Nonetheless, the dialogues of his young lovers are always interspersed with expressions that clearly allude to such relations, e.g., in the first scene of *The Miser*:

> *Valère*: Eh, what! Charming Elise, you are growing melancholy, after the kind assurances which you were good enough to give me of your love! Alas! I see you sighing in the midst of my joy! Tell me, is it with regret at having made me happy? And do you repent of that engagement to which my affection has induced you?
>
> *Elise*: No, Valère, I cannot repent of anything that *I do for you*. I feel myself attracted to it by too sweet a power, and I have not even the will to wish that things were otherwise. But, to tell you the truth, our success causes me uneasiness; and I am very much afraid of *loving you a little more than I ought*.
>
> *Valère*: Eh! what is there to fear, Elise, in the affection you have for me?
>
> *Elise*: Alas! a hundred things at once: *the anger of a father, the reproaches of my family, the censure of the world*; but more than all,

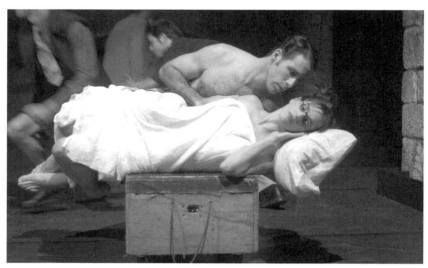

3 Élise and Valère in explicit sexual scene, in the Khan Theatre *The Miser*. *Photo*: Gadi Dagon. Courtesy of the Jerusalem Khan Theatre.

Valère, the change of your heart, and that criminal coolness with which those of your sex most frequently repay *the too ardent proofs of an innocent love.* (I, i; my italics)

These protests of too much love indicate imprudent behavior and, from an ironic viewpoint, they allude to sexual relations. Nevertheless, these are not ludicrous in themselves. It is the allusion to such foolish behavior in front of a prudish audience that is meant to lift an inhibition, and thereby produce both anxiety and laughter.

Moreover, comedy, farce in particular, deals not only with tabooed sexual relations, but also with pregnancies and even illegitimate babies, which ignore the conventional parental blessing. Such innuendos too presuppose dramatic irony.

Breaking conventions

Comedy often presupposes the rules underlying a convention in order to thwart them. Such a procedure is intended to arouse laughter. For example, the soliloquy of Harpagon in *The Miser*:

> *Harpagon*: (alone) — It is certainly no small trouble to keep such a large sum of money in one's house; and he is a happy man who has all his well laid out at interest, and keeps only so much by him as is necessary for his expenses. One is not a little puzzled to contrive, in the whole house, a safe hiding-place; for, as far as I am concerned, I distrust safes, and would never rely on them. I look upon them just as a distinct bait to burglars; for it is always the first thing which they attack. For all that, I am not quite sure if I have done right in burying in my garden these ten thousand crowns, which were paid to me yesterday. Ten thousand golden crowns in one's house is a sum sufficient. . . . (*aside, perceiving* Elise *and* Cléante). Oh, Heavens! I have betrayed myself! The excitement has carried me too far, and I verily believe I have spoken aloud, while arguing to myself. (*To* Cléante *and* Elise). What is the matter?
>
> *Cléante*: Nothing, father?
> *Harpagon*: Have you been there long?
> *Elise*: We were just coming in.
> *Harpagon*: You have heard . . .
> *Elise*: What?
> *Harpagon*: What I said just now.

> *Cléante*. No.
> *Harpagon*: Yes, You have.
> *Elise*: I beg your pardon.
> *Harpagon*: I see well enough that you overheard some words. I was talking to myself about the difficulty one experiences now-a-days in finding money, and I was saying how pleasant it must be to have ten thousand crowns in the house. (I, iv)

Like the aside, the soliloquy's convention implies that what is articulated by it is not overheard even by characters present on stage. In this case, Harpagon breaks the convention in assuming that he might have been heard by his children and, therefore, he attempts to distort what he has been saying, which is an additional indication of Harpagon's suspicious and foolish nature, which is a flaw that derives from his stinginess, and which is manifested in ludicrous actions. Ironically, it is possible that this would-be secret soliloquy in effect reveals the hiding place of Harpagon's money, which enables the eventual marriages of his children, and thus the satisfaction of the spectator's spontaneous expectations (cf. the overheard soliloquy of Euclio in *The Pot of Gold*: p. 33). This device too presupposes dramatic irony.

Potentially this principle applies to all stage conventions. Another example is that of breaking the confidant convention: when a character confides his stratagems to the wrong confidant. In various ways, the revealed secret is always to the butt's detriment. For example, in Molière's *The School for Wives*, Agnès, the naïve young ward, confides her experiences with her young lover Horace to Arnolphe, her old guardian, in contrast to his plan to educate her as his future wife as a simpleton in order to prevent her infidelity.

> *Arnolphe*: . . . But tell me what followed, and how the young man behaved during his visits.
> *Agnès*: Alas! if you but knew how delightful he was; how he got rid of his illness as soon as I saw him, the present he made me of a lovely casket, and the money which Alain and Georgette have had from him, you would no doubt love him, and say, as we say . . .
> *Arnolphe*: Yes. But what did he do when he was alone with you?
> *Agnès*: He swore that he loved me with an unequalled passion, and said the prettiest words possible, things that nothing ever can equal, the sweetness of which charms me whenever I hear him speak, and moves I know not what within me.
> *Arnolphe* (*aside*): Oh! sad inquiry into a fatal mystery, in which

the inquirer alone suffers all the pain. (*Aloud*) Besides all these speeches, all these pretty compliments, did he not also bestow a few caresses on you?

Agnès: Oh, so many! He took my hands and my arms, and was never tired of kissing them.

Arnolphe: Agnès, did he take nothing else from you? (*Seeing her confused*) Ugh!

Agnès: Why, he . . .

Arnolphe: What?

Agnès: Took . . .

Arnolphe: Ugh!

Agnès: The . . .

Arnolphe: Well?

Agnès: I dare not tell you; you will perhaps be angry with me.

Ironically, despite knowing from Agnès her plans to keep meeting her lover, Arnolphe cannot preclude their encounters (cf. the confidences of Lubin, the servant of Clitandre, to George Dandin).

Parody

'Parody' *applies to a target-text that maintains an intertextual relation with a serious source-text and indicates the intention to mock the latter.* In general parody is a laughter device that presupposes dramatic irony, on condition that the source-text is part of the spectator's cultural baggage; e.g., Alfred Jarry's *Ubu Roi*, which is a grotesque parody of Shakespeare's *Macbeth* (cf. Weitz: 178–83). The narrative follows the source-text: Ubu's aim is to become powerful and rich. He plans to kill King of Poland Vencelas and his family, and crown himself in his place. He succeeds, and only Vencelas's son Bougrelas survives to hunt the usurper. Finally Ubu flees the country. The grotesque mood reflects the intention to shock the audience through sheer cruelty and vulgar language.

Nicoll employs 'burlesque' for possible farces that treat established serious myths through laughter devices: 'burlesque of divine or heroic legend has always been associated with all forms of mimic drama' (p. 25; cf. p. 40). Under the assumption that myths command (serious) belief, their burlesque treatment should be conceived of in terms of 'parody', because of referring to a preexisting, serious and known myth; e.g., Plautus' *Amphitryon*, which presents Jupiter (Greek Zeus) in his trickeries and unbridled sexual appetite.

While a dramatic parody usually relates to an entire text, this is not always the case; e.g., the words of Guard in Ionesco's *Exit the King*:

> *Guard*: . . . It was he who invented gunpowder and stole fire from the gods. . . . He was the one who fitted up the first forges on earth. . . . As an engineer he made the first balloon, and then the Zeppelin. And finally, with his own hands, he built the first aeroplane. . . . he'd invented the wheelbarrow. . . . Then rails and railways and automobiles. He drew up the plans for the Eiffel Tower, not to mention his designs for the sickle and the plough, the harvesters and the tractors. . . . He built Rome, New York, Moscow and Geneva. He *founded* Paris. He created revolutions, counter-revolutions, religion, reform and counter-reform. . . . He wrote tragedies and comedies, under the name of Shakespeare. (pp. 71–2)

This is a parodic version of the first *stasimon* in Sophocles' *Antigone* (332–72), through which the chorus praises various inventions that reveal the genius of the human race, especially in the domains of science and technology, in order to stress, in contrast to the gods, human mortality: 'There's only death / that he [man] cannot find an escape from' (*Antigone*: 359–60). Against the background of this source-text, Ionesco highlights the ludicrous gap between King Bérenger as representing the great achievements of mankind and his shortcomings as an individual; e.g., in Queen Juliette's words: 'He was never any good with his hands! He used to call the plumber at the slightest sign of a leak!' (p. 72). In particular, the parodic intent of this partial parody is discerned in that the list of admirable human inventions and feats, as in the source, puts on the same level the wheelbarrow and Shakespeare's play-scripts. The parody of this *stasimon* is part of Ionesco's grotesque treatment of the extremely serious theme of individual death. It also depicts death not as a passage to the "real" world, but as an absolute ending. It can also be claimed that by the same token he presents a parodic commentary and critique on the dead-seriousness of the anonymous *Everyman* (Rozik, 2009: 116–18).

Another example: the opening speech of Sganarelle in Molière's *Don Juan*, which is a parody of a dead serious speech wasted on a trivial matter. It begins with 'Whatever Aristotle and the entire philosophy could say: there's nothing in this world like tobacco' (I, i). The reversal of mood is already in the opening words (cf. Weitz: 29).

A good example of cinematic parody is Mel Brooks' film *Blazing Saddles*, which is a parody of Western films, of Fred Zinnemann's *High Noon* in particular.

Plautus' *Amphitryon*

Amphitryon, the commander of the Theban army, sets out to fight a war against the Teleboans, leaving behind his pregnant wife Alcmena. In his absence, Jupiter fancies Amphitryon's proverbially faithful wife and disguises himself as her husband; while Mercury, Jupiter's son, disguises himself as Amphitryon's servant Sosia. Jupiter is then welcomed by Alcmena, who becomes pregnant from the god too. Upon their return, after seven months, the true Amphitryon and Sosia face ludicrous confusions. Sosia is beaten and driven away by Mercury under the pretence that the real servant is an impostor. Sosia, confused at being beaten by "himself", tells Amphitryon, who does not believe him and decides to inquire into the story. At home he is met by Alcmena's suspicion, as she believes that her husband had just left for the war. Amphitryon infers that somebody has stolen his identity and charges her with infidelity. He then leaves for the harbor to find a witness to his arrival; but upon his return he is driven away by Mercury and Jupiter under the pretence that he is impersonating Amphitryon. Belpharo, the pilot of the ship, is asked to determine who is the real Amphitryon, but is unable to tell the one from the other. Alcmena gives birth to Iphicles and Hercules, the sons of Amphitryon and Jupiter respectively — with the latter immediately indicating his divine nature by killing two serpents with his bare hands. Eventually, Jupiter discloses the mystery, and Amphitryon, in contrast to his legal right to even kill his wife for infidelity, happily reconciles with his god and his wife. (cf. Molière's *Amphitryon* and Jean Giraudoux's *Amphitryon 38*).

Segal contends that this is not a happy ending on the grounds that a cuckold cannot reconcile (p. 216). But Amphitryon's final words show differently: 'By Polux, I'm not troubled in the least / If I am blessed to share my goods with Jove.'

Comic acting

All the devices noted above would not work unless substantiated by a particular kind of acting, often labeled 'comic acting', which is characterized by exaggerated, crooked and bold physical gesture, particularly grimace, and distorted intonation. Basically, actors that intend to produce laughter in this way usually enact physical deformity, which should be understood as a metaphor of psychical deformity. This principle is corroborated by the classical comic mask, probably shared by comedy and satire in ancient Greek theatre, which is distorted and ugly, and also by that actors who enact ludicrous characters are often ugly, bodily deformed and/or speak in a contorted voice; e.g., Molière himself.

Comic acting is also characterized by a kind of detachment between actor and character, possibly supporting Brecht's notion of '*verfrem-dungseffekt*'; and a kind of complicity between character and audience, as if all the actions of the former are performed in a playful manner. This also applies to the buffoon.

Students often question the comic nature of comedies, including those of Molière. Indeed, reading comedies, such as Menander's *The Arbitration* and Terence's *The Brothers*, may create the impression that they are not written in the comic mood and with no intention to produce comic laughter; and that apart from their lowly mode they could be perceived as subspecies melodrama. Often, only the existence of stock-types such as the cook and the parasite indicates their comic nature. The only sensible answer is that they should be mentally read as being performed in the comic mood; i.e., complemented through ludicrous acting. In the last two centuries such comedies have usually been enacted in the acting style or, rather, what is thought to have been the acting style, of *commedia dell'arte* (see CHAPTER 9). However, it is not at all clear whether or not comedies of all periods were complemented by such acting.

In this sense, there is no point in reading a play-script as a comedy unless firm information or clear indications of a synchronic performance are available. As I have suggested elsewhere, a play-script is an incomplete notation of a description of a fictional world in that it lacks the nonverbal elements of interaction, which determine its nature — with these being conveyed solely by the performance-text (Rozik, 2008a: 90–101). Moreover, it is widely accepted that comic acting can transform a scripted melodrama into a comedy, and serious acting can transform a scripted comedy into a melodrama, which means that the resulting mood is a matter of directorial interpretation, rather than a necessary feature of a play-script.

Comic atmosphere

A significant means of producing laughter is the preparation of the spectator for laughter: 'Before people will burst out laughing they have to be prepared to burst out laughing. The only sure preparation is a particular state of expectation and sensitivity that amounts to a kind of euphoria. . . . A stage of excitement can be reached at which people will laugh at anything' (Bentley: 234). A successful comedy probably signals from the beginning that the fictional world is in the humorous mood: 'The most favourable condition for the production of comic pleasure is a generally cheerful mood in which one is "inclined to laugh". In a toxic mood of cheerfulness almost everything seems comic . . . A similarly favourable effect is produced by an *expectation* of the comic, by being attuned to comic pleasure' (Freud, 1989: 271–2).

All the laughter devices, which aim at producing laughter regardless of genre, presuppose dramatic irony, and constitute a set open to additions depending on the inventive talent of an author. Although comedy shows a clear predilection for laughter devices, these are also employed in satiric and grotesque fictional worlds, albeit for different purposes. Comic acting and comic atmosphere are the main laughter devices that condition the expected effects on receivers.

Fictional Structure 4

For more than two millennia, commencing with Aristotle's remarks in the *Poetics*, attempts have been made to determine whether or not comedy evinces a particular and typical fictional structure. The *Poetics*, which focuses on tragedy, presumably considers that comedy shares several structural features with tragedy; and that its specific remarks on comedy are necessary only where this genre departs from their common ground. I have suggested elsewhere that Aristotle's structures of action characterize not only tragedy (*Poetics*: XIII, 2), but are potentially shared by all fictional genres; i.e., reflect the particular mode of fictional thinking. It is only their specific moods that make the difference (Rozik, 2009: 67–78).

However, the extreme diversity of kinds of what is usually perceived under the category of 'comedy' seems to lead to the opposite conclusion. Corrigan claims that 'we must resist falling victim to . . . the "formalistic fallacy" in the study of dramatic genres. This is a kind of thinking about drama based on the assumption that there are certain formal and structural characteristics which all comedy of all ages must share in common' (p. 3). Against the background of the broad sense of 'comedy' this claim is sound, especially because this term also applies to a set of tangential genres, which evince different moods and often preferences for different fictional structures (see CHAPTER 8); even the humorous mood is not always combined with a particular fictional structure (see CHAPTER 7).

This chapter is devoted to the fictional structure of action in general. It ponders Aristotle's remarks, presuppositions and implications, and subsequent theories of fictional structure, and concludes that the specific difference of comedy is to be found not on the level of structure of action, but on the level of mood. The next chapter is devoted to the overall structure of comedy, in the narrow sense, including its characteristic mood and its typical preference for the structure of action that satisfies the spectator's archetypal expectations.

The fictional mode

This study endorses Frye's distinction between the thematic (pp. 33–52 & 367) and the fictional (pp. 52–67 & 365–6) modes of expression. Whereas the fictional mode is characterized by the creation of fictional worlds that mediate between authors and spectators, the thematic mode is characterized negatively by the lack of such mediation. As suggested above, whereas this study adopts the notion of 'fictional world', it does not adopt this notion of 'thematic', because fictional worlds too evince thematic aspects (see Introduction). The expression of the single psyche of an author, and potentially of a receiver, through a multiple world of characters and their interactions, implies that a fictional world reflects the spontaneous partition of the psyche into psychical agencies and/or drives, and their personification. Since personification is a particular kind of metaphor, which draws its connotations from the human sphere, *a fictional world, which is build upon this basic layer, is a potentially metaphoric description of the spectator's amorphous psychical state of affairs* (Rozik, 2009: 141–50).

If a fictional world is a potential self-referential description of a single psyche through a multiple world of characters, the receiver's identification cannot relate to a single character, as usually assumed, but to an entire fictional world; i.e., it is a pluri-identification with all its characters, including the ethically good, the depraved, and the ludicrous. There is a fundamental advantage to the principle of 'multiple identification': it explains the appeal of negative and ludicrous characters, albeit rejected by consciousness, and the anxiety in confronting them. Such a negative identification supports the claim that a ludicrous or depraved character is a metaphoric description of an inhibited drive of the spectator.

Basically, a fictional world reflects the psyche of its author. In this sense, it is self-referential. It can be conjectured, nonetheless, that in experiencing a description of a fictional world the receiver takes over the function of referent (Rozik, 2009: 122–3). This principle is fully acknowledged in the theory of lyric poetry. The deictic terms of a poem, such as 'I', 'you', 'here' and 'now', assumedly refer to the poet, his/her attitude to an object and the circumstances of his/her lyric utterance, and *because of the abstract nature of such deictic words, their referential function can be diverted to the receiver, who thus becomes their actual referent*. This explains why readers of poems deem and praise such ready-made texts as expressions of themselves; e.g., a prayer.

If the principle of 'substitution of referents' adequately describes the

63

relationship between an 'I' poet and an 'I' receiver, it is sensible to conjecture that *in experiencing a comedy too a similar substitution of referents
takes place — with the receiver substituting for the author.* This is facili-
tated by that the subject of a fictional expression, the author of the
ready-made fictional text, is usually not marked ('0' sign); i.e., there is
no obstacle to such a substitution. In general, there is no need for making
a subject explicit, if it is self-understood.

Structure and thematic specification

In order to determine the typical fictional structure of a dramatic genre
the first step is to establish the meaning of 'structure'. A 'structure' is a
pattern of relations that organizes several functions underlying the unity
of a text or component unit of any extent; i.e., it is a kind of complex
syntactic principle on the holistic level. The notion of 'structure' implies
the notion of 'function' and vice versa. In particular, in the fictional
domain, the notion of 'structure' applies to a fictional interaction, which
leads from a motive to either its final success or failure, to its meaning,
and to its possible effect on an audience. 'Motive', 'success' and 'failure'
are basic categories of 'action' (Dijk: 175–6; cf. Austin) or, rather, functions in a holistic fictional action. According to the structural approach,
a whole fictional world is thus perceived as a complex and organized set
of functions.

Both 'structure' and 'function' are empty principles. Therefore, in
order to generate a particular fictional world each function needs to be
thematically specified; and, conversely, the function of each thematic
specification in the overall structure has to be determined. In principle,
function and thematic specification are mutually independent, in the
sense that different thematic specifications may fulfill the same function, and the same thematic specification may fulfil different functions.
For instance, different drives can specify the function of 'motive'; e.g.,
recovering the stolen money in Plautus' *The Pot of Gold* and precluding
the infidelity of a wife in Molière's *George Dandin*; and different
outcomes can specify the functions of 'success' such as that of Euclio in
The Pot of Gold and 'failure' such as that of George Dandin.

A structure determines the hierarchical contributions of all its
thematically-specified functions, thus bestowing definite meaning on
them, in the sense of the whole being more than the sum of its parts. The
aim of a fictional world is to bring about the experience not of a blank
structure, but of a structured set of thematic specifications. It follows that

not only is determining the exact function of each thematic component vital to the interpretation of a fictional world, but also that this must be done in the context of at least an intuition of the overall meaning of such a world and its possible impact on the spectator.

Aristotle's structural approach

Aristotle's *Poetics* is the first known attempt to determine the structure of tragedy, and by implication of comedy, under the assumption that, in some respects, these are opposite genres. He derives his view on the structure of tragedy from what is perceived as its ultimate and essential end, which is a specific emotional experience: 'through pity and fear effecting the proper purgation [catharsis] of *these* emotions' (*Poetics*: VI, 2; my italics); while presupposing that all the structural components of a tragedy should be subordinated to this end. Accordingly, Aristotle discerns four functions in the deep structure of tragedy that combine in achieving catharsis: (a) the ethical nature of a character and/or its motive ('virtuous man', 'villain' or '*hamartia*-afflicted'); (b) the performative nature of the outcome (success/prosperity or failure/adversity); (c) the *philanthropon*, probably in the sense of the spectator's 'ethical sense', according to which characterization and action are assessed; and (d) the emotional nature of the concluding experience: catharsis of fear or shocking effect (*Poetics*: XIII, 2). I contend that this deep structure of action is shared by all fictional worlds, including comedies.

Aristotle correctly presupposes that beyond the amazing diversity of fictional worlds, and themes in particular, there is a single deep structure and a rather small set of surface structures, which are generated by all the possible combinations of the said four functions, and underlie the generation of all fictional worlds. Accordingly, he suggests five such surface structures (*Poetics*: XIII), which are:

Nature of character	ultimate success or failure	*philanthropon*	effect
1. 'A virtuous man'	'from prosperity to adversity'	[satisfies it not]	'it shocks us'
2. 'A bad man'	'from adversity to prosperity'	'satisfies' it not	[it shocks us]
3. 'An utter villain'	his 'downfall'	'satisfies' it	similar to comedy
4. [A virtuous man]	[his success]	[satisfies it]	similar to comedy
5. An error or frailty	'misfortune'	[satisfies it]	catharsis

(Square brackets = implications)

The term *'philanthropon'* has been diversely understood and translated; e.g., 'moral sense' by Butcher (*Poetics*: XIII, 2; cf. XVIII, 5) and 'humane sympathy' by Halliwell (p. 52). I suggest that this term refers to the spectators' 'ethical sense', based on their communal system of values. Much has been said about the *Poetics* possible moral bias. I believe that this criticism is justified. Moreover, since it also refers to a religious *hamartia*, it is clear that the notion of '*philanthropon*' cannot be restricted to moral values alone, and should include additional ones. *I thus suggest that this notion applies to all that is valuable in the eyes of a cultural community, including religious, moral, aesthetic and even epistemic values.* It is in this wide sense that I employ 'ethical' in this study. Aristotle's distinction between 'villainous' and 'virtuous' characters has obviously been made against the background of the contemporary value system in the wide sense. It is also clear that Aristotle employs 'virtuous man' and 'villain' in the wide sense of observation or violation of the *philanthropon*. Assumedly, *this system of values is shared by tragedy and comedy.* It follows that any fictional world should be analyzed against the background of its synchronic *philanthropon*.

All the above functions thus reflect the *philanthropon* of the synchronic audience who naturally categorize the fictional interaction in their own terms. Whereas Aristotle presents them as static elements, a dynamic account of them is possible and even necessary: a character that aims at achieving a goal is assessed from the viewpoint of the spectators' contemporary system of values; and, on such grounds, they also generate spontaneous expectations for either its success or failure; and the either gratification or frustration of such expectations produces either a cathartic or a shocking effect respectively. This principle applies also to comedy, albeit its motives and their corresponding values are of less consequence.

This dynamic account reveals that Aristotle presupposes that the spectators develop spontaneous expectations, as otherwise neither gratification nor frustration can be explained. These expectations are 'archetypal' in the sense of being grafted upon the biologically determined and culturally-conditioned wishful and fearful expectations; i.e., in both serious and comedic fictional worlds, archetypal expectations arise not from instinctual drives that aim at realizing themselves such as killing a father or marrying a mother, but are umbilically-linked to ethically-conditioned motives such as the absurdity of an old man's wish to marry a young girl; i.e., they are based on *a priori* archetypal models in the spectators' minds, and not on personal experiences. It should be noted that the notion of 'archetype', as understood by the psychoanalytic school, does not contradict cultural conditioning, as in the Jungian terms 'positive' and 'negative' archetypes (cf. Franz: 158ff). I believe that

Aristotle's presupposition of 'spontaneous expectations' is a fundamental contribution to a theory of fictional worlds: *whereas value systems interchange, the mechanisms of generating archetypal expectations and their gratification or frustration remains the same in all cultures.*

It follows that structures that reflect and gratify the spectator's spontaneous expectations should be termed 'archetypal structures'; and the worlds structured by them 'archetypal fictional worlds'. The notion of 'archetypal ending' is thus wider than 'happy ending', in also applying to 'unhappy endings' for ethically negative and ludicrous characters; i.e., in harmony with the spectator's archetypal expectations. Accordingly, structures that reflect and frustrate the spectator's spontaneous expectations should be termed 'absurdist structures', 'shocking' in Aristotle's terms (*Poetics*: XIII, 2); and the worlds structured by them 'absurdist fictional worlds'. I suggest that, in the narrow sense, comedy shows an unqualified preference for archetypal structures. Pavis correctly contends that 'The *fabula* [narrative] in comedy goes through the phases of *balance, imbalance* and *new balance*' (Pavis: 64), which is an alternative description of the archetypal structure. Such a structure is materialized also by archetypal tragedy. It is noteworthy that there is a kind of tragedy that reflects an absurdist structure; e.g., Euripides' *Hippolytus* and *Medea*.

Archetypal expectations are structural principles in the sense of projecting themselves onto the time axis, towards a possible gratification or frustration, not of the character's wishes, but those of the spectator. It is not only the wishful expectation that something desired will succeed, but also the fearful expectation that something undesired will prevail. Culturally-conditioned wishful and fearful expectations are thus two sides of the same coin. *It is this duality that underlies 'suspense', which is too a euphemism for 'fear'.*

Aristotle erroneously considers that only the archetypal surface structures 3, 4, and 5 can generate tragedies. He contends that the structure that best reflects the *essence* of tragedy is that based on a *hamartia* (5), in satisfying all his four conditions: increment of fear and pity, catastrophe, satisfaction of the ethical sense, and catharsis. Since these are not completely satisfied by those dramatis personae that are characterized on the extremes of the ethical scale, the virtuous and villainous characters, '[t]here remains, then, the character between these two extremes, — that of a man who is not eminently good and just, yet whose misfortune is brought about not by vice or depravity, but by some error or frailty [*hamartia*]' (*Poetics*: XIII, 3; cf. 4). To be detected, a *hamartia* should thus be set against the background of a basically positive character, as otherwise its distinction from 'utter villainy' would be impossible. Since the catastrophes that befall *hamartia*-stricken and negative characters are the same, it is implied that the *hamartia* must be severe to such a degree as to both elicit extreme fear and bring about a proportional catastrophe. In this sense, such a catastrophe gratifies the spectators' expectations; i.e., the fictional world that substantiates structure (5) is archetypal too.

Aristotle also claims that '[i]n the second rank comes the kind of tragedy which some place first. Like the Odyssey, it has a double thread of plot, and also an opposite catastrophe for the good and the bad. It is accounted the best because of the weakness of the spectators; for the poet is guided in what he writes by the wishes of his audience' (*Poetics*: XIII, 7). This structure is based on the conflict between a virtuous man and a villain that leads to opposite endings for both, according to their ethical characterization, while both satisfy the archetypal expectations of the synchronic audience. The ending of such a double-surface structure has usually been termed 'poetic justice'. In Aristotle's view, this kind of tragedy, which combines archetypal structures 3 and 4, does satisfy the ethical sense of the audience, but does not elicit fear — thus precluding catharsis. I believe that this reflects a misunderstanding of the relation between fictional structure and 'catharsis': also the conflict between virtuous and villainous characters produces additional fear, which is the raw material of catharsis.

The term 'catharsis' too has been variously understood and translated; e.g., against the background of the traditional 'purification' (Butcher: 243), Butcher translates it into 'purgation' (*Poetics*: VI, 2) and Halliwell uses '*katharsis*', with no translation (p. 37). The problem is that while Aristotle employs this term in the *Poetics*, he neither defines nor explains it. He also employs it in his *Politics* for the effect of a kind of music, but again with no explicit explanation. He even refers its readers to the *Poetics* for its meaning (VIII, vii, 4). Following J. Bernays (1857), it is now widely accepted that 'catharsis' is a dead metaphor, whose source lies in the medical domain in which it is used to explain the effect of laxatives in causing the evacuation of harmful matters through the intake of less harmful ones (Butcher: 244–5). Indeed, in *Politics*, Aristotle clearly draws an analogy between purgation and this kind of music, which restores the listeners to their normal state 'as if they had received medical treatment and taken a purge', and affords them 'harmless delight' (VIII, vii, 5–6; cf. Butcher 249). The application of this term to the arts is thus based on a *weak* analogy between the intake of materials foreign to the body in order to remove *different* and harmful materials, and the arousal of fear and pity in order to remove an excess of the *similar* emotions, perceived as harmful to social and individual life.

In general, no analogy should be stretched beyond its limits. First, in contrast to purgation, Aristotle's perception of the cathartic mechanism in tragedy stresses the similarity between the emotions aroused by a fictional world (fear and pity) and the removed emotions (*Poetics*: VI, 2). Second, this analogy does not explain the mechanism underlying this psychical process, which is obviously different. On such grounds the mere transference of 'catharsis' from the physical to the psychical domain implies difference that may justify its translation into 'purification'. The therapeutic connotation, possibly advocated by Aristotle himself, is clearly supported by the psychoanalytic approach; e.g., 'our actual enjoyment of an imaginative work proceeds from a liberation of tensions in our minds' (Freud, 1990: 141).

Anxiety is produced not only by harmony being overthrown by evil or unintended harm, but also by foolishness and even clumsiness. In fact, any action that threatens to unbalance psychical harmony, whatever the cause, can produce additional anxiety, which is the precondition for holistic catharsis. Even real events that evince similar conditions can produce catharsis; e.g., the catharsis of a soccer fan when his team eventually wins.

Theory of drama should explain why increased and accumulated tension should lead to its eventual release (holistic catharsis). In fact, there are fictional worlds that end in increased tension, which are shocking in Aristotle's terms (*Poetics*: XIII, 2); i.e., in an absurd final accord. He thus implies that anxiety is produced by a sense of disharmony between spontaneous expectations and momentary or final outcomes of actions. I suggest, therefore, that *a fictional world produces holistic catharsis only through a peripeteia, i.e., the final reversal of the fictional situation from its temporary absurdity, in contrasting the spontaneous expectations of the audience based on their held values, which augments the anxiety accumulated in real life, to their eventual gratification.* Such a peripeteia can be brought about by diverse means such as *anagnorisis*, a character's change of mind, a change in external circumstances, and even by *deus ex machina*.

Since holistic catharsis depends on the accumulation of anxiety, a euphemism for fear, and presupposes it, there is every reason to suggest that comedy too potentially produces anxiety, which is a pre-condition for its holistic catharsis. Indeed, comedy often presents an irrational situation that potentially augments the spectator's anxiety and, therefore, may bring about the total release of accumulated tension through a peripeteia from initial absurdity to eventual harmony. Fundamentally, the principle of 'holistic catharsis' entails that *fearful thinking is the emotional raw material of drama, whether tragedy or comedy*.

It follows, therefore, probably *in contrast* to Aristotle's view, that *comedic catharsis does not differ from tragic catharsis*. When he claims that each art or, rather, genre 'ought to produce, not any chance pleasure, but the pleasure proper to it' (*Poetics*: XXVI, 7; cf. XIV, 2), he presupposes that different genres differ in their kinds of holistic catharsis. This view is supported by his contention that the 'second rank' tragedy produces a kind of pleasure that 'is not the true tragic pleasure. It is proper rather to Comedy, where those who, in the piece, are the deadliest enemies — like Orestes and Aegisthus — quit the stage as friends at the close, and no one slays or is slain' (*Poetics*: XIII, 8). He clearly implies thereby the possibility of a specific kind of comedic holistic catharsis. I suggest that this implication does not stand to reason: it is unthinkable that the human psyche affords a cathartic mechanism for each possible genre. It is more reasonable to assume that catharsis is a single psychical mechanism that can be triggered by different archetypal structures, following a peripeteia from a situation that contrasts archetypal expectations to their gratification (Rozik: 2009). In other words, in contrast to Aristotle, I suggest that there is no difference between tragic and comedic holistic catharsis (cf. *Poetics*: XIV, 2 & XXVI, 7).

In all the archetypal structures it is the peripeteia toward harmony that triggers the forceful discharge of harmful anxiety, which sweeps away *all* the spectators' fears, like the opening of a valve for the release of excessive pressure (cf. Freud: 1990: 141). Assumedly, the higher the anxiety the stronger is the catharsis. Therefore, the cathartic principle also explains why the climax of suspense must be deferred almost to the ending (Lope, 1965: 20, p. 66; cf. Corneille: 180). It should be noted that the phenomenon of catharsis has also been demonstrated experimentally (Kreitler), albeit not given a final explanation.

Aristotle employs the verb 'shock' for a structure that eventually frustrates the spectators' spontaneous expectations (*Poetics*: XIII, 2), while implying that the opposite surface structures gratify them. While the shocking structures include those in which a virtuous character ends in failure and a villain or *hamartia*-stricken character ends in success, the gratifying structures include those in which a positive character ends in success and a negative or *hamartia*-afflicted character ends in catastrophe. In other words, it is the eventual disharmony that is 'shocking', in the sense of ending in augmented anxiety, in contrast to catharsis. Comedy definitely avoids shocking structures.

Attempts have been made to arrive at a formula for comedic catharsis in parallel to that suggested by Aristotle for tragedy. For example, the *Tractatus Coislinianus* suggests that '[c]omedy is an imitation of an action that is ludicrous and imperfect . . . through pleasure and laughter effecting the purgation of the like emotions' (Cooper: 224). It should be stressed that this formula echoes the similarity between the emotions elicited by tragedy and those purged by it. However, there is no point in the catharsis of either laughter or pleasure. There is no reason to cathart pleasure, because it is not a harmful emotion, and it is as absurd as saying that comedy catharts a cathartic mechanism. Similarly, Wylie Sypher claims: 'Like tragedy, comedy is homeopathic. It cures folly by folly' (p. 222). However, although this formulation too is parallel to that of Aristotle, it lacks its necessary implication: it is the anxiety caused by folly that is catharted by comedy's dénouement. It is more sensible, therefore, to claim that comedic catharsis too presupposes anxiety in the spectator, because it is the absurd behavior of the ludicrous character that lifts the inhibitions, which produces anxiety. Therefore, as I have suggested for laughter (see CHAPTER 2), there is nothing to prevent the use of Aristotle's same formula for comedy: it is the catharsis of anxiety, increased by the comedic action, that is released by the final peripeteia, which brings about the gratification of the spectators' archetypal expectations; e.g., the youngsters' wedding. In the context of comedy, there is no point in suggesting pity as an additional emotion that is produced and purged by the comedic action, because, as suggested above, it is irrelevant to the comic mood, laughter in particular (see CHAPTER 2).

If holistic catharsis presupposes that a fictional world is capable of increasing anxiety, in addition to the anxiety that the spectators harbor prior to their exposure to a fictional experience; that this increment depends on the irrational nature of a fictional narrative; and that the total release of anxiety necessitates a peripeteia from an imminent frustrating dead end to a gratifying one, then there is no reason to deny potential holistic catharsis to the combination of structures 3 and 4. Although Aristotle scorns this double structure, because the playwright is guided 'by the wishes of his audience' (*Poetics*: XIII, 7), he still categorizes it as tragic, which indicates that in Aristotle's view the common denominator of structures 3, 4 and 5 is not their structure of action, but their tragic mood.

Aristotle rejects surface structures 1 and 2 as fit for tragedy for being shocking; i.e., contrasting archetypal expectations. Nevertheless, on the grounds of the serious mood being the specific difference of tragedy, absurdist structures too generate tragedies, as Aristotle himself implicitly admits in his praise of Euripides' tragedies (*Poetics*: XIII, 6). Paradoxically, he fails to envisage the theoretical possibility of absurdist structures generating tragedies, despite their actual existence in his own time. Neither did he envisage the possibility of absurdist structures aiming at reaffirming the absurdist expectations of synchronic audiences. Nonetheless, structures leading to the experience of the absurd can be derived from Aristotle's archetypal structures by simple inversion, on the grounds of eventually frustrating archetypal expectations, as Aristotle himself posits in regard to his 'shocking' structures (*Poetics*: XIII, 2). I suggest that *the absurdist structures not only contrast the archetypal ones, but also presuppose them: only against the background of archetypal expectations can their frustration be experienced as absurd.* Although absurdist structures are irrelevant to the discussion of comedy, they are highly relevant to the nature of tangential genres, satiric and grotesque drama in particular, as we shall see below (see CHAPTER 8).

I suggest that the archetypal structures of action, posited by Aristotle, while taking into account his presuppositions and the above qualifications, are also shared by comedy, and that its specific difference lies in its typical humorous mood. It is this mood that affects all the levels of the structure of action and determines comedy's consistent lowering of motives, values and effects. Following Aristotle, the theoretical tradition has focused on the comedic structure based on the comic *hamartia*, which is the humorous counterpart of the tragic *hamartia*. However, there are additional ways of implementing the humorous mood, as shown above; e.g., the sitcom (see CHAPTER 3).

Although Aristotle's approach is limited in various regards, the inclusion of the spectators' value judgments and their archetypal expectations as decisive structuring factors are major theoretical achievements in the understanding of both tragedy and comedy.

In principle, Lope de Vega (e.g., 1965: 5, p. 64), Corneille (e.g., p. 170) and John Dryden (e.g., pp. 142–7) accept and implement Aristotle's structural approach. Nonetheless, in contrast to Aristotle's essentialist attitude, based on what tragedy should be according to its ultimate aim, holistic catharsis, they offer a hedonist approach to fictional creativity and reception, in the sense of considering the gratification of the spectator's taste of supreme importance. In fact, there is no necessary contrast between holistic catharsis and gratification of the spectators' expectations. Accordingly, in contrast to the *Poetics*, they show a clear predilection for his second-rank structure (3 & 4), while supporting their positions with the very same reason employed by Aristotle for condemning this structure: the gratification of the audience's expectations (*Poetics*: XIII, 7). Probably following Aristotle's remark to the effect that the dénouement of this double structure is 'proper rather to comedy' (XIII, 8), Lope also advocated the use of 'comedy' for his serious play-scripts that, even according to the dominance of their 'serious mood', as implied in the *Poetics*, deserve to be labeled 'tragedies'.

Hegel's structural approach

G.W.F. Hegel made a substantial contribution to the structural approach by emphasizing the cognitive intent of the fictional experience, which is marginalized by Aristotle, particularly by his notion of 'catharsis'. Hegel presupposes the existence of an 'ethical substance', which is a kind of Platonic idea of 'ethos', and contends that, in any culture, each particular value both shares the nature of the ethical substance and is a reductive version of it. A particular value is thus partially valid and partially violates the absolute validity of the ethical substance. A tragic character that abides by a particular value, and disregards the validity of any other value, thus violates the ethical substance, especially in the case of conflict, despite both parties deriving their justifications from the very same absolute source of validity. Therefore, the typical tendency of the ethical substance is to expose the partiality of each particular value and to reestablish its own unqualified unity, which is achieved through the tragic catastrophe: 'However justified the tragic character and his aim, however necessary the tragic collision, the . . . thing required is the tragic resolution of this conflict. . . . [which] restores the substance and unity of ethical life with the downfall of the individual who has disturbed its peace' (p. 1197). Such a dénouement brings about a sense of 'reconciliation' (*ibid.*), which explains the paradoxical nature of the spectator's pleasure at the tragic dénouement: pleasure despite the main character's suffering. In addition to 'reconciliation' (pp. 83 & 91), Bradley employs 'restitution' and 'affirmation' (p. 91); and Krook uses 'reaffirmation' of the ethical order (p. 8) in the sense of reinstituting its absolute validity, which is a cognitive act in nature. This study employs Krook's term.

Hegel applies a general theory of historical change to the ancient Greek culture, whose basic pattern is thesis, antithesis and synthesis, and contends that the idea of an ethical substance, and the conflicts and reconciliations that it generates, is a discovery not of Greek philosophy, but of Sophocles' tragedies, particularly his *Antigone*. Allegedly, this play-script attained the peak of ancient cognitive achievements. It is hard to believe, however, that Sophocles was interested in exploring principles of historical change. In general, it is not the aim of a theory of fictional creativity to search for epistemic achievements sanctioned by philosophy as such, but to understand the mechanisms of generating meaning through fictional worlds.

Nonetheless, with appropriate modification, Hegel's theory can enrich the theory of comedy by providing a beneficial insight into the cognitive nature of the dramatic experience. Accordingly, I suggest, first, that *what is actually at stake in each fictional world is not the 'ethical substance', but the synchronic ethical system of an audience*, what Aristotle probably means by '*philanthropon*': despite possible partiality, the aim of a fictional world is to bring about the reaffirmation or confutation of its validity. I suggest that this applies to both tragedy and comedy, albeit the latter relates to values that are perceived as less significant by contemporary culture, thus reflecting the latter's lighthearted mood. For example, in Sophocles' *Oedipus the King*, Oedipus' endeavor to live in contrast to Apollo's prophesy questions the god's divinity, committing thereby the sin of hubris. This is corroborated by his attempt to invoke Tyche, the goddess of chance, instead of Apollo. Consequently, according to contemporary beliefs, the catastrophe that befalls him restores the cosmic order, and reconfirms them. In comedy, in contrast, the values at stake are less central to the spectator's beliefs; e.g., the golden mean in Terence's *The Brothers*.

In a tragic archetypal fictional world a character may endanger the audience's synchronic ethical system — thus leading to its own catastrophe (cf. Hegel: 1196); Bradley: 69ff; & Krook: 8–9); or a character may comply with this system — thus leading to a happy ending. Both such endings reflect the archetypal expectations of a synchronic audience and are conducive to a sense of reaffirmation. In all genres, therefore, such endings convey a verdict on such a system of values; e.g., in tragedy, *a final catastrophe is a metaphor of the negative nature of evil or a hamartia, as determined by the synchronic philanthropon.*

On such grounds, it is possible to understand how a catastrophe becomes a metaphor of order or, rather, what is viewed as order by a synchronic audience. This principle too applies to comedy; e.g., the frustration of a ludicrous father, which gratifies the spectator's spontaneous expectations, is a metaphor of the negative nature of his comic hamartia. Correspondingly, a final wedding is a metaphor of the positive nature of the lovers' shared motive — thus conveying the reaffirmation of their values. In contrast to both, the eventual frustration of archetypal expectations is meant to subvert established values through the spectator's experience of the absurd. As suggested above, whereas comedy avoids absurdist structures, these are usually implemented in satire and grotesque drama (see CHAPTER 8).

Second, there is little point in the use of 'conflict' only for double actions in which the confronting characters are equally justified; especially if we take into consideration that these may be perceived differently from either naïve or ironic viewpoints; e.g., Sophocles' *Antigone* (Rozik, 2009: 229–33). From the viewpoint of theoretical efficiency it is preferable to use this term for any clash between characters, whether both parties are justified, or not; and whether both parties are assessed from either naïve or ironic viewpoints.

Hegel's approach complements Aristotle's *Poetics*: first, acting in accordance with a particular value, while disregarding the validity of another value, can be perceived as a case of *hamartia*; and second, Hegel's theory reveals the crucial epistemic function of the fictional world, which is marginalized by the *Poetics*, probably because of its focus on tragedy's emotional effect. In this sense, catharsis should be seen as the emotional counterpart of cognitive reaffirmation in both tragedy and comedy.

The combination of Aristotle's and Hegel's approaches provides, therefore, the necessary tools for a synthetic theory of the deep and surface structures of action that, in principle, are shared by all genres. It is, therefore, the specific mood that determines their specific differences (see CHAPTER 1). It follows that the structures of action and moods are mutually independent and that, in principle, any mood can attach to any structure of action, and vice versa, including two moods within the same fictional world; e.g., the mixing of moods in Shakespeare's *Romeo and Juliet* (see CHAPTER 1).

The psychoanalytic approach

Ludwig Jekels reports that the analysis of several classical comedies led him to the conclusion that they are characterized 'by a mechanism of inversion: *the feeling of guilt which, in tragedy, rests upon the son, appears in comedy displaced on the father; it is the father who is guilty*' (p. 264). Moreover, 'this infantile phantasy of the father as the disturber of love is nothing but a projection of the son's own guilty wish to disturb the love of the parents. By displacing this phantasy on the father, by endowing him with this specifically filial attitude, it becomes clear that the father is divested of his paternal attributes, and thus is removed as a father and degraded into a son' (p. 268; cf. Grotjahn: 273). It is certainly the case that in some comedies the father's endeavor to block his son's love match is eventually frustrated, and the son has the upper hand. However, first, a quite limited set of comedies features such a theme, which does not characterize comedy as a genre on structural grounds, not to speak of comedies in which only father-daughter relations are involved. At most this theme can explain its wide appeal for certain audiences. Second, a very limited set of tragedies too features the theme of children's guilt, which definitely has nothing to do with the structure of tragedy as a genre. It is noteworthy that in Sophocles' *Oedipus the King*, Oedipus is not guilty of killing his father, but of hubris and *miasma* (pollution) (Rozik, 2008a: 118–19 & 129–31).

Third, the blocking role of a father in a fictional world can also be explained on different grounds, which are closer to the nature of comedy's structure. In some societies, while the fathers enjoy power, including wealth, their children are dependent on them for their livelihood and marital choices. Against this background, the combination of a defective character and power is critical: in endangering the welfare of those who depend on him and frustrating the spectators' wishes for their success: excessive power produces anxiety, which is exacerbated by the father's foolish behavior. Therefore, the reversal of the situation, when the father is reduced to frustration, potentially releases anxiety. It is both the initial absurdity and the final peripeteia toward harmonization that better explains the appeal of such a theme. In comedy such a reversal is humorous and carnivalesque in nature (see CHAPTER 10). This theme also explains the aggressive nature of satire when deriding an individual on whom the welfare of the spectators depends (see CHAPTER 8). Jekels claims that '[o]nly this reduction of the father to a son can explain how writers of comedies can unleash so wide a range of aggression (scorn. derision, etc.) against the father' (Jekels: 169). In contrast, I suggest that aggressiveness is the hallmark not of comedy, which is lighthearted in nature, but of satire, which is not (see CHAPTER 8).

An interesting fact is that in many a comedy fathers are not accompanied by mothers but, at most, by stepmothers. According to the psychoanalytic approach, it might have been expected that the alleged 'mechanism of inversion' would also apply to sons' guilt for wishing to marry their mothers, and thus constitute a very attractive theme for comedy. The fact is, however, that it is not. This too supports the claim that the appeal of this theme is better explained by the conflict of power between fathers and children. Mothers are not involved in such a

struggle — thus being, possibly, superfluous characters. Extreme dependence creates anxiety, which is a precondition for holistic catharsis.

Jekels contends that:

> Not only has psycho-analysis made us recognise that the "tragic guilt"
> of the hero, . . . actually stems from the repressed Oedipus-wishes of
> the dramatist but it has also drawn our attention to the interrelation of
> dramatist and audience; that is, to the fact of a common guilt as the
> decisive psychological factor which, on the one hand, enables the
> dramatist to create his work and, on the other, produces Aristotelian
> catharsis, or "purging of the passions". (p. 263)

Grotjahn too endorses Jekels' interpretation of comedy as an inversion
of the myth of Oedipus: 'The psychodynamics of the comedy can be
understood as a kind of reversed Oedipus situation in which the son does
not rebel against the father but the son's typical attitudes of childhood
longing are projected upon the father, The son plays the role of the victorious father with sexual freedom and achievement, while the father is
cast in the role of the frustrated onlooker' (p. 273). Nevertheless, just as
the myth of Oedipus does not characterize the genre of tragedy, its inversion too does not characterize the genre of comedy. Unfortunately,
Jekels' theory reflects the typical fallacy of the traditional psychoanalytic school of criticism in its attempt to reduce all tragedies (and all
comedies) to a single myth, in clear contrast to their vast thematic diversity.

Jekels wonders how the same impulse results in 'such completely,
even diametrically opposite effects . . . tragic guilt and expiation arise in
one case, and effervescent high spirits in the other?' (p. 268) This is an
excellent question. For the right answer, however, it is necessary to look
not into the thematic features of comedy, but into the different treat-
ments, moods in particular, of the very same myths.

Frye's thematic approach

In contrast to Aristotle and Hegel, and under the influence of the psychoanalytic school, Northrop Frye too suggests a structure for the action of
comedy on thematic grounds: '*What normally happens* is that a young
man wants a young woman, that his desire is resisted by some opposition, usually paternal, and that near the end of the play some twist in the
plot enables the hero to have his will' (p. 163; my italics). However, such

a thematic structure can also be implemented by a serious fictional world.

On a more abstract level, Frye suggests a model that comes closer to the notion of 'structure' as promoted in this study: 'The obstacles to the hero's desire . . . form the action of the comedy, and the overcoming of them the comic resolution'. (p. 164) Indeed, this formula applies to a wider range of comedies, even to those that do not feature the theme of parental obstruction to youngsters' love. Furthermore, the principles of 'desire' and 'opposition' determine the existence of two types of characters: that which features a positive motivation and that which obstructs it. Frye continues: 'The obstacles are usually paternal, hence comedy *often* turns on a clash between a son's and a father's will' (p. 164; my italics). However, this widening of the set does not abolish the qualifications raised above. Indeed, this model reverts to thematic terms. 'Paternal' implies that not only fathers fulfil this function, but also their equivalents such as guardians. Furthermore, an action that brings about the frustration of a ludicrous father or guardian greatly suits the archetypal endings that characterize comedy; e.g., Molière's *The School for Wives*.

Frye also suggests that 'Comedy usually moves toward a happy ending, and the normal response of the audience to a happy ending is "this should be", which sounds like a moral judgment. So it is, except that it is not moral in the restricted sense, but social. Its opposite is not the villainous but the absurd' (p. 167). Such a 'happy ending' is implied in Frye's 'overcoming of the obstruction'. Moreover:

> [t]he movement of comedy is *usually* a movement from one kind of society to another. At the beginning of the play the obstructing characters are in charge of the play's society, and the audience recognizes that they are usurpers. At the end of the play the device in the plot that brings hero and heroine together causes a new society to crystallize around the hero, and the moment when this crystallization occurs is the point of resolution in the action, the comic discovery, *anagnorisis* or *cognitio*. (p. 163; my italics)

Furthermore, '[t]he tendency of comedy is to include as many people as possible in its final society: the blocking characters are more often reconciled or converted than simply repudiated' (p. 165). This is a remarkable insight that reflects the overall effect of the comic mood.

The appearance of this new society is *frequently* signalled by some kind of party or festive ritual, which either appears at the end of the play or is assumed to take place immediately afterward. Weddings are most common. . . . As the final society reached by comedy is the one that the audience has recognized all along to be the proper and desirable state of affairs, and an act of communion with the audience is in order. . . . The resolution of comedy comes . . . from the audience's side of stage.' (pp. 163–4; my italics)

'An act of communion with the audience' probably means that eventually the fictional world gratifies the archetypal expectations of the audience, and is synonymous with Aristotle's 'the poet is guided . . . by the wishes of his audience' (*Poetics*: XIII, 7). An interesting question is: Why does the audience identify with a society that often contrasts their real one? The answer lies, I believe, in that the spectators do not relate to a fictional world on the grounds of their own life experience, but on those of psychical (archetypal) models of harmony, and on the metaphoric meaning of such worlds. This approach may explain how even real blocking fathers may identify with the wishes of fictional young lovers.

Basically '[t]here are two ways of developing the form of comedy: one is to throw the main emphasis on the blocking characters; the other is to throw it forward on the scenes of discovery and reconciliation' (Frye: 166).The former way is typical of a substantial set of comedies: 'In Molière we have a simple but fully tested formula in which the ethical interest is focused on a single blocking character, a heavy father, a miser, a misanthrope, a hypocrite, or a hypochondriac' (p. 167). Nonetheless, Frye's opposition is quite odd, unless we assume that his intention is to accommodate romantic comedy, in which the blocking characters are not necessarily ludicrous; e.g., Shakespeare's comedies. Nonetheless, there are also other alternatives (see CHAPTER 6).

Frye distinguishes between the 'villainous' and the 'absurd'. However, following Hazlitt's approach, since the blocking characters are often ludicrous, absurdity is their main trait; if so, the correct distinction should be made between the 'villainous' and the 'ludicrous'. Whereas a villainous character consistently violates the values of the synchronic ethical system, a ludicrous character contrasts a model of harmony in the spectator's mind.

Frye's model of a comedic fictional world indeed suits many a comedy, possibly justifying his 'what normally happens'. The problem is that there are also comedies that do not implement this model. The main problem of his approach lies in that his model is formulated in thematic terms, i.e., in the terms of thematic specification, which contradicts the notion of 'structure' as suggested above. The fact is that the themes of 'comedy' are not restricted to obstructed love, e.g., Menander's *The Arbitration*. Moreover, comedic drama often relegates this theme to a secondary role, e.g., Plautus' *The Pot of Gold*; and even serious drama occasionally features it, e.g., Corneille's *Oedipe*.

In the structural terms of a combined Aristotelian/Hegelian approach, Frye's alleged structure of comedy or, rather, 'typical narrative', should be reformulated as follows: from the viewpoint of the audience's *philanthropon*, the parallel and legitimate motives of two positive characters are blocked by a negative or ludicrous character, and a peripeteia enables them to materialize their wish — thus gratifying the archetypal expectations of the audience, reaffirming the synchronic *philanthropon* and potentially producing catharsis. This description implements the structure of an archetypal fictional world.

Plautus' *The Pot of Gold*

Euclio, a miser, obstructs his daughter Phaedria's love. There is only one day left before she must marry old Megadorus, instead of Lyconides, her lover and the father of her baby. The only way to prevent this odd wedding is to steal the father's pot of gold, which is done by a slave who also trades it for his freedom. The probable dénouement (the end of the text is missing) is: the young lover returns the pot of gold in exchange for Euclio's consent to the youngsters' marriage. In the end, the young lovers marry, Euclio gives the pot of gold to his daughter Phaedria as a dowry, and the slave goes free (cf. Molière's *The Miser*).

It is the combination of Aristotle and Hegel's poetics that provides the grounds for a sound theory of the 'structure of action'. In principle, all genres share the entire set of structures of action, and only differ in their typical moods; in particular, the specific difference of comedy lies in its humorous mood. In addition, comedy shows a clear predilection for archetypal structures of action, and definitely avoids absurdist ones. In principle, structures of action and moods are mutually independent, in the sense that all combinations are possible, even within the very same fictional world from different viewponts.

Structure of Comedy 5

The above-considerations lead to the conclusion that there is no difference between tragedy and comedy on the level of structure of action, and that the specific difference of a genre lies in its mood. Therefore, without negating the valuable insights of Aristotle's and Hegel's poetics, there is a need for a more complex model of structure that includes the specific function of the comic mood within the overall structure of comedy, and acknowledges its dominant function in determining the nature of the spectator's experience. I thus suggest a distinction between the structure of action and the structure of a genre, which includes its typical mood. In this respect, I contend that (a) comedy is characterized by absolute preference for an archetypal structure of action; (b) the specific difference of comedy lies in the humorous mood, which explains the said preference; and (c) the dominant role of the humorous mood is manifested in all the structural levels of the structure of action. It should be stressed that the combination of the humoristic mood and a structure of action is not one of necessity. The following sections offer such a complex model.

A model of fictional/comedic structure

This section suggests a model of fictional deep structure that, through the application of additional optional rules, generates all the fictional surface structures. On the level of deep structure, this model both applies to all major genres — tragedy, comedy, melodrama and farce — and enables the distinctions between them on the grounds of specific moods. The model is integrative, in the sense of being basically Aristotelian/Hegelian in nature, and enriched by their presuppositions and implications, while incorporating subsequent theories.

I distinguish here between inner and outer structure: while the former applies to a fictional world in isolation from its possible effect on an audience, the latter focuses on the intended effect, which subordinates the inner structure and determines its nature.

The inner structure

The overall deep structure of a fictional world comprises seven basic layers: personified, mythical, praxical, naïve, ironic, aesthetic and modal (for an expanded discussion of these layers see Rozik, 2009).

(A) *The personified layer:* The fact that a single psyche is represented by a world of characters implies that *the psyche is split into several partial agencies and/or drives, which are represented by a set of human characters; i.e., it is a phenomenon of personification;* which is a particular kind of metaphor that draws its associations from the human sphere. The enactment of these characters by live actors on stage lends additional support to the personified nature of the fictional world. Personification is thus the fundamental layer on which the entire structure of a fictional world is built. This layer characterizes fictional thinking.

Personification is shared by all genres, including comedy, with no differential options. The existence of this layer is based on the insights of psychoanalytic theory.

(B) *The mythical layer* is a kernel narrative, which is grafted upon personification and consists in bestowing minimal characterization on personifications, such as 'father–son'; schematic categorization of actions, such as 'son kills father'; and basic temporal order such as before and after. Even on this abstract level, the essential property of this layer is the ability to produce extreme anxiety, due to embodying the spectator's embarrassing or suppressed irrational drives. 'Anxiety', which is a euphemism for 'fear', *is the vital stuff of drama, including comedy.* The basic principle is: minimal characterization/action and maximal impact on the spectator. On this level, any minimal narrative, which satisfies these conditions, may constitute the nucleus of a meaningful fictional world in any genre.

'Mythical' does not mean here 'myth'. A myth never exhibits the schematic and neutral form of the mythical layer, but is further organized by additional cultural layers, as in any piece of fiction or dramatic narrative. 'Mythical' reflects here the distinction between 'mythos', which is the basic and neutral core of a narrative (including in myth), and 'logos', which consists in the additional layers that lend cultural meaning to a narrative, and can transmute deeply disturbing narrative materials even into an enjoyable experience. It is the substratum of *mythos* that corresponds to 'mythical' here. In this sense, the mythical layer is the simplest and most distressful narrative element. This layer develops Aristotle's intuitions on family animosity (*Poetics*: XIV, 4) and those of the psychoanalytic school, especially in their (biased) treatment of the myth of Oedipus (Rozik, 2009: 149).

This layer offers several options depending on the expected degrees of anxiety, which constitute a continuum ranging from the most trivial entanglements to the most severe infringements of cultural taboos — with their common denominator being their irrational nature. Comedy opts for the lighter end of this continuum. Indeed, the mythical materials at stake in comedy are of less consequence and easier to settle; e.g., in contrast to Oedipus killing his own father, in Molière's *The Miser* father and son compete over the same young maiden, Mariane. Due to his advantage in wealth and cunning, Harpagon threatens to obstruct the realization of the youngsters' mutual love. This nucleus constitutes a source of anxiety in contrasting the archetypal expectations of the audience on two grounds: parents are supposed to care for their children more than for themselves, and love and marriage are supposed to engage people of reasonably similar age; i.e., the opening situation is inherently absurd (obviously, depending on culture).

(c) *The praxical layer* further structures the mythical layer by bestowing thematic specification upon the motive that underlies an action — with each motive aiming at realizing itself, whether it finally succeeds or fails. This performative layer is, therefore, already part of the fictional logos in imposing an axiomatic structure on the mythical layer (*mythos*), in the sense of all the actions of a character deriving from its macro-motive, and in allowing their interpretation by it, which explains the arousal of the spectators' archetypal expectations and their sense of unity. It also determines the temporal boundaries of a fictional world, from the inception of a macro-motive to its consummation or frustration — thus producing a sense of wholeness; e.g., despite his own death, Hamlet's motive to avenge the murder of his father, and his final success, in Shakespeare's *Hamlet* and Dandin's attempts to prevent his wife's infidelity, and his final frustration, in Molière's *George Dandin*. This layer is based on Aristotle's remarks on the centrality of action: 'Hence the incidents and the plot are the end of a tragedy; and the end is the chief thing of all' (*Poetics*: VI, 10). It is also the sole concern of the theories of Vladimir Propp, Étienne Souriau and Algirdas Greimas (Rozik, 2009: 44–6).

Motive and action are mutually independent, in the sense that the same action may reflect different motives, and the same motive may be indicated by different actions. The existence of an overall motive produces two simultaneous archetypal expectations: to either succeed or fail — with one possibility being desired and the other dreaded by the spectator, depending on the nature of the character. These concurrent and contrasting expectations lie at the heart of 'suspense', which too is a euphemism for fear.

In contrast to Aristotle, I suggest that the analysis of this layer should focus on a single macro-action, reflecting a single macro-motive, of a single character. The advantage of isolating a single action lies in that a complex action can be analyzed in the terms of simple ones (e.g., Aristotle's second rank tragedy on the grounds of structures 3 & 4; cf. *Poetics*: XIII, 7–8); e.g., two characters having a common end or pursuing ends that exclude one another; i.e., being in conflict. This principle too applies to all genres (*ibid.*: VI, 10; cf. VI, 5). It also applies to comedies that feature parallel actions on the levels of masters and servants; e.g., Molière's *Don Juan*.

This layer offers two basic choices: (a) between specific macro-motives that range from the most trivial to the most consequential — with comedy revealing a consistent predilection for the trivial end of the continuum, e.g., to receive wages from two masters in Goldoni's *The Servant of Two Masters*; and (b) between macro-motives that end in either success or failure — with comedy revealing a consistent predilection for happy endings for the positive characters and unhappy ones for the negative or the ludicrous characters; i.e., for endings that gratify the spectators' archetypal expectations; e.g., Menander's *The Arbitration*.

Flawed macro-motives also motivate ludicrous characters, but their faults are lighter; e.g., in Molière's *The School for Wives*, Arnolphe believes that he has developed a method to prevent a future wife from betraying her husband through educating her as a simpleton. Eventually, he is made to experience the absurdity of his own idea. Indeed, his "method" reflects a ludicrous *hamartia*. Furthermore, in contrast to tragedy that often ends in disastrous consequences, without necessarily contradicting the archetypal expectations of the audience, a comedy usually ends in (the prospect of) a happy ceremony such as a wedding and/or festive meal; e.g., Plautus' *The Pot of Gold*, and Molière's *The Trickeries of Scapin*.

(D) *The naïve layer* further structures the praxical layer in terms of the ethical/epistemic categorization of the characters' motives and actions, from their own independent and naïve viewpoints. 'Ethical' is used here in the sense of any principle that is valued in the eyes of a character, an author and/or a synchronic audience (see CHAPTER 4). The term 'naïve' presupposes the operation of an ironic perspective — with the latter reflecting authorial authority; i.e., a perspective is naïve from an ironic viewpoint.

A 'viewpoint' is reflected in the terms through which a motive or act/action is perceived. Such terms represent an ethical/epistemic system. There is, usually no need for a full and orderly exposition of such a system due to its being part of the audience's cultural baggage. The system is, rather, represented by key terms, which should be seen as its metonyms, on the grounds of a part/whole relationship. Through these metonyms an entire ethical/epistemic system thus becomes an integral part of a fictional world. The ethical and/or cognitive neutrality of the mythical and praxical layers are thus lent a dimension of cultural meaning. Since characters tend to justify their motives even if negative, the naïve layer might increase the sense of absurdity induced by the mythical layer; e.g., the positive reasons given by Knemon in favor of his misanthropy in Menander's *Old Cantankerous*. This layer is not accounted for in any of the major theories of comedic structure.

The naïve layer offers two basic choices: (a) between a naïve viewpoint that conforms to the synchronic *philanthropon* or is alternative to it; and (b) between a naïve viewpoint that is anchored in an established epistemic/ethical value system or in an innovative one. These options hold for all genres. Nonetheless, whereas the naïve viewpoints of tragic characters are capable of undermining crucial beliefs and/or values of the synchronic audience, those of ludicrous characters are usually simply ridiculous and support foolish macro-motives.

(E) *The ironic layer* further structures the previous layers by re-categorizing the fictional interaction, including the naïve layer, from the viewpoint of the author's ethical system, which is expected to be adopted by the synchronic audience. Whereas the mythical and naïve layers stress the irrational nature of the narrative (*mythos*), the praxical and ironic layers foster a sense of rationality (*logos*). Indeed, the ironic layer underlies the experiences of reaffirmation or confutation of held beliefs and values (Hegel: 1194–7; cf. Bradley: 69–95), the *philanthropon* in Aristotle's terms (*Poetics*: XIII, 2).

The structural gap between the ironic and naïve perspectives constitutes 'dramatic irony', which is the sense of advantage that spectators experience in their better knowledge, understanding and evaluation of the characters' worlds (see CHAPTER 3). Although the natural propensity of the spectators is to categorize the fictional world in their own terms of reference, most fictional worlds feature key terms (metonyms) of the established epistemic/ethical system, which aim at guiding the spectators towards the expected categorization. These terms are conveyed by ironic conventions — functional characters and/or inter-acting characters in functional situations (e.g., the soliloquy) — which represent the author within a dramatic text. The analysis of this layer requires, therefore, knowledge of the synchronic spectators' cultural background.

While both the naïve and ironic perspectives converge on the praxical level, the latter enjoys authorial authority; namely, it is the one expected to be adopted by the receivers. On such grounds, a fictional world should be perceived as a mechanism that manipulates the audience into a preconceived perspective on a fictional world. The ironic layer is thus at the heart of the logos. This layer develops the notion of 'dramatic irony' as suggested by G. G. Sedgewick (pp. 32–3) and Styan (1967: 48–63).

The ironic layer offers three basic choices: (a) between positive, nega-tive and (tragic or comic) *hamartia* characterization from the ironic viewpoint; (b) between sharing the ironic viewpoint with the spectator or not, who in the latter case becomes the object of dramatic irony; and (c) between an ending that either gratifies or frustrates the receivers' archetypal expectations, thus reaffirming or confuting respectively their *philanthropon*.

This layer is shared by all fictional genres. However, (a) whereas in serious fictional worlds flawed motives are reconsidered in terms of, for example, hubris, theomachy, and heresy, in comedic fictional worlds they are in terms of, for example, absentmindedness, foolishness, and clumsiness. And (b) whereas in the former the values at stake are highly consequential and their confutation may jeopardize the spectator's basic orientation in the world, in the latter the values are "lighter" such as 'moderation' (e.g., Terence's *The Brothers*), honesty (e.g., anonymous *Maître Pathelin*) and matrimonial fidelity (e.g., Molière's *The School for Wives*). Furthermore, comedy shows a consistent preference for arche-typal endings; i.e., endings that reaffirm the spectator's held values and beliefs.

(F) *The aesthetic layer* re-structures all the previous layers in terms of 'harmony' or 'disharmony', which in my view are the main aesthetic categories, with the archetypal expectations of the spectator. This layer develops aesthetic principles, whose discovery and application are rela-tively recent in comparison to Aristotle's *Poetics*. Rather than reflecting poetic rules, this layer imposes aesthetic rules of its own on fictional worlds. These rules thus require a basic familiarity with aesthetics (cf. Rozik, 2009: 79–89).

Inter alia, fictional endings are reconsidered in terms of 'proportion' or 'disproportion', which are aesthetic sub-categories of harmony and disharmony. 'Proportion' presupposes that the audience exercises an intuitive model of harmony in regard to the relation between the ethical meaning of a motive/action and the performative meaning of its success or failure; e.g., between Truffaldino's attempt to gain wages from two masters, which is unethical, and the eventual proportional punishment: being beaten by both masters. Even real outcomes are usually examined in such terms; e.g., the perennial question: why do the righteous suffer and the wicked prosper? (*Babylonian Talmud*, Berakhot, 7a; cf. *Ecclesiastes*: 8, 14). Following the methodical preference for the analysis of single actions, in comedy there is a proportional ending for each kind of character such as the young lovers, the villain, the astute servant and the ludicrous *senex* (old man). On the cognitive level, whereas an experience of proportion is archetypal and reaffirms the audience's value system, an experience of 'disproportion' is absurd and questions the system's validity.

Although all fictional genres equally feature this layer, there are differences, which reflect the dominant function of their specific moods. Both archetypal tragedy and comedy aim at a proportional ending that gratifies the spectator's spontaneous expectations; but, whereas in the former this is often achieved by the catastrophe that befalls a villainous or *hamartia*-afflicted character, in the latter this is achieved by lighter misfortunes; e.g., in Molière's *The Trickeries of Scapin*, Scapin is only reprimanded, and eventually pardoned. Whereas in archetypal tragedy the virtuous character ends in success, comedy usually harmonizes with the spectators' spontaneous expectations through a felicitous event; e.g., the eventual marriage of Sostratos and Knemon's daughter in Menander's *Old Cantankerous*. Nevertheless, d*espite these differences, the experience of proportion is the same, in similarly reflecting archetypal models of proportion in the spectator's mind.*

As Frye correctly observes: 'The tendency of [the fictional] society is to include as many people as possible in its final society: the blocking characters are more often reconciled or converted than simply repudiated' (p. 165). For example, in Molière's *The Miser*, although frustrated in his attempt to marry Mariane, Harpagon still recovers his money and participates in the final weddings. In general, comedy shows a consistent preference for archetypal fictional worlds and avoids disproportional or, rather, absurdist endings, which also reflects the dominant role of the humorous mood.

This layer offers two choices: (a) proportion or disproportion in the relation between the ethical nature of a character/motive and the character's final lot; and (b) gratification or frustration of the archetypal expectations of the audience, which in fact reconsiders the either reaffirmation or confutation of their held beliefs and values in aesthetic terms. Whereas proportion and gratification of the spectators' archetypal expectations are reconsidered in terms of 'harmony', disproportion and frustration of such expectations are in terms of 'disharmony' or, rather, 'absurdity' in Esslin's terms (p. xix). *While each cultural audience operates its own value system and standards of harmony and disharmony, the mechanisms of harmonization or absurdization (reaffirmation and confutation) are the same across cultures.* In reflecting the authorial attitude, this layer too fulfills an ironic function.

The harmonious or disharmonious nature of the fictional experience also explains the either cathartic or shocking effect on the audience, which should be seen as the physical counterpart of the experience of cognitive harmony or disharmony.

The aesthetic nature of comedy is also manifested in its typical tempo. It presupposes various intuitive models of tempo that characterize different personalities, occupations and activities, which can be harmonized with or not. In this sense, a particular enacted behavior can be faster or slower than expected; e.g., tragedy is usually slower than usual and comedy faster than usual — with farce bringing tempo to paroxysm. In this respect too, a particular genre also creates definite expectations that can be either harmonized with or not (see CHAPTER 4)

(G) *The modal layer* further structures all the previous layers, which together constitute the structure of action, through the optional prism of a serious, comic, satiric or grotesque mood, or a calculated combination of them. There is an unbridgeable gap between the serious and the humorous moods, and gradation is found only within each of them. Whereas the sublime mood of tragedy is the highest pole of the serious continuum, e.g., Aeschylus' *The Oresteia*, the 'true to life' mood of melodrama is probably the lowest, e.g., C. H. Hazlewood's *Lady Audley's Secret*; and whereas the romantic atmosphere of Shakespeare's comedies is probably the highest pole of the lighthearted continuum, e.g., *Twelfth Night* (see CHAPTER 7), the crude means of farce is the lowest; e.g., *The Three Cuckolds* (a scenario of *commedia dell'arte*; Lea: 582–4. See CHAPTER 9).

Since a mood circumvents the characters' viewpoints, and often permeates entire fictional worlds, it should be perceived as fulfilling an ironic function, in reflecting the author's perspective on the fictional world and conditioning the audience's attitude to it. For the same reason, in the case of a single mood, it is sensible to speak in terms of 'unity of mood'.

Although mood is accounted for in all theories of fictional genres, it has never been seen as a structural layer in the structure of a fictional world, comedy in particular.

The humorous mood is reflected in each of the previous layers in the consistent lowering of levels: e.g., the kinds of macro-motive, the types of success or failure, and the values and beliefs that underpin the characters' actions. The lowering tendency of comedy is also reflected in the nature of its deities; e.g., Aphrodite's prologue in Euripides' *Hippolytus*, as opposed to the *lar familiaris'* prologue in Plautus' *The Pot of Gold*.

This layer offers two basic choices: (a) between the serious, the humorous, the satiric and the grotesque moods; and (b) between pure and mixed moods. As suggested above, there are two basic kinds of mixed moods: (a) the *linear*, in which the moods alternate, without hindering one another; e.g., in Molière's *Don Juan*: whilst the serious mood is promoted by Don Juan the humorous mood is promoted by Sganarelle. Whilst Don Juan deserves the fires of hell, his comic servant is left to bemoan his lost wages: 'Mes gages! Mes gages!' Another example: in Shakespeare's *Romeo and Juliet* there is a clear transition from the humorous mood of the beginning to the extremely serious mood of the ending (see CHAPTER 1). And (b) the *grotesque*, in which what appears to be a comic mood or, rather, a set of laughter devices, is imposed on an extremely serious theme (see CHAPTER 1). In such a case, these devices undercut the serious associations of a certain theme; e.g., the theme of individual death in Ionesco's *Exit the King* (see CHAPTER 8).

T.G.A. Nelson contends that 'there is a potential for *conflict* between the subversiveness of comic action and dialogue, full of pratfalls, insults, ridicule, defiance, and irreverence, and the steady movement towards harmony in the comic plot' (p. 2; quoted by Weitz: 12; my italics). Indeed, there is an inherent tension between the action of a comedy, which is serious in nature, such as the theme of obstructed love, and the comic mood that constitutes the prism through which such an action is meant to be perceived. Nonetheless, in contrast to Segal, who tends to find tragic elements in most comedies (e.g., pp. 219, 317 & 358), this is not a matter of conflict but of function: the serious action fuels the tension necessary for both comic laughter and holistic catharsis (see CHAPTER 2).

This layer develops Aristotle's remark that second-rank tragedies do not fully realize the essence of tragedy (*Poetics*: XIII, 8); while still these being categorized as tragedies. This implies that this is due to both the sharing of the serious/sublime mood, and that the mood is the main consideration in generic categorization. He also sees the absurdist fictional worlds of Euripides as tragedies, most probably because of their ending in catastrophe, which is perceived by Aristotle as essential to tragedy (cf. *Poetics*: XIV, 7), and because of sharing the serious/sublime mood (*ibid.* XIII, 6). Since the specific modal layer is the only one that is not shared by tragedy and comedy, there is every reason to see that the specific differences of these genres lie in their different moods.

In general, *the distinction between tragedy and comedy, on the grounds of their difference on the level of mood, does not affect the nature of holistic catharsis:* the manipulation of anxiety is a common denominator of all genres, and the eventual pleasurable release of tension assumedly reflects the operation of the very same psychical mechanism. Comedy, however, usually operates laughter as an additional cathartic mechanism, which distinguishes it from tragedy and melodrama (see CHAPTER 4).

It is only against the background of similarity on the level of structure of action and difference of mood that comedy can be seen as the inverted version of tragedy.

Menander's *Old Cantankerous*

Old Knemon obstructs his daughter's innocent love for Sostratos, and their possible happiness. Knemon, a bad-tempered and misanthropic *senex*, rejects everyone in his naïve belief that unselfish people do not exist, and that he can live without the help of others. In the meantime, the nurse loses a bucket in a well, and in his attempt to rescue the bucket, without any help from others, Knemon too falls into the well. Eventually, he is rescued by his foster son, Gorgias. He then acknowledges that there is also altruism in the world, and willingly gives his daughter to Sostratos in matrimony. It should be borne in mind that this is Menander's only remaining complete play-script.

On the mythical level, Knemon jeopardizes the happiness of his only daughter, which is absurd. On the praxical level, she wishes to marry Sostratos, but Knemon initially withholds his agreement, and eventually changes his mind, thus enabling the consummation of the youngsters' desire. On the naïve level, he is entrenched in his belief that people are not to be trusted — thus justifying his misanthropy, which is a potentially comic *hamartia*. He is blind to the fact that while there are untrustworthy people, there are trustworthy ones too, which is his anagnorisis on the ironic level. On the ironic level, his *anagnorisis*, which enables the dénouement, reaffirms the 'golden mean', which was assumedly already cherished by the synchronic audience. On the aesthetic level, the action leads to the wedding, which is in harmony with the archetypal expectations of the audience, who also witness Knemon's acknowledgment of his error. The consummation of the youngsters' love indicates that this is an archetypal fictional world. On the modal level, although the main action reflects a fairly serious mood, despite the quite inconsequential value at stake, the servants' dialogues and the cook's actions and remarks indicate a prevailing humorous mood.

On the level of Knemon's action, the blocking character ends in the frustration of his own macro-motive, to prevent the wedding of his daughter, and in the collapse of his erroneous perception of humanity. Such an ending too, despite final frustration, is archetypal. In contrast to Frye's model of comedic structure, this fictional world marginalizes the action of the youngsters.

The outer structure

On the level of relationship between a fictional world and its spectators, I suggest, a structured and thematically specified fictional world is potentially experienced as an overall metaphor of harmony or disharmony of their psychical states of affairs (see CHAPTER 4; cf. Rozik, 2009: 141–50). The metaphoric thesis is already substantiated by the fundamental layer of personification, which is a particular kind of metaphor upon which the entire fictional world is constructed, and without which the entire fictional structure would collapse. The metaphoric thesis is corroborated by the inherent difference between such a fictional world and the world of the spectator. *A fundamentally different description cannot make sense unless the principle of 'metaphor' is invoked.*

Exposure to recurrent experiences of temporary violation of values and their eventual reconfirmation, in the contexts of different fictional worlds, is intended to reinforce the overall metaphor of harmony that spectators wish for as their mental image of the real world, which makes their lives possible. These experiences also explain the frustrating nature of overall images of disharmony. *Fictional worlds are, therefore, potentially complex metaphors of harmony or disharmony. Theatre is one of the arenas where the perennial struggle between order and chaos can be addressed.*

Whereas a character may initially endanger a synchronic value system, due to the momentary success of its evil intention or serious/ludicrous *hamartia*, the eventual reversal may produce a sense of reaffirmation of this system, even at the cost of the character's catastrophe/frustration (Hegel: 1195–1205; Bradley: 80; cf. Krook: 8–9). An archetypal ending thus becomes a metaphor of order and is potentially enjoyable. Similar considerations apply to the initial suffering of a character that complies with the synchronic value system and eventually succeeds. In contrast, the eventual frustration of these archetypal expectations is meant to subvert established values and beliefs and to produce an experience of the absurd.

It is the rhetoric aim of a fictional text to persuade the spectators to adopt such an overall metaphor as a true description of their own psychical states of affairs. The intended gratification or frustration of the audience's archetypal expectations, which are generated against the background of their own beliefs and values, implies that a fictional world is not an objective test for their contemporary ethical system. Such a world is, rather, pre-structured to achieve such a definite rhetoric effect by taking for granted what is held to be true by the audience. 'Happy endings do not impress us as true, but as desirable, and they are brought about by manipulation' (Frye: 170). This manipulation aims not at 'truth' in the scientific or philosophic sense, *but at producing an 'experience of truth', which is essentially metaphoric.* (Rozik, 2009: 162–72)

The metaphoric and rhetoric principles thus constitute the outer structure of a fictional world, which are two additional structural layers of the total fictional experience. I suggest that the rhetoric structure subordinates not only the metaphoric, but also all the layers of the inner structure. In other words, the entire structure of the fictional world is subordinated to the effect the playwright intends to produce in the synchronic audience.

This outer structure too is shared by all genres, including comedy. The aim of comedy is to persuade the spectators to accept (rhetoric layer) the overall metaphor of a comedic fictional world (metaphoric layer), which is harmonious with their archetypal expectations (aesthetic layer); and to reaffirm their philanthropon (ironic layer), which undermines the validity of the character's viewpoint (naïve layer), in regard to its fictional action (praxical layer), based upon a mythos (mythical layer) and the personification of their psychical states of affairs (personified layer). All this is perceived through the prism of the humorous mood (modal layer), which reflects the lighthearted attitude of the playwright and is expected to be adopted by the audience. For example, in Menander's *Old Cantankerous*, it is Knemon's new insight that not all people are selfish that is at the heart of the benevolent metaphor that Menander probably wished to offer for the spectator. In fact, this overall metaphor only reaffirmed a held value of the contemporary audience, because Knemon's insight was probably already accepted by them prior to the comedic experience. His prejudice was in all probability perceived as an unwelcome deviation from the golden mean.

Terence's *The Brothers*

Whereas obstructed love is not the unique theme of comedy, as suggested above, the fictional structure usually remains the same. For example, in Terence's *The Brothers*, Demea is a farmer who had given one of his sons to be adopted and raised by his bachelor brother Micio. The brothers are characterized by two diametrically opposed excesses: whereas Demea is conservative, narrow-minded and tight-fisted, Micio is liberal, broad-minded and extravagant. Demea's son Aeschinus, to his father's distress, behaves according to his adoptive father's perception of life. He enjoys life with no restraint, while Micio pays the bills. Demea then adopts his brother's way of life in order to demonstrate that Micio only gains sympathy from others out of weakness, indulgence and reckless spending, and that moderation is the appropriate way of life. Eventually, both Micio and Aeschinus are persuaded to adopt the golden mean, which assumedly reaffirms the synchronic *philanthropon*.

The main line of action is conducted in a consistent serious mood. There are, nonetheless, several comic complications, orchestrated by Syrus, Micio's servant, which indicate that the humorous mood is not absent. The narratiive also features young lovers, a blocking parent, and an archetypal ending. However, the theme of obstructed love is marginalized by the central one that focuses on the value of moderation. This fictional world constitutes an overall metaphor of reaffirmation and harmony with the spectator's archetypal expectations, which reflect the rhetoric/educational intent typical of Terence.

Deus ex machina

Against the background of shared structures of action, comedy evinces a clear predilection for archetypal endings, even at the "risk" of '*deus ex machina*'. Such an ending is defined as a dénouement that contrasts the logic of characterization and/or situation, which is brought about through an external intervention, usually divine, capable of imposing an ending that, albeit irrational in nature, gratifies the archetypal expectations of the synchronic audience.

The literal meaning of '*deus ex machina*' is 'a god from a machine'. It originally meant the typical dénouement of an action, probably common in ancient Greece, through the theatrical epiphany of a god descending from a machine onto the stage. Aristotle already employs this term in the abstract sense for an ending that does not derive from the characterization of the dramatis personae and/or the nature of the action, and illustrates this principle through the salvation of Medea by means of a chariot drawn by dragons sent by the god Sun (*Poetics*: XV, 7).Aristotle condemns *deus ex machina* for its irrational nature: 'the unraveling of the plot, no less than the complication, must arise out of the fictional action itself, it must not be brought about by the *Deus ex Machina* [. . .] Within the action there must be nothing irrational' (*Poetics*: XV, 7; cf. Horace: 85). Corneille advises that *deus ex machina* should be avoided absolutely, because it indicates the weakness of an author who has failed to find an appropriate conclusion to the overall interaction (p. 246).

Nevertheless, due to both its frequent use and the spectators' appreciation, *deus ex machina* deserves theoretical attention. Indeed, such an ending contrasts the axiomatic nature of characters' behavior, which is part of the logos of a fictional world. It might appear therefore, that such an ending would frustrate the archetypal expectations of the spectators. However, it is not only accepted by them, but is often expected and always enjoyed. It follows that, despite Aristotle's condemnation, any explanation of *deus ex machina* should proceed from this fundamental fact.

On such grounds, I suggest *that the mechanism of deus ex machina reflects a logic of its own.* An archetypal fictional world needs to initially increase the anxiety that the spectators harbor prior to their exposure to a fictional world, and finally to release it all. Such a world generates additional anxiety if the spectator believes that a dreaded ending is possible. This belief is achieved by bestowing advantageous power and even possible immunity on characters that can frustrate the spectators' expectations. The more the odds are in favor of such characters, the more the suspense increases and the prospects of archetypal dénouement diminish. Therefore, *a fictional world that aims at increasing anxiety to the extreme must prevent any clue to a possible wished-for dénouement, and instead produce a sense of dead end. Deus ex machina is then the only option left for gratifying the archetypal expectations.* Maximum anxiety requires a sense of dead end, which in turn requires *deus ex machina*.

It would appear that the characterization of a positive character as a hero, such as a knight, a cowboy or a detective, reduces suspense through positing his power to reverse any adverse development. Although such a character usually suffers temporary defeats at the entanglement, it is its axiomatic superiority that enables the expected dénouement. It would appear, therefore, that such a character precludes additional anxiety and undermines any prospect of powerful catharsis. Nonetheless, it is possible to produce a sense of dead end, to increase anxiety to the extreme, and to trigger a powerful catharsis even for such a hero. However, such an ending is not *deus ex machina*, because it materializes the axiomatic structure of the fictional world. *Deus ex machina* should thus be defined as *the intervention of a power that is not part of the axiomatic buildup of a fictional world, in order to bring about a peripeteia that enables the gratification of the spectator's spontaneous expectations and catharsis.*

Whereas the *deus-ex-machina* dénouement contrasts the archetypal expectations for manifest causation, it does not frustrate these expectations from the perspective of the spectators' need for the synchronic cultural ethos to prevail. Under such conditions, *a deus ex machina too constitutes a metaphor of the infallibility of an ethical system — thus inducing a sense of its reaffirmation.* In traditional cultures, this is accomplished by divine agents, but these are not of necessity. *Facing the choice between either axiomatic behavior and confutation, or irrational intervention and cathartic reaffirmation, the spectator clearly prefers the latter.* Consequently, *deus ex machina* is a specific form of the realization of the spectators' archetypal expectations.

Aristotle condemns the authorial tendency to cater for the spectators' taste through irrational means (*Poetics*: XIII, 7–8). Nonetheless, from the viewpoint of the archetypal fictional experience, gratifying the spectators' wishes is the very aim of an archetypal fictional world. In this sense, *deus ex machina* is a possible means for achieving this goal: 'If he [the author] describes the impossible, he is guilty of an error; but the error may be justified, if the end of the art be thereby attained' (*ibid.*: XXV, 5; cf. Horace: 85). Even for the purpose of the frustration of the spectators' wishes an author can employ *deus ex machina* such as Medea's escape despite her horrendous deeds. The ending of Euripides' fictional world was undoubtedly meant to shock the synchronic spectators who believed in the gods of the Greek pantheon.

In some fictional worlds, *deus ex machina* is employed, even though a happy end could have been reached by rational means. For example, in Molière's *The Miser* it is possible to bring about Harpagon's agreement to the marriages of his son and daughter by merely manipulating his avarice, which is done in any case through the stealing of his safe.

4 Anselm's *deus ex machina*, in the Khan Theatre *The Miser*.
Photo: Gadi Dagon. Courtesy of the Jerusalem Khan Theatre.

Nonetheless, Molière adds the unexpected arrival of Anselm, the lost father of Mariane and Valère — thus implementing the principle of *deus ex machina* with no structural need.

It is possible, therefore, that the spectators love *deus ex machina* precisely because of its irrational nature. Dead ends are common fare in their lives and existential cravings for miraculous dénouements would seem, therefore, only natural. *A fictional deus ex machina should thus be perceived as a metaphor of reestablishment of order and harmony even by unexpected and miraculous means.*

The modern spectator might seem to be suspicious of *deus ex machina*, but this is an optical illusion. In the last hundred years the basic reaffirmative function of theatre and literature has been taken over by cinema and TV drama; and the 'consumption' of fictional worlds, including comedies, which gratify archetypal expectations even by miraculous means, has increased enormously, e.g., westerns, detective and war movies; the advent of TV series and telenovelas bear witness to the persistent magnetism of *deus ex machina in all dramatic genres.*

Mood is an integral part of the overall deep structure of the fictional world, and comedy reflects the preference for a specific surface structure, which is archetypal in nature, and whose specific difference is its humorous mood. This mood is also a crucial factor in conditioning the nature of the fictional experience; i.e., the comic mood is a fundamental category of experience.

Comedy is a cathartic genre, often combining comic laughter and holistic catharsis. However, not all comedies are generated by fictional structures; e.g., the sketch comedy (see CHAPTER 7).

Comedic Character   **6**

In principle, a character can be characterized in any way, even paradox-ically; e.g., as a character on stage that is not enacted by an actor on stage in Luigi Pirandello's *Six Characters in Search of an Author*. It might appear, therefore, that characters are not necessarily structured, and that the determination of their traits is merely a matter of thematic specifi-cation, left totally to the discretion of the author; as otherwise it is difficult to account for their immense diversity. Nonetheless, a character is not merely a bundle of casually related traits.

In regard to tragedy, Aristotle correctly contends that in affecting the audience 'most important of all is the *structure* of the incidents' (*Poetics*: VI, 9; my italics); that 'character comes in as subsidiary to the actions' (*ibid.*: VI, 10); and that '[t]he Plot, then, is the first principle, and, as it were, the soul of a tragedy: Character holds the second place' (*Poetics*: VI, 14). He thus suggests and supports the principle of subordination of character to the structure of the action, as does Frye:

> [i]n drama, characterization depends on function; what a character is follows from what he has to do in the play. Dramatic function in its turn depends on the structure of the play; the character has certain things to do because a play has such and such a shape. The structure of the play in its turn depends on the category of the play; if it is a comedy, its structure will require *a comic resolution and a prevailing comic mood*. (pp. 171–2; my italics)

The principle of 'subordination' thus holds not only for tragedy, but also for comedy. It is sensible to conjecture, therefore, that if the character's structure is subordinated to the inner structure of the fictional world, characterization reflects all its inner structural levels (see CHAPTER 5). And if the inner structure of the fictional world is subordinated to the outer structure, i.e., to the overall metaphor and the rhetoric effect that a synchronic audience is expected to experience, although through the mediation of the inner structure, characterization is subordinated to them too. This two-fold subordination prevents any possible reduction of characterization to a single quality.

In other words, *the comedic character is not a bundle of casually related traits, but a structured unit subordinated to the overall layered structure of the fictional world.* I employ here 'comedic character', because not all characters of comedy are comic, in the sense of being lighthearted or aiming at producing comic laughter, and not all fictional worlds aiming at producing laughter are comedies.

Structure of comedic character

The notion of 'characterization' should be perceived in a wider sense than usual, and as applying to the configuration of all the permanent traits of a character, which are recurrently reflected in *all* its actions such as its qualities, motives, values from naïve and ironic perspectives, and modal and aesthetic traits. The main reason for conceiving of all these as a complex single unit lies in their stratification, hierarchical structure, particular configuration, and unified dramatic functions that, in addition to thematic specification, are: (a) to bestow meaning on each action of a character, with no need for the constant reiteration of characterization, under the assumption that the same action may have different meanings in the context of different characterizations; (b) to elicit definite expectations in the audience, which underlie their suspense, because only on such grounds is it possible to anticipate the future moves of a character; and (c) to contribute to the ironic advantage of the audience. In other words, only the appropriate authorial command of characterization can ensure the spectators' correct reception of and response to a fictional world.

(A) *The personified layer.* A character is a fictional construct and the result of a process of personification that reflects the spontaneous creativity of the psyche; i.e., the basic and essential trait of a character is its humanity. This trait justifies the interpretation of its behavior as human, unless specified otherwise. Even if a character does not eat or sleep on stage, it assumedly does so in the non-represented parts of the fictional world. Even its psyche should be presupposed, on condition that inferences are restricted to the pertinent psychological notions of a synchronic culture; e.g., one cannot attribute an unconscious to a character conceived of in a period for which this concept was beyond the cultural horizon. The analysis of a comedic character should strive, therefore, to reveal the concept of 'human nature' that underlies each character on synchronic grounds, and the questions asked about it should be constrained accordingly. Moreover, for any particular culture, even if the analysis of both characters and real human beings are made in the very same terms, the distinction between a character, as a fictional construct, and a real person, remains valid.

On a different level, e.g., in theatre and cinema, there is a fundamental correspondence between the personification of a character and its embodiment by a flesh and blood actor, which adds a concrete physical dimension to personification. However, no human image can be created on such a level of abstraction; i.e., no actor can be asked to perform a role on the level of bare personification. In order to become a concrete source of metaphoric associations, personification requires additional specific human traits. In principle, *the more a character resembles a human being, the more the principle of 'personification' materializes.* On this level, there is no difference between tragedy and comedy.

(B) *The mythical layer.* This layer creates a kernel narrative through grafting upon personification some minimal characterization such as mother and son; schematic categorization of motives and actions such as son marries mother; and basic temporal order. Despite its abstract nature, such a narrative is able to produce extreme anxiety in the spectator due to the lifting of inhibitions such as a severe taboo; i.e., in being extremely irrational. For example, 'being a mother' means loving and caring for a son, and 'being a son' means loving and honoring a mother — with both characterizations precluding sexual relations. In general, family relations are constrained by definite taboos. Such a minimal characterization and motivation, therefore, is basically irrational and explains both the additional anxiety produced by a fictional world, and its possible catharsis. If such traits (mother and son) were changed (e.g., step-mother and step-son), the action being equal, the meaning of the resulting fictional world would change substantially (e.g., Racine's *Phèdre*). On this level too, there is no difference between tragedy and comedy; e.g., Arnolphe's maltreatment of his ward, young Agnès, in Molière's *The School for Wives*.

(C) *The praxical layer* is grafted onto the mythical layer, attributes a definite macro-motive to a character, and determines the nature of the outcome; e.g., the competition between a father and a son over a girl. Such a macro-motive should be perceived as an integral component of characterization, in being a permanent element, which, similarly to a quality, is manifested in all of a character's actions, even if not explicitly stated. The assumption is that even the same action should be understood differently against the background of a different motive. Such a macro-motive strives for success and persists until its goal is finally either achieved or frustrated.

On this level, characterization is axiomatic in the sense that each action of a character is expected to reflect it — thus underlying and explaining the expectations of a synchronic audience and their basic sense of unity. Moreover, since a motive usually ranges from its inception to its eventual success or failure it also underlies the spectator's experience of wholeness. On the praxical level, comedy is basically serious, and usually produces anxiety prior to the dénouement. On this level, there is no essential difference between comedy and tragedy, while the specific difference of comedy lying in that the character's motives are of lesser cultural repercussion; e.g., Arnolphe's motive to prevent the infidelity of his future wife, Agnès, in Molière's *The School for Wives*.

(D) *The naïve layer* is grafted onto the previous layer. It reflects a character's own perspective in bestowing ethical meaning on all its qualities, motives and actions throughout an entire interaction; and it too is a permanent element of characterization. This "personal" perspective applies not only to the meaning of a character's own motives and actions, but also to the nature of the entire fictional world of which it is a denizen. Such a perspective is indicated by the key-terms or, rather, metonyms of an ethical system that a character employs in describing its own predicament; i.e., the analysis of this layer should focus on the verbal component of a character's speech interaction.

A character usually acts under the assumption that its macro-motive is justified, or at least reasonable, whether its viewpoint is accepted by the fictional culture or strictly personal, and whether it is accepted by the spectators' synchronic culture or not. Indeed, a naïve perspective may be strictly personal. Even if a character deviates from its own aim and justification, such a deviation too bestows meaning on its acts; e.g., Euclio's change of mind in Plautus' *The Pot of Gold*. On this level too, there is no essential difference between tragedy and comedy, while the specific difference of comedy lies in that the character's values are of less consequence in regard to the validity of the synchronic ethos; e.g., Arnolphe's macro-motive is to educate Agnès as a simpleton as the best way to prevent future marital infidelity, in Molière's *The School for Wives*.

(E) *The ironic layer* is grafted onto all the previous layers, and bestows ethical meaning on a character's macro-motive and actions from an authorial perspective, which is expected to be adopted the synchronic audience. Both archetypal and absurdist fictional worlds presuppose such a viewpoint, which is usually conveyed by functional characters and/or interactive characters in functional situations, and indicated through the metonyms of an established ethical system, which is usually part of the synchronic spectator's cultural baggage. Such an ironic categorization of a character is meant to be perceived as its definitive ethical characterization.

In principle, the ironic viewpoint positions a character as an object of dramatic irony. Since both the naïve and ironic perspectives converge on the same mythical and praxical characterization, the meaning bestowed upon them from the latter perspective should also be seen as a genuine and permanent trait of a character's construct. On this level too, there is no essential difference between tragedy and comedy; while the specific difference of comedy lies in that the values applied are lower in the synchronic hierarchy of values; e.g., from such a viewpoint, Arnolphe's idea of ensuring his future wife's fidelity is obviously absurd. It indicates a ludicrous *hamartia* against the background of what is presented as the expected normal behavior by Chrysalde, the 'honest man', in Molière's *The School for Wives*.

(F) *The aesthetic layer* is grafted onto all the previous layers and is pertinent to characterization, particularly on the level of the character's inner harmony or disharmony and, in poetic terms, coherence and incoherence — with both incoherence and inconsistency being kinds of inner disharmony. However, whereas consistency and inconsistency pertain to the axis of action, which is temporal in nature, coherence and incoherence pertain to characterization, which is atemporal in nature. Both these levels reflect the ironic viewpoint of the author.

Aristotle relates to the principles of probability and necessity underlying characterization:

> it is not the function of the poet to relate what has happened, but what may happen, — what is possible according to the law of probability or necessity. . . . Poetry, therefore, is a more philosophical and a higher thing than history: for poetry tends to express the universal, history the particular. By the universal I mean how a person of a certain type will on occasion speak or act, according to the law of probability or necessity. . . . In Comedy this [the tendency to express the universal] is already apparent: for here the poet first constructs the plot on the lines of probability, and then inserts characteristic names; — unlike the lampooners who write about particular individuals. (*Poetics*: IX, 5)

It should be noted that 'probability' and 'necessity' relate to the degree of constraint upon the behavior of a character according to its axiomatic characterization, while necessity means 'no leeway' whatsoever. I suggest that these observations relate to the inner logic of a character or, rather, to the models of coherence and consistency in the spectators' minds.

The *hamartia*-afflicted characters in both tragedy and comedy are characterized by a consistent incoherence, due to the flaw existing in the context of a basically positive characterization. The sensible conclusion is that the synchronic spectator operates models of coherence that relate not to separate traits, but to their configurations. Similar considerations apply to consistency of the *hamartia*-afflicted character on the time axis — with consistency preserving the incoherence of a character; e.g., the consistent incoherence of Arnolphe, who is afflicted by an obsessive fear of marital infidelity, in Molière's *The School for Wives*. 'Obsession' implies a consistent flaw.

While it is the initial disharmony that determines the expectations of the audience, especially in regard to ludicrous characters, their final frustration is meant to reinstate harmony. There is, usually, no difference on this level between a comic and a tragic character. Nonetheless, the ending of comedy is milder than that of tragedy — thus reflecting too the predominance of the lighthearted mood.

(G) *The modal layer* bestows permanent modal traits on a character, as characterized so far, through the prism of the typical mood of each genre, the humorous mood in particular. Since the comic traits are attributed to a character by an author, mood characterization is an additional aspect of the ironic perspective, which determines how the character is expected to be perceived by an audience.

Aristotle contends: 'Comedy is [. . .] an imitation of characters of a lower type, — not, however, in the full sense of the word bad, the Ludicrous being merely a subdivision of the ugly. It consists in some defect or ugliness which is not painful or destructive. To take an obvious example, the comic mask is ugly and distorted, but does not imply pain' (*Poetics*: V, 1; cf. Halliwell: 36). He suggests thereby a combination of lowly characterization, which is a specific kind of mode, and a comic equivalent of the tragic *hamartia* whose specific difference is 'being ludicrous', which reflects a specific kind of mood. However, the ludicrous character is not the only one to produce laughter. Albeit not envisaged in the *Poetics*, the buffoon too does so by exposing the ludicrous nature of the objects of derision or by pretending foolish failure. While spectators laugh *at* the ludicrous character when failing foolishly, they laugh *with* the latter when causing others to fail foolishly, even if not ludicrous in themselves, or when pretending foolish behavior (cf. Olson: 21).

5 Harpagon's instructions for Mariane's visit, in the Khan Theatre
The Miser.
Photo: Gadi Dagon. Courtesy of the Jerusalem Khan Theatre.

In principle, a character is ludicrous not on the level of characterization; e.g., although Harpagon is a miser, such a character can also be serious and even produce pity for its suffering (see CHAPTER 2). Basically, what makes a character ludicrous is the foolishness of its actions; e.g., Harpagon in his parsimonious preparations to meet Mariane, which are foolish in nature (Urian: 21).

Laughter is a cathartic mechanism that presupposes several basic conditions: failure, foolishness, anxiety, pitilessness and change of mood (see CHAPTER 2). It is the incoherent violation of a lesser value, which is manifested in foolish actions, that reflects a comic *hamartia* (cf. Potts: 201: on Ben Jonson's Prologue to *Every Man in his Humour*). It is highly probable that spectators invest a great deal of psychical energy in inhibiting drives that might make them laughable in the eyes of others, which involves a great deal of anxiety, and that the mere confrontation with a character that embodies such lifted inhibitions augments anxiety, which is released in the guise of comic laughter, when following the intuition that this is done in a humorous mood.

Failure is shared by both serious and comic characters, but foolish failure, which does not reflect authorial aggressiveness, only characterizes comedy (see CHAPTER 2). Whereas on the level of its macro-motive a character is serious, its way of implementing this motive may reveal a ludicrous nature. It is not stupidity but stupid actions that make spectators laugh. Nonetheless, a permanent disposition to such failures is integral to comic characterization.

It is on this level that the main difference between the serious and the comic genres becomes prominent; e.g., in Molière's *The School for Wives*, Arnolphe's attempts to prevent infidelity are ludicrous, while he is always outwitted by Agnès. Although unaware of her own tactics: love has been her true school.

To conclude, in principle, *there is a total correspondence between comedic characterization and the overall structure of the comedic fictional world, which includes its specific mood*. These are two basic forms of organization of the same fictional material: whereas fictional action is a temporal form of organization, characterization is an atemporal one While each particular action of a character is an instance of its characterization, the latter is an abstraction of its recurrent traits reflected in all its actions, including those that take place in the non-represented parts of the action, usually presented through an exposition.

Verbal characterization in the exposition or elsewhere is a highly expedient means in that it requires neither enactment of all its manifestations in previous events, nor repetition in the context of each fictional event — thus enabling the short scope of drama, whether theatrical or cinematic. Moreover, in presupposing permanence, characterization also triggers and shapes the spectators' expectations regarding the possible actions/reactions of a character under foreseeable changing circumstances.

Again, in pre-structured fictional worlds, whether archetypal or absurdist, all the layers of characterization are subordinated to the overall metaphor that an author wishes to create, and to persuade the spectators to adopt as a suitable description of their psychical states of affairs.

Kinds of comedic characters

In comedy, the ludicrous character is only one of the possible kinds of character. Aristotle views the ludicrous character as 'being merely a subdivision of the ugly' and 'consists in some defect or ugliness, which is not painful or destructive' (*Poetics*: V, 1). In this definition too he employs the term '*hamartia*' (see Greek source), which justifies the expression 'comic *hamartia*'. Such a *hamartia* is comic because of promoting the comic mood and possibly also comic laughter. For example, in Molière's *Tartuffe*, Orgon is afflicted by gullibility, which is a ludicrous flaw — with this being both incoherent and foolish. He is ready to believe without question anything that Tartuffe, who pretends to be a holy man, preaches. To his surprise, he is made to witness the fraudulent nature of Tartuffe from beneath a table, in a carefully machinated and farcical scene. Orgon is thus exhibited as a fool — with credulity being a kind of mental blindness, which is the comic counterpart of tragic mental blindness; e.g. Oedipus. Although Aristotle does not employ 'painful and destructive' as the differential qualities of the tragic *hamartia*, these are implied in his parallel description of the comic *hamartia*.

It is from an ironic viewpoint that a character can be perceived as afflicted by a comic *hamartia*. It is difficult to believe, however, that any modernist scholar would consider the ludicrous to be a subspecies of the ugly. Nonetheless, if the 'ugly' is perceived as an instance of disharmony, Aristotle's dictum may make sense. As suggested above, harmony and disharmony should be seen as the main aesthetic categories (see CHAPTER 5); and, as an instance of incoherence, the ludicrous should be perceived under the category of 'disharmony'. The ugly, which is disharmonious, can only be a central category in the context of an aesthetics that views beauty as the main category.

On the one hand, in contrast to monolithic characters, such as the villainous and the virtuous, the *hamartia*-afflicted characters are incoherent by definition. On the other hand, such characters also breach a value — with the difference between the tragic and the comic character lying in the degree of significance that a culture bestows on this value. Whereas the former violates a crucial value for the audience, which impinges on their orientation in the world, such as hubris, theomachy and heresy, the latter breaches a less significant value such as the golden mean and even trivial ones. Furthermore, there are serious dramas that also focus on lesser values — with the additional difference being that the comedic violation is also ludicrous.

Corrigan claims that '[i]n making this distinction between the ludicrous and the serious, Aristotle was not denying the potential seriousness of comedy, rather, much like Plato, he was postulating the idea that comedy — as well as tragedy — derives from positive attitudes toward value. For something to be serious we must assign serious value to it, and this can occur only when there exists a larger system of values which we accept as valid and of which the specific value is a part' (Corrigan: 5).

Indeed, in regard to value comedy too is serious. It is in the manner of violating a value that a character is either serous or ludicrous. A comic character thus features a two-fold ethical and aesthetic transgression; e.g., Orgon breaches not only a model of coherence in the spectators' minds, which is aesthetic in nature, but also the value of rationality in frustrating the expectation that a human being discern between what makes sense and what does not. Other examples: the incoherence in the coexistence of erudition and absent-mindedness in a professor; and that of a beautiful woman who speaks in a squeaky voice 'because she fails *to measure up to the standard* which her appearance had previously established' (Corrigan: 5–6; my italics).

Corrigan correctly claims that incongruity alone cannot explain the comic *hamartia* because the tragic *hamartia* too is a case of incongruity: it can be 'a terrible act committed by a character from whom we expect love' (p. 6; on the grounds of *Poetics*: XIV, 4). He concludes, therefore, that '[w]hat is operative in the ludicrous is not a question of mere incongruity, but a perceptible falling short of an already agreed upon standard of seriousness which we have set for the object, or which is set by the object for itself' (p. 6). I suggest that instead of 'standard of seriousness', the 'mental model of coherence' should be used; in that it is more sensible to adopt the simpler thesis that there is a spontaneous model of coherence in the spectators' minds, and that both the comic and serious afflicted characters contravene it. Whereas a standard can be social or cultural, a mental model can be neutral in these respects. Indeed, models of coherence apply to both serious and comic *hamartia*-afflicted characters, and both equally depart from them, albeit in opposite directions. Only monolithic villainous and virtuous characters do not contravene models of coherence. It follows that a serious character or a comic character may depart from a model of coherence without impairing its seriousness or lightheartedness. Consequently, the standard or, rather, model cannot be of seriousness or lightheartedness in itself. If 'incoherence' is employed instead of 'incongruity' and 'model of coherence' instead of 'standard', Corrigan's assertions can be accepted.

In both serious and comic archetypal fictional worlds the ironic layer takes for granted the validity of a particular *philanthropon*, which determines what kind of behavior either complies with it or not. In many a case, the comic *hamartia* is a kind of excess in regard to what is usually termed the 'golden mean'. Indeed, typical human excesses presuppose such a yardstick, without knowing precisely what validates it; e.g., in Terence's *The Brothers*, 'stingy' and 'squanderer' refer to opposite excesses that presuppose a golden mean in regard to the way money is spent. Other opposite excesses are, for example, the pedant and the careless, the coward and the imprudent, and the irascible and the phlegmatic. Language usually provides names for these parallel and opposed excesses, and each of them may be treated either comically or seriously. Furthermore, in contrast to the tragic or, rather, serious *hamartia*, which presupposes a background of positive and coherent characterization in order to distinguish it from sheer evil, it is possible that a comic *hamartia* presupposes a background of traits that fit models of normality. Because of Harpagon is flawed not only in avarice but also in suspicious nature and a lack of care for his own children he looks more as a monolithic comic character; namely, he is comic in all respects.

A ludicrous character is also equivalent to a tragic *hamartia*-afflicted character on the level of ultimate consequences. However, whereas eventually both are "punished", the punishment of the comic character is less severe; he is only deprived of his wish, and usually even reintegrated into society.

Whereas Aristotle focuses on the existence of a ludicrous character, afflicted by a comic *hamartia*, which is meant to explain the fact that a comedy elicits laughter, comedy can also elicit laughter through additional characters, such as the buffoon and the boor, and even through entanglements of serious characters in ludicrous situations. Basically, in comedy there are laughed-at characters and laughed-with characters. Even the young lovers have something ludicrous in their characterization.

In principle, an evil character is serious in nature. Nonetheless, there are comedies that mix characters designed in the spirit of humor and characters designed in the spirit of melodrama, in the sense of being serious in nature. For example, Tartuffe is an evil character in disguise who manages to deceive gullible Orgon by merely pretending sanctity in Molière's *Tartuffe*. Similar considerations apply to the villainous and serious character of Don Juan and the comic character of his servant Sganarelle in Molière's *Don Juan*. In comedy too, evil characters are severely punished, according to their nature. It should be noted that ludicrous characters too are ethically negative on the level of action. If a comedy entangles basically serious characters, it is usually dubbed 'situation comedy' or 'sitcom', e.g., *Friends*, in contrast to 'comedy of character'.

Aristotle contrasts comedy to tragedy only on the shared grounds of *hamartia*. An interesting question is whether or not tragic homogeneous (virtuous and villainous) characters also have counterparts in comedy. It is difficult to envisage a ludicrous character that is fully ludicrous, in that this would contradict its lack of coherence. In contrast, buffoons and boors are homogeneous characters if only in promoting the humorous mood. Moreover, since there is an element of violation of values in the actions of ludicrous characters, which is a serious matter, a serious character that sets the ethical standard in comedy is possible, such as the honest man; e.g., Chrysalde in Molière's *The School for Wives*.

Bergson's approach

Bergson's perception of the comic character derives from his theory of laughter, under the (erroneous) assumption that such a character is the only one capable of producing laughter. He thus suggests two elements of characterization that combine in creating a comic character: first, its unsocial nature: '[c]onvinced that laughter has a social meaning and import, that the comic expresses, above all else, a special lack of adaptability to society, and that, in short, there is nothing comic apart from man, we have made man and character generally our main objective' (p. 146); and second, its automatic nature: '[a]ny individual is comic who automatically goes his own way without troubling himself about getting into touch with the rest of his fellow-beings. It is the part of laughter to reprove his absentmindedness and wake him out of his dream' (p. 147). 'In *laughter* we always find an unavowed intention to humiliate, and consequently to correct our neighbour, if not in his will, at least in his deed' (p. 148; my italics).

Bergson goes on to claim that 'it follows that the elements of comic character on stage and in social life will be the same' (p. 149). The question is: How can the spectator's laughter humiliate and correct a character or, rather, what is the point of laughing at a character? In fact, a character cannot be humiliated: laughter external to its world cannot affect and/or correct it, unless it is assumed that a character is a (metaphoric) representation of an undesired and inhibited proclivity in the spectator, even if the latter attributes it to somebody else or outright denies it. I suggest that it is the purposeful embodiment of an undesired and inhibited trait or drive in the spectator that distinguishes a comic character from a comic real human being.

Moreover, such a representation cannot be literal because ludicrous characters display an array of ludicrous traits that, most of which at least, do not characterize the spectator. It follows that it can only be metaphoric. In other words, Bergson fails to explain how laughing at a character impinges on the spectator. As we shall see below, the use of laughter for humiliation is typical not of comedy but of satire (see CHAPTER 8).

Second, Bergson argues that the comic is not always an indication of a fault, in the moral sense: 'what is essentially *laughable* is what is done automatically. In a vice, even in a virtue, the comic is that element by which the person unwittingly betrays himself — the involuntary gesture or the unconscious remark. Absentmindedness is always comical' (p. 155; my italics). Again, Bergson is consistent with his theory of laughter, which indeed, is not necessarily an indication of a moral fault, but an indication of a foolish failure, whether rooted in characterization or situation. Nonetheless, Bergson cannot avoid the conclusion that it is a social fault: 'To sum up, whether a character is good or bad is of little moment; granted he is unsociable, he is capable of becoming comic' (p. 154). However, in principle a social fault is ethical: whether moral or other, it is always a matter of value.

Bergson concludes: 'Rigidity, automatism, absentmindedness and unsociability are all inextricably entwined; and all serve as ingredients to the making up of the comic in a character' (p. 156). In the spirit of his approach, it should be added: because these make us laugh. However, first, rigidity and automatism also characterize tragic characters; second, laughter does not characterize only comedy; and third, it is not the necessary aim of comedy to elicit laughter (see CHAPTER 2). What characterizes this genre is the comic mood and optional comic laughter, which is triggered by the comic potential of foolish behavior with no intention of correction — with this intention only characterizing the satiric mood. It follows that one should never derive comic characterization from a reductionist theory of laughter.

Bergson also claims that 'if critics insist on seeing a fault, even though a trifling one, in the ludicrous character, they must point out what it is here that exactly distinguishes the trifling from the serious' (p. 149). Here Bergson advances a thought-provoking distinction: 'maybe it is not because a fault is trifling, that it makes us laugh, but rather because it makes us laugh that we regard it as a trifling; for there is nothing [that] disarms us like laughter' (p. 149). Nevertheless, a fault is trifling according to psychical models in the spectators' minds and, therefore, it is the possible cause of laughter. Foolishness is trifling. I believe that Bergson fails to distinguish between two aspects of laughter: the reaction to a fault that is perceived as intrinsically trifling, and the consequence of satiric laughter that exhibits a serious proclivity in a person under a trifling light.

Characterization and function

A comic character is defined here by its promotion of the comic mood, and occasionally of laughter and, usually, within the context of a comedic fictional world. The set of comic characters includes at least the ludicrous old man, the buffoon, the boor, the churl and the young lovers. The latter are comic characters because of their extreme innocence and dependence on the servants in their confrontations with their usually ludicrous fathers.

Frye suggests a pair of characters or, rather, functions that polarize the comic mood: the buffoon (*bomolochos*) and the churl (or *agroikos*) respectively (p. 175). Whereas the buffoon's function is 'to increase the mood of festivity rather than to contribute to the plot' (*ibid.*), the churl's role 'is that of the refuser of festivity, the killjoy who tries to stop the fun' (p. 176). This suggestion indicates a sensible reading of '*bomolochos*' in the *Tractatus Coislinianus*, which does not mention any 'churl' or '*agroikos*' (Cooper: 226). In this respect Frye follows Aristotle's *Nicomachean Ethics*: (IV, vii, 1 — viii, 12). I believe that the addition of the churl reflects a felicitous insight: e.g., Malvolio in Shakespeare's *Twelfth Night*.

The oldest known buffoon is the 'parasite' who 'does nothing but

6 Malvolio receives Olivia's letter, in the Khan Theatre *Twelfth Night*. *Photo*: Yael Ilan. Courtesy of the Jerusalem Khan Theatre.

entertain the audience by talking about his appetite' (Frye: 175). This type is closely related to the 'cook' who appears to be 'not simply as a gratuitous addition like the parasite, but as something more like a master of ceremonies, a center for the comic mood' (*ibid.*).

Without denying the function of the churl, the buffoon enjoys making fun of several butts; e.g., the churl, the boor, which is coarse, ignorant and innocent, and the ludicrous character, which is ridiculous in nature. I suggest that the buffoon and its three butts, who are usually not aware of being laughable, promote the lighthearted mood, and even laughter, each of them in its own way. While the spectators laugh *with* the buffoon, they laugh *at* the ludicrous butts.

In fact, neither the buffoon nor the butts are comic characters but, rather, comic functions. Indeed, there are characters that fulfill the function of promoting the humorous mood alongside other functions.

Frye also suggests two dramatic characters or, rather, functions that polarize the advancement of the action of both comedy (p. 172) and tragedy (pp. 216ff): while the function of the *eiron* is to hatch 'the schemes which bring about the hero's victory' (p. 173; cf. the 'trickster' in Stott: 51), the function of the *alazon* is to obstruct the *eiron*'s intent. Frye identifies the comedic *eiron* in the hero and the cunning servant; and the comedic *alazon* in 'the *senex iratus* or heavy father' (*ibid.*) Although he claims allegiance to the *Tractatus Coislinianus* (Cooper: 226), in this case his interpretation reveals a simple misreading (p. 172). I suggest that in place of using the pair 'eiron' and 'alazon' for the polarization of the interactive functions, these should be employed for the polarization of dramatic irony, in accordance with the use of these terms for these functions in traditional (and modernist) theory: 'eiron' as the subject of dramatic irony and 'alazon' for its object (see CHAPTER 3).

There are indeed comedic characters that attempt to promote the action and those that attempt to block the action of another character; but both kinds do so in trying to crown their own motives with success. These functions are conspicuous in the case of conflict in which both characters promote their own goals by blocking those of the others. In other words, the same character may fulfill both functions. Therefore, advancing and blocking an action are not kinds of characters, but fictional functions, which should be properly named, possibly in terms of 'agential' and 'blocking' functions.

It would appear that in certain comedies the servant is in charge of advancing the action toward its expected ending. Indeed, in some cases, young lovers ask a servant to help them in overcoming parental obstruction, and they do help; e.g., La Flèche's stealing of the safe in Molière's

The Miser, which enables all the eventual youngsters' weddings (IV, vi). However, occasionally, the servants make matters even worse; e.g., Scapin in Molière's *The Trickeries of Scapin*. Often they are not given any function in the action; e.g., Cario, Chremylus' servant, in Aristophanes' *Plutus*.

The use of 'function' in this context is justified in that the same character usually fulfils more than one function; e.g., Harpagon combines the functions of blocking the actions of his children, advancing his own action, initially being the subject of irony and eventually its object, and being throughout the object of derision. Several characters may fulfil the very same function; the blocking function of both Géronte and Argante in Molière's *The Trickeries of Scapin*. And a single character may fulfil contrasting functions, whether simultaneously, as in cases of inner conflict, or not, as in cases of anagnorisis; e.g., Knemon in Menander's *Old Cantankerous*.

Emphasis on each kind of comedic character, which embodies a configuration of functions, generates a different type of comedy: (a) emphasis on the ludicrous and blocking old man generates what is usually termed 'comedy of character', e.g., Argan in Molière's *Le Malade Imaginaire*; (b) emphasis on the servants/buffoons, 'comedy of zanni', e.g., Truffaldino in Goldoni's *The Servant of Two Masters*; and (c) emphasis on the young lovers, 'romantic comedy', e.g., Orsino and Viola in Shakespeare's *Twelfth Night*.

Stock-type characters

The notion of 'stock-type character' refers not to a function but to a recurrent kind of character, which exhibits a stable configuration of functions, has a stage tradition, and re-appears in different fictional worlds under the same mask and costume, and often also under the same name; e.g., Harlequin. In this sense, an author of comedy can recycle not only pre-existing actions but also pre-existing characters. This is typical not only of *commedia dell'arte* (see CHAPTER 9). A character can be seen as a stock-type even if it does not wear the same mask and bear the same name. The only condition is a recurrent configuration of traits and functions; e.g., Molière's ludicrous fathers who are basically modeled after the *Pantalone* stock-type.

Following his singular structural approach, Frye suggests the stock-type as the infrastructure of a character, which becomes a lifelike character only if additional traits are attributed to its dramatic functions:

when we speak of typical characters, we are not trying to reduce life-like characters to stock-types, though we certainly are suggesting that the sentimental notion of an antithesis between lifelike character and the stock-type is a vulgar error. All lifelike characters, whether in drama or fiction, owe their consistency to the appropriateness of the stock-type which belongs to their dramatic *function*. That stock-type is not the character but it is as necessary to the character as a *skeleton* is to the actor who plays it. (p. 172; my italics)

Indeed, a comedic character may embody such a skeleton while accorded additional traits that make it into a life-like character to a certain degree. However, this does not apply to all characters in comedy; e.g., Micio in Terence's *The Brothers*. In contrast, as a recurring configuration of functions and thematic specification, it is its ready-made nature that underlies its recyclable nature. Comedy capitalizes on the existence of stock-type characters: such a character can elicit laughter even when entering the stage or screen, prior to any intervention, because of the spectator's familiarity with it from previous productions of different plays. It thus creates the right atmosphere for the comic mood to take off.

Nicoll tries to identify the comic stock-types of Dorian mime, the Phlyakes and the Fabula Atellana through the analysis of contemporary statuettes and vase paintings of comic actors. He finds that in antiquity comic stock-types are characterized by their quite consistent appearances, such as a mask, a tight fitting vest, padded stomach and buttocks, and a leather phallus (pp. 20–134); and suggests that this tradition persisted in the scripted comedies of Menander, Plautus and Terence, such as the parasite and the cook, and up until *commedia dell'arte*, which has continued to influence comedy to the present day.

It is in *commedia dell'arte* that all the characters are stock-types. Such characters were called 'masks' because they could be enacted by different actors not only in different productions, but even in the same one — thus being identified by the audience as recurrent characters (see CHAPTER 9).

Static characterization

My definition of characterization as a set of constant traits, which mirror the various structural levels of a fictional action, presupposes the principle of 'consistency'. Comedy shows a clear preference for unchanging characterization, especially in regard to ludicrous characters, which is probably responsible, *inter alia*, for its lighthearted mood. The spectator can thus count on the character's propensity to commit similar ludicrous acts over and over again. Development is usually not an option in comedy. A comedic character may change his mind, but as a result of coercing circumstances, not of mental growth. For example, Harpagon remains the same miser despite relinquishing his attempt to marry Mariane. Such a change can be detected only against the background of an axiomatic model of characterization. The permanence of his avarice also explains the dénouement, following the recovery of his money.

The chorus as comic character

The chorus is not a typical character of comedy. Whereas Aristophanes employs choruses, apparently, this is more a sign of status than a structural necessity: 'Comedy has had no history, because it was not at first treated seriously. It was late before the Archon granted a comic chorus to a poet' (*Poetics*: V, 2). I have suggested elsewhere that in tragedy the chorus is a residue of its origin in the choral dithyramb: whatever story-telling function that could not be dramatized was left for the chorus, usually conveying the ironic viewpoint (Rozik, 2001). If comedy existed as a drama prior to its chorus, the implication is that the residual principle does not apply to comedy.

Aristotle claims that '[t]he chorus too should be regarded as one of the actors [characters]; it should be an integral part of the whole, and share in the action' (*Poetics*: XVIII, 7). It is implied, therefore, that *the chorus should be thematically characterized.* This is typical of Greek tragedy; e.g., the Fates in Aeschylus' *The Eumenides*, the sailors in Sophocles' *Philoctetes*, and the Asian bacchae in Euripides' *The Bacchae*. In contrast, the choruses of Aristophanes' comedies look, rather, as parodies of the tragic models; e.g., in *Frogs* the chorus is a group of frogs.

There is a fundamental correspondence between the structure of a fictional action and the structure of a comic character, and the subordination of the latter to the former reveals that these are two forms of organization of the same fictional material: temporal vs. atemporal, which are two sides of the same coin. The complex structure of the comedic fictional world implies that *no character can be reduced to a single trait.* Comedy features various kinds of comic characters that promote the humorous mood.

The Range of Comedy 7

Over the last few decades scholars have often abstained from attempting to define comedy. This tendency is probably explained by the extreme heterogeneity of the range of fictional worlds usually perceived as belonging in this genre. Indeed, scholars have generally not distinguished between comedy, satiric drama and grotesque drama (e.g., Segal, Stott and Weitz). However, in the light of the clear distinction made in this study, which aims at bestowing a high degree of homogeneity on each genre, a definition becomes possible. The following definition by Pavis complies with this criterion: '[c]omedy is traditionally defined by three criteria that oppose it to its elder sister, tragedy. It has characters of humble origins and happy endings, and is intended to make the spectators laugh' (p. 63). Although such a definition is widely accepted, it is problematic, because: (a) it is not the low class of the characters that characterizes comedy, but its lowly mode (see CHAPTER 1); (b) the ending is not necessarily happy, but always satisfies the spectator's archetypal expectations, i.e., there are also frustrations and punishments (see CHAPTERS 4 & 5); and (c) the intention to elicit laughter is optional, and characterizes other genres as well: only comic laughter is purely cathartic (see CHAPTER 2). I suggest, therefore, that 'comedy' refers to a fictional world characterized by an archetypal structure of action; a lowly mode, regardless of class; a comic mood; and optional comic laughter.

It should be emphasized that a particular mood reflects the intention of the author. However, in creating a stage production of a certain playscript, a director may choose to change its original mood, which results in a particular creative interpretation; e.g., Molière's *The Miser* has been performed as a comedy, a farce and a melodrama (Urian: 43)

So far this study has focused on comedy proper. There are additional genres, however, usually perceived as different, which, according to the said definition, should be seen as subspecies 'comedy'. They share with comedy proper the lowly mode, the humorous mood, the eliciting of anxiety (due to the lifting of inhibitions), the repression of pity, the cathartic effect of possible laughter, and usually the archetypal structure of action, which aims at reaffirmation of the established value system and holistic catharsis. These genres are farce, romantic comedy and sketch comedy. I suggest that in fact all these belong in the same genre, because their differences are only a matter of emphasis and/or degree.

Farce

Basically, there is an unbridgeable gap between the serious and the humorous moods, and gradation is found only within each mood. Similar to the relation between tragedy and melodrama, the boundaries between comedy proper and farce too are not clear-cut. Nonetheless, it is clear that both these genres operate the lighthearted mood, leading to the thesis that their differences are only a matter of degree. The following considerations are attempts to establish the nature of these boundaries.

(A) Farce is characterized by the lifting of severe inhibitions. Bentley claims that '[i]n farce we can never be in the mood to feel sorry for the victims. We are having too good a time doing the victimization. Toward both the attacker and the attacked farce is unemotional as it is unreflective' (p. 298). Indeed, farce gives the impression that the suffering of the victim is enjoyable; e.g. Molière's *George Dandin*. Moreover, whereas farce 'is "unfeeling"', in comedy 'feeling is not only present but abundant' (*ibid.*). Indeed, farce is quite violent, crude and highly uninhibited in lifting the audience's inhibitions: it touches themes, such as jealousy, adultery and cuckoldry, which both produce additional anxiety and enable powerful catharsis. This indicates that, indeed, the difference is only a matter of degree.

Bentley also contends that '[i]n farce what lies beneath the surface is pure aggression, which gets no moral justification, and asks none' (p. 296). However, analyses of farces indicate that it is indeed crude and violent, but not aggressive. In order to be aggressive there is a need for an extra-fictional object, as in satire. Bentley is aware that violence is shared by all fictional genres, including tragedy and melodrama, but observes that '[f]arce is perhaps even more notorious for its love of violent images' (p. 219) — with the reason being that 'if art did not treat violence, it could not go to the heart of things' (p. 221). Does farce excel in going to the heart of things, perhaps even more than tragedy? Is tragedy not more violent?

Bentley's approach to farce is inspired by psychoanalysis, particularly in its thesis that laughter involves the lifting of inhibitions. It is precisely thus that farce both coerces the spectator to confront the shameful and even suppressed contents of the psyche, and potentially leads to extreme pleasure. It does so through a fictional world that disregards these inhibitions, under the safe conditions of theatre's permissive atmosphere; i.e., of a collective experience that tacitly permits such exposure to usually inhibited and even suppressed contents of the psyche. 'Farce affords an escape from living, a release from the pressures of today, a regression to the irresponsibility of childhood' (p. 298). The problem is that catharsis is not an escape from life, especially not to childhood, but a mechanism that enables release of the tension that is produced by merely living under normative inhibitions — thus making life possible. This principle applies also to comedy proper, despite differences in degree.

(B) The extremely uninhibited nature of farce indicates that its peculiarity is a matter of synchronic decorum. Lanson explains farce's (temporary) tendency to disappear by the middle of the seventeenth century for reasons of decorum: 'Mme. de Rambouillet, says Tallemant, who blamed her for it, could not listen to an obscene word; and farce put precious ears to a cruel test' (p. 384). Bentley remarks that in one of Noel Coward's plays 'a man slaps his mother-in-law's face and she falls in a swoon. Farce is the only form of art in which such an incident could normally occur' (p. 240). Is this a reason for "decent" people to shun farce? On the contrary, farce is especially designed for them, who are the typical spectators of farce. In tragedy too mothers are killed, even by their own children; e.g., Aeschylus' *The Libation Bearers*.

The extreme lifting of inhibitions also applies to the typical language of farce: for example, the use of words that allude to sex in a culture that inhibits mentioning them. Whereas comedy proper tends to employ sexual innuendos, e.g., the lovers in Molière's plays (see CHAPTER 3), farce tends to be explicit to the verge of sheer crudeness and vulgarity. According to Bakhtin, this liberty is highly conspicuous in the imagery characteristic of carnival literature and art, which he views as grotesque. This imagery mainly alludes to the functions of the human body: making love, eating, drinking, defecating and urinating (p. 19). In this, farce and grotesque drama concur. I suggest that this is the very reason why farce is so powerful in its cathartic effect.

Whereas comedy proper shows a tendency to make us laugh by addressing social types and typical excesses through profound insights and witty dialogue, i.e., by exploiting the ludicrous potential in human nature, farce achieves this effect through indecent situations, licentious language, and vulgarity of gesture, while seemingly subverting any rule of decorum. Whereas comedy proper may or may not produce laughter, farce is usually characterized by aiming at making people laugh regardless of means. If farce does not succeed in making the spectator laugh, it is a flop. This does not mean that farce promotes indecency. On the contrary, these departures from decency are employed for the sake of cathartic laughter, which paradoxically enables the continued rule of the contemporary decorum. In this respect too, the difference between comedy and farce is only a matter of degree.

(c) Both comedy proper and farce reflect a fictional structure, which, in principle, is shared by all the basic genres (tragedy, comedy, melodrama and farce). On this level, both kinds of fictional world are generated by the same archetypal surface structures and arouse the same kind of archetypal expectations. Moreover, both genres incorporate and subordinate episodes aimed at producing laughter. As suggested by Lanson, laughter is essentially episodic (p. 389).

Both comedy proper and farce show a clear predilection for archetypal structures, which gratify the audiences' spontaneous expectations, and potentially produce catharsis. Both thus trigger the mechanism of catharsis on both the levels of component units (cathartic laughter) and entire fictional world (holistic catharsis). On this level the specific difference of farce probably lies in its kind of ending: whereas comedy proper shows a clear predilection for weddings or other festive events, farce may choose to gratify even odd expectations; e.g., the final laments of George Dandin.

(d) There is a difference also on the level of tempo. The notion of 'tempo' applies to the sense of measured pace produced by a certain kind of behavior. It presupposes various mental models that characterize different personalities, occupations and activities. Tempo can be sensed not in a play-script, but only in a stage performance. An enacted narrative may be in harmony with these models or not. Whereas tragedy tends to be slower, as befits sublime behavior, comedy proper tends to be faster than expected — with farce bringing tempo to paroxysm. Such a tempo can create the impression of automatism, which is laughter-eliciting in itself, and probably supports Bergson theory of laughter, because farcical actors may produce the image of a machine. Nonetheless, this study presupposes the distinction between tragic and comic automatism (see CHAPTER 2). Change of rhythm and/or tempo, in regard to previous productions of a certain play-script, may radically change the spectators' perception of a fictional world.

Farce is thus a comedic genre whose specific difference lies in its extremely uninhibited nature. In this sense, it challenges more deeply the ethical sensibility of the spectator. In other words, the difference between comedy proper and farce is rather a matter of gradation. The most salient quality of farce is its focus on the cathartic function of laughter — which is enabled by its unbridled tapping into the most shameful inhibitions of the audience. It is noteworthy that, in addition to the audience's *philanthropon*, farce presupposes even the validity of their stereotypes and prejudices, and may reaffirm them without questioning them. The emphasis on producing cathartic laughter in open disregard of means makes farce the generic correlative of melodrama, whose main aim is to produce cathartic crying, regardless of means.

It should be noted that the typical distinction between comedy proper and farce conveys connotations of value, in the sense that comedy proper is superior to farce because of its refined means. Whereas comedy proper is usually characterized by elements of social type-characterization, social criticism and even satire, witty dialogue and verbal innuendo; farce is characterized by crudity of gesture, extremely coarse language, and bawdiness of speech; i.e., by aiming at making people laugh even by contemptible means. Comedy proper is thus deemed more prestigious than farce, despite the existence of poor comedies and excellent farces. However, *in any attempt to determine the nature of farce, such evaluative elements should be disregarded.*

Gustave Lanson contends that '[f]arce is at the root of all Molière's comedy, even in its highest forms, the comedy of manners and comedy of character' (Lanson: 380). There are indeed farcical elements in Molière's comedies, and even entire fictional worlds should be seen under this category, e.g., *George Dandin*. However, if indeed the difference between comedy proper and farce is only a matter of degree, most of his comedies are not farcical.

A good example of cinematic farce is Brian Robbins film *Norbit*, 2007, with Eddie Murphy playing the lead.

Molière's *George Dandin*

George Dandin is a rich commoner who has married a poor maiden of noble ancestry in order to join his wealth to her status. Presumably, her parents shared the same design.

Act I: Lubin (servant of Clitandre) confides to George Dandin that his master is having a love affair with Dandin's wife Angélique. She denies this and claims that her husband is a "jaloux" (tormented by fear of infidelity). Dandin complains to her parents, M. and Mme. de Sotenville, who do not believe him. They question Clitandre, who denies the affair. In front of them all Angélique ironically promises Clitandre to receive him 'comme il faut' (ambiguous: 'as it should be'). Madame de Sotenville scolds Dandin for not deserving such a wife and forces him to apologize. Angelique then declares her "feminist" credo: she had not got married in order to renounce life; whereas Dandin had not asked her whether she agreed to renounce life; and had only spoken to her parents, she wishes to continue to enjoy life. Dandin bemoans his lot.

Act II: Claudine (servant of Angelique) helps Clitandre to meet her mistress. Lubin again tells Dandin that his master had given money to Claudine to this effect; and again Dandin complains to his wife's parents, who are called to witness the encounter. Angelique pretends to reject Clitandre. Mme. de Sotenville praises her behavior and obliges Dandin to apologize. Dandin expresses his distress in a soliloquy.

Act III: Night. Dandin suspects that his wife has left home to meet Clitandre. She indeed meets her lover; but, upon returning home, she finds that the door is locked. She admits to having done something wrong and, in exchange for letting her in and not exposing her deed to her parents, she promises Dandin to renounce 'toutes les galanteries'. He refuses. She threatens to commit suicide and to make people think that he had killed her. Dandin still refuses. Eventually she pretends to kill herself. He then opens the door and Angelique and Claudine sneak in and lock the door, leaving him outside. Angelique then reverses the situation and admonishes her husband for returning home so late. M. and Mme de Sotenville witness the scene and demand Dandin's apology. Again, he is left to lament his bad luck: 'George Dandin, George Dandin, you've committed the greatest stupidity in the world!' (translation: Segal: 341)

George Dandin is a typical farce in its characterization of Dandin and Angelique and theme of conjugal infidelity. Its main intention is to present the ludicrous husband as a '*cocu*' (a cuckold), a typical butt of derision in a male-oriented culture. Similarly to other comedies of Molière, the ludicrous character is eventually frustrated (and suffers), which, in gratifying the spectators' archetypal expectations, should be seen as potentially cathartic. It should be noted that Dandin's reintegration into the final society is missing — thus indicating the less indulgent nature of farce.

This fictional world is an extreme instance of the enthymematic principle (see CHAPTER 12 & Rozik, 2008: 139–40). Its farcical characterization, the laughter that it intends to produce in particular, can be understood only if a certain stereotype is presupposed in the synchronic audience: the justification of conjugal infidelity to a commoner who has purchased social status through marriage, which was perceived as a kind of fraud. The oddity of this "value", which betrays the nature of our present perspective, reveals the enthymematic nature of the fictional experience, in considering that what is held to be valid and/or true by a particular audience is the basis for both comedy proper and farce. It follows that this fictional world does not reflect an absurdist structure because it satisfies the archetypal expectations of the audience. The recurrence of the same pattern three times (suspicion, denial, parents' reproach, apology and final lamentation) reflect a cyclic structure that implies infinite repetition — with Beckett's *Waiting for Godot* being a modernist example.

Farce is inconceivable without its enactment on stage. In *George Dandin* the few stage directions notated in the play-script, which probably indicate that the stage business was well-known to Molière's troupe, do reflect the importance of nonverbal acting in comedy; e.g., at the end of Angelique's monologue, through which she seems to castigate Clitandre's insolence, the stage direction states: 'She takes a stick and slaps her husband instead of Clitandre (II, viii; my trans.). In general, in promoting the comic mood, the comic acting is the main laughter device of farce (see CHAPTER 3)

Feydeau's *A Flea in the Ear*

Raymonde suspects that her husband Chandebise is betraying her because of his sexual indifference to her. Together with her friend Lucienne, she plans to prove it by sending him a love letter, inviting him to a hotel of ill repute. The letter is written by her friend in order to prevent the husband from recognizing his spouse's handwriting. Chandebise, who is totally devoted to his business, passes on the invitation to his friend Tournel, who is a known womanizer. Tournel is also fervently courting Raymonde, who hints that she is prepared to reciprocate his love on condition that he proves that her husband is faithful, as otherwise there is no point in betraying him (p. 374). The husband receives the letter and shows it to Lucienne's husband, Homénidès, a Spaniard, who is very jealous of his honor and his wife, recognizes her handwriting.

The second act takes place in the hotel, which is suitably equipped for discretion, and is a parody of a respectable hotel. For various reasons all the characters arrive at the place, including several comic characters, such as Camille, a youngster who because of a cleft palate mispronounces everything, an English tourist who keeps repeating the same question in a corrupt foreign accent, Homénides the jealous husband who in his amusing "Spanish"-French wishes to kill his wife, and a drunken servant. The action becomes a kind of whirlpool of entrances and exits, opening and closing doors, entire rooms swirling on hinges, misunderstandings, unexpected encounters and misidentifications, which reach a climax in the confusion between Poche the porter and Chandebise (enacted by the same actor), because of their complete resemblance and because, following the porter's mugging, they have exchanged outfits. The tempo reaches paroxysm as typical of farce.

In act three all settles down. Étienne, the servant's wife, denies categorically having betrayed him. She invokes the help of the porter, who for a small sum is prepared to vow that she had not left the house. The confusion of identities between Poche and Chandebise is cleared up. Raymonde reconciles with her husband, who has proven to be innocent. She reveals the truth of the letter to Homénidès, who reconciles with his wife. Happy ending for all.

The theme of the play-script is suspicion, betrayal and cuckoldry. In general, the action is serious and the comic mood is promoted by secondary characters. The name of the play-script, *La Puce à l'Oreille* (A Flea in the Ear), is a French idiom that roughly means a 'sudden *idée fixe*' that probably relates to Raymonde's suspicion, which is groundless as in fact her husband is impotent.

Chaplin's *Modern Times*

Although this silent film is widely perceived as the epitome of cinematic farce, it is more probably an offspring of the comedy of zanni.

Charlie is characterized as unfit for modern times, a *schlemiel*, who fails in every task, which is a kind of comic *hamartia*; e.g., he fails as a factory worker, a shipyard hand, and even in his attempts to be imprisoned. His failures are always foolish and funny. The film is an example of unity of character and episodic structure. Each episode is autonomous and reflects the intention to elicit comic laughter. The order of the episodes can thus be interchanged, any episode can be left out and/or a new one inserted. Charlie is the unique connection between them. In itself, each episode is hilarious, typical of comedy proper. There is also an overarching action: that of his affection for the orphan girl, the 'gamine'.

In addition to humorous failures, there is also an humorous fantasy:

while sitting with the gamine in front of a typical bourgeois home, Charlie imagines their future home; e.g., when returning from work he eats an apple from a tree growing outside the window; the gamine prepares dinner; Charlie calls a cow, milks it into a jug, and puts the jug on the table. Eventually, he returns to reality and exclaims (title): 'I'll do it! We'll get a home, even if I have to work for it.' The spectator knows that this will not happen: Charlie is the antithesis of the petit bourgeois. This piece of imagination is indeed foolish and ludicrous.

The film ends with the image of Charlie and the gamine walking together toward the horizon, which is parody of the clichéd image that hints at a new and promising beginning, and which characterizes many serious narratives. It is lent a comic innuendo by Charlie's clownish walking and the spectators' certainty that he will continue to be the very same *schlemiel* wherever he goes.

Modern Times focuses on a character afflicted by a ludicrous *hamartia*: Charlie's unfit nature, which is reflected in each of his actions. In contrast to farce, the episodes are characterized by their mild humor and their inconsequential results, which preclude pity, and promote comic laughter. It is comedy proper at its best.

Romantic comedy

Shakespeare's typical comedy should be seen as the extreme opposite of farce — with both being part of the comedic continuum. Rather than focusing on the ludicrous nature of the blocking character, or on the clownish nature of the servants, romantic comedy focuses on the lovers' yearnings to consummate their love. The ludicrous characters and the buffoons (cunning servants) do not entirely disappear, but are relegated to secondary roles. It is the romantic atmosphere that Shakespeare weaves around the lovers' narratives that bestows such an unprecedented quality upon them: e.g., *Twelfth Night*. The specific difference of romantic comedy lies in its emphasis on certain comedic characters.

The relegation and even abolition of the blocking father and the help of the cunning servants, needed for the wished-for happy ending for the young lovers, probably opened the way to modernist romantic comedy in which the blocking function is typically attributed not to an external character but to a blocking proclivity in the mind of one of the lovers or an extreme incompatibility between them. An example of the former: in Garry Marshal's film *Runaway Bride*, Maggie Carpenter (Julia Roberts) is known for recurrently running away from her wedding ceremonies in churches, leaving the grooms frustrated, before eventually marrying Ike Graham (Richard Gere) not in a church but in a private ceremony on a beautiful hill — with true love being the antidote of her odd drive. An example of the latter: Garry Marshal's film *Pretty Woman* arouses the archetypal expectation that two equally beautiful people and equally despised occupations (a hooker and a corporate raider) will eventually find the way to consummate their love and marry.

Shakespeare's *Twelfth Night*

Viola is the survivor of a shipwreck who believes that her twin brother Sebastian has drowned. Under the name Cesario, she disguises herself as a young page in the service of Duke Orsino. He is in love with the bereaved Lady Olivia, while she, mourning for her late brother, rejects all suitors. Viola, in turn, has fallen in love with the Duke who, to her despair, believes that she is a man and his confidant. Orsino employs Cesario (Viola), *inter alia*, to send him as his messenger to Olivia who, believing that Viola is a man, falls in love with the handsome and eloquent messenger. Nonetheless, Orsino is fascinated by Cesario. The dénouement: Sebastian, Viola's brother, arrives on the scene, sowing

7: Viola and Olivia, in the Khan Theatre *Twelfth Night*.
Photo: Yael Ilan. Courtesy of the Jerusalem Khan Theatre.

more confusion. Mistaking him for Cesario, Olivia asks him to marry her, and they are secretly united.

Then, when both twins appear in the presence of Olivia and the Duke, there is awe and wonder at their similarity, at which point Viola reveals her true identity, and that Sebastian is her lost twin brother. Olivia in fact has wedded Sebastian; and, when Orsino discovers that Cesario is a woman, everything falls into place: the play-script ends in the announcement of the marriage of the Duke and Viola. It is learned that Sir Toby and Maria too have married.

In parallel, there is a comic subplot. Olivia's servants Maria and Fabian, her uncle Sir Toby Belch, Sir Andrew Ague-cheek, and her father's favourite fool, Feste, conspire to make Olivia's pompous steward, Malvolio, believe that she is secretly in love with him. They forge a letter imitating Olivia's handwriting, asking Malvolio to wear yellow stockings to show his agreement. In an act of naïve pride and wearing bright yellow stockings, detested by Olivia, he declares his love for her and she, to the amusement of his victimizers, disdainfully ignores him.

Under the pretence of his insanity, they lock Malvolio up in a dark cellar. Feste, disguised as a priest, exploits his visits to mock him. In the end, Malvolio learns of their conspiracy and promises revenge. In

8 Exhilarated Malvolio in yellow stockings, in the Khan Theatre
Twelfth Night.
Photo: Yael Ilan. Courtesy of the Jerusalem Khan Theatre

contrast to Frye's theory, he is not accepted into the final society. Nonetheless, the ending is meant to satisfy all the spontaneous expectations of the audience — thus enabling holistic catharsis.

It is probably the cancellation of the ludicrous *senex*, who obstructs the happines of the youngsters, that enables this romantic narrative to stand on its own. Due to the lovers not necessarily being naïve and helpless, the playwright was free to emphasize the romantic atmosphere of their loving relationship. This playwriting move also explains the disengagement between the serious and comic actions — with the latter not interfering in the former, while still providing comic relief. In this narrative, Malvolio is the butt of the buffoons. This comedy thus preserves the duality of serious and comic moods, which is typical of comedy proper, but with the balance tipping toward the serious mood and lofty mode, in its high language and manners (see CHAPTER 1).

Sketch comedy

'Sketch comedy' refers to the series of short comedies or, rather 'sketches', whose common denominator is usually the intention to produce pure laughter, albeit occasionally being used in the spirit of satire. A sketch is a self-contained unit that usually lasts a few minutes; for example, a program by the Israeli troupe Hagashash Hakhiver (The Pale Tracker) and British *Monty Python*. Weitz correctly describes a sketch as a 'freestanding lazzo' (p. 108). Sketches are strung together to form a whole program, which may also include other performative components such as playing music instruments, singing and dancing. Such a series can be performed by either actors or puppets; e.g., the British programs *The Sketch Show*, 2001–3 and *Spitting Image*, 1984–96, respectively.

The Mobilized Vehicle

This sketch, by the Hagashash Hakhiver troupe, relates to the period after the Israeli War of Independence, in which private and commercial vehicles were mobilized in times of war in exchange for a substantial tax reduction. The sketch opens with two soldiers entering the stage telling jokes and performing comic routines — thus establishing the comic atmosphere for the main part of the sketch: the dialogue between them and a reserve duty soldier who arrives to release his car. The two soldiers, who are in charge of the operation, are extremely delighted with their job, and receive the reserve soldier in a humorous mood. He is permitted to take away his car, which is parked beneath a tree just opposite the office; but, soon enough he returns complaining that this is not his car, which was a gray Chevrolet 66. The two soldiers explain that the car had been repainted in order to camouflage it, and end with: "drive away in peace, the keys are inside." From then on, the reserve soldier keeps returning and complaining that something else is missing such as the seats, the radio, and even the engine. The two soldiers, who always provide a humorous explanation, tell him that it is only a matter of a minor expense, and repeat "drive away in peace, the keys are inside." Eventually, in deepest frustration, the soldier asks: how is he supposed to drive the car away? And their answer in unison is: "What, you didn't bring a tow track?"

The audience laughed with the two buffoons and at the victim, who is depicted as a tearful and extremely worried character, which is a kind of comic *hamartia*. Laughter increased with each "drive away in peace, the keys are inside", which is (intentionally) foolish, because no key can start such a wreck. The sketch is not a satire on the Israeli Army, and the laughter is comic. The sketch neither features ethical characterization, nor fictional structure; but ends in a punch line, like a joke. It is indeed a dramatized joke (see CHAPTER 11).

There are additional genres that share with comedy proper the humorous mood, the eliciting of additional anxiety (due to the lifting of inhibitions), the absence of pity, the cathartic intent of laughter, and often the archetypal structure of action and holistic catharsis. These genres are farce, romantic comedy and sketch comedy. Their differences are only a matter of emphasis on different kinds of character and/or degree in lifting inhibitions. Despite being usually perceived as different genres, they should more correctly be seen as sub-genres of 'comedy', including comedy proper. Henceforth I employ 'comedy' for this entire set.

Tangential Genres   8

The previous chapter focused on comedy proper, farce, romantic comedy and sketch comedy, all of which share the humorous mood, possible comic laughter, and the basic aim of satisfying the spectators' expectations for archetypal ending and holistic catharsis. In this sense, they should be conceived of as sub-species 'comedy'. In contrast, this chapter deals with additional genres, which share with the former only the use of laughter devices, and give the wrong impression that, because of this, they too belong in the category of 'comedy'. However, they employ these devices in order to promote completely different moods. In this sense, they are only tangential to comedy. If indeed the specific mood is the key to generic categorization, it is sensible to claim that these additional genres (satiric drama, grotesque drama and satiric stand-up comedy) deserve reading and experiencing according to their own rules. The theoretical aim of this chapter is, therefore, to establish their specific differences on the levels of mood and kinds of laughter.

Satiric drama

Lehmann correctly observes that 'what has been written about the subject [of comedy] is, except for incidental insights, not about comedy. It is about satire. . . . The laughter, it is said, is corrective; we are invited to believe that the chief end of comedy is to reform manners and dispositions' (p. 163). He contrasts thereby the general attitude of scholars , such as Segal, Stott and Weitz, who do not make any distinction between these genres on the grounds of mood. Lehmann thus clearly implies that comedy and satire are different dramatic genres. Aristotle had already hinted at such a conclusion in making a distinction between 'dramatizing the ludicrous' and 'writing personal satire' (*Poetics*: IV, 9) Indeed, whereas comedy is characterized by its lighthearted attitude, in the sense of being sympathetic, benevolent, tolerant, and even merciful, satire is characterized by its severe attitude, in the sense of being aggressive, unsympathetic, intolerant and often even vindictive. Indeed, satiric drama is basically a serious genre, despite its use of laughter devices. It employs these devices in order to deride personalities, institutions or ideas that are not necessarily ludicrous in themselves. Indeed, any sacred cow is potentially an object of satire.

That comedy and satire share the use of laughter devices should not confuse us. Whereas comedy *aims* at producing comic laughter, which is purely cathartic, satire *uses* laughter in a castigating capacity. Satiric laughter too can be cathartic, but for a different reason: it gratifies an aggressive impulse. In contrast to humorous laughter, satiric laughter is derogative and humiliating — thus reflecting a different rhetoric intention. Moreover, 'large numbers of play-scripts today merely *use* the mechanism of laughter without granting its expected release of tension. ... The comic [satiric] may be no laughing matter' (Styan, 1968: 47). The implication is that laughter is hardly a common denominator of comedy and satiric drama. It should be noted that, in this sense, Aristotle's notion of 'ludicrous' is ambiguous, because it fits both comic and satiric drama.

In contrast to Bergson, each kind of laughter should be explained by the fundamental difference between humorous and corrective laughter (see CHAPTER 2). The explicit aim of satire is to expose imperfection and possibly to amend it. Since laughter presupposes a foolish fault, it can also be used for satire, by merely attributing such a fault to a real object, even if arbitrarily. Aristotle already makes this observation: 'In Comedy ... the poet first constructs the plot on the lines of probability, and then inserts characteristic names; — unlike the lampooners who write about particular individuals' (*Poetics*: IX, 5).

'Comedy of manners' is a particular kind of satiric drama; e.g., Congreve's *The Way of the World*, whose aim was to criticize the admixture of romantic and economic concerns that characterized the English upper class in his own days. Similar considerations apply to Oscar Wilde's *The Importance of Being Earnest* and Shaw's *Pygmalion*, whose aim was too to deride and discredit the manners of the upper class. Moreover, whereas 'comedy of character' presupposes a distinction on structural grounds, 'comedy of manners' is a grouping on thematic grounds.

The problem is that the notion of 'comedy of manners' is often wrongly applied to comedies, especially to the comedies of Molière, possibly because the borderline between these genres is not clear-cut. In many a case, the specific difference of satiric drama hinges not on textual clues but on different intentions: while satire is characterized by the intention to deride a real person, class, institution or idea; i.e., aims at a real referent, which is not necessarily ridiculous, comedy reverses this relationship: it aims at employing comic flaws in human nature for the purpose of laughter. This probably explains what happened with Molière's *Tartuffe*, which features nothing to suggest its interpretation as a satire on the clergy. Tartuffe is not a priest, but merely a spiritual mentor, who violates trust as a private person. He is a plain fictional villain.

Satire is extremely aggressive when addressing *real* personalities, such as fathers, teachers and politicians, who elicit anxiety due to the spectators' dependence on them. Persons in control are thus downgraded by attributing foolish behavior to them, whether they are foolish in themselves, or made foolish by the intentional exaggeration and even distortion of their inclinations and actions. Similar considerations apply to real institutions. The traits that can be ridiculed include anything that is different such as nationality, accent, skin color, social class, occupation, gender and the like. In general, being different produces anxiety. Satire is particularly aggressive in addressing racist, sexist and homophobic ideas and attitudes.

Freud contends that 'One can make a person comic in order to make him become contemptible, to deprive him of his claim to dignity and authority' (1989: 234). The implication is that, in contrast to comic characters, which are laughable in embodying a suppressed ludicrous tendency in the human nature, the victims of satiric treatment must not be ludicrous in themselves. In regard to Aristophanes, Corrigan claims that Aristophanes' 'satiric wit is, of all forms of wit, the most ephemeral. [In his play-scripts], [t]he basic comic gesture is universal in its appeal based on immediate, topical references — usually the absurdities of current political or social behavior — and almost impossible to translate or pass on to future generations' (p. 360). Indeed, the references to a synchronic extra-fictional reality make satiric drama dependent on time and place.

Moreover, what is usually called the 'happy idea' in Aristophanes' play-scripts, which lends unity to his topical references, is not only a platform for satiric remarks, but also satiric in itself (cf. Weitz: 42 & 79). For example, in *Lysistrata*, the idea of ending a war through a sex strike by women implies that war is a male foolishness that can be cured by a female foolishness that hits close to the males' hearts. In *Frogs*, the happy idea is that in order to restore the glory of Athens one of the great tragedians should be rescued from Hades, preferably Aeschylus. This is not only a blow to Euripides' prestige, but also an implicit criticism of Aristophanes' contemporary Athens, including its theatre. In *Plutus*, the happy idea relates to the absurd thought that the arbitrary distribution of wealth can be amended by curing Plutus, the god of wealth, of his blindness, which is a satiric metaphor on the dream of a new social formula.

The effect of satire is often achieved by exaggerating existing slight imperfections and failures in a derisive and even grotesque spirit. In this sense, satire is a kind of stage caricature (cf. Freud, 1989: 249); e.g., making a political leader seem stupid by exploiting his credulity or gullibility (cf. *ibid.*). Bergson notes that '[t]he art of the caricaturist consists in detecting [some favorite distortion towards which nature seems to be particularly inclined], at times, imperceptible tendency, and in rendering it visible to all eyes by magnifying it' (p. 77) Olson too observes: 'Aristophanes' plays are cartoons in dramatic [enacted] action' (p. 69).

'Ridicule is a particular kind of *depreciation*. We cannot ridicule someone by showing that he is extremely *good* or *better* than most, or even *ordinary*; we must show that he is *inferior*' (Olson: 12). Satiric laughter thus conveys a sense of superiority. This sense of superiority is not the contrived one that characterizes dramatic irony, but a real sense of superiority in regard to a real person or institution. In contrast, laughing at a miser or hypochondriac is not social criticism. Whereas in watching comedy there is no point in feeling superiority in regard to a ludicrous character, in satire it crowns the satiric intent with success.

The difference between comedy and satiric drama is also reflected in their preferences for different surface structures. Whereas the former tends to prefer archetypal endings, the latter tends to prefer absurdist endings, which best suit its critical intention. While the comic mood moves to final harmony through the gratification of the spectators' archetypal expectations, the satiric mood inherently moves to final disharmony through the frustration of their archetypal expectations. Satire may be generated by an archetypal fictional structure, but it is in the interest of the satirist to eventually shock the audience through the ultimate revelation of what is deemed to be a hidden truth.

Satire shares its criticism with critical serious fictional worlds, e.g., Büchner's criticism of the military and scientific establishments in *Woyzeck*. However, the specific difference of satiric drama lies in that criticism takes the form of derision. Whereas serious or satirical, criticism can be painful; it may create the conditions for the reconsideration of what is held to be true and/or valuable. This is viewed as a commendable quality of satire: 'the best comedy [satire] teases and troubles an audience; it can be painful. Comic [satiric] method can serve to create an imaginative but dispassionate attitude; to create the conditions for thinking; to free the dramatist in his attempt to tap certain rational resources of mind in his audience' (Styan, 1968: 46).

A typical surface structure of comedy can be employed as a platform for satire; e.g., in *The Importance of Being Earnest*. Similar considerations apply to personal diatribe in Aristophanes' play-scripts; e.g., in *Frogs*. As Corrigan claims '[t]here is really very little plot to most of Aristophanes' plays . . . only a series of episodes which serve as the occasions for his wit and satiric thrusts. His plays move from moment to moment and have a sense of spontaneity rather than structure' (p. 359). In my view, it is clear that Aristophanes does not structure his play-scripts in the manner of fictional thinking. He is a discursive thinker.

The satiric intent is supported by considerations of value. The satirists usually claim that they are motivated by a system of values, whether accepted by the audience or not, and that their intentions are honest. This is in all probability true. However, this argumentation also reveals a weak point, because their means are fundamentally aggressive. In R. C. Elliot's view, '[a]ccording to the image [which the satirist projects of himself and his art he] is a public servant fighting the good fight against vice and folly wherever he meets it; he is honest, brave, protected by the rectitude of his motives; he attacks only the wicked and then seldom or never by name; he is, in short, a moral man appalled by the evil he sees around him, and he is forced by his conscience to write satire' (p. 334). Nonetheless, society usually suspects the purity of the satirists' intentions. I believe that this too is justified:

> Society has doubtlessly been wise, in its old pragmatic way, to suspect the satirist. . . . his relation to society will necessarily be problematic. He is of society in the sense that his art must be grounded in his experience as social man; but he must also be apart, as he struggles to achieve aesthetic distance. His practice is often sanative, as he proclaims; but it may be revolutionary in ways that [established] society cannot possibly approve, and in ways that may not be clear even to the satirist. (Elliot: 342)

'From the beginning the satirical poet has skated on the thin edge of censorship and legal retribution' (*ibid.*: 330). The relation between the satirist and society is, therefore, basically ambiguous (*ibid.*: 338), which is not the case in regard to comedy.

Corrigan observes that the purpose of the writer of satire '*is* always corrective. . . . the satirist is either seeking to restore values and patterns of behavior which he believes have been lost, forgotten, or debased, or he is urging us to discover new ideals and ways of living. Therefore, all of his jibes — no matter how bitter — are ultimately directed at the restoration or preservation of the social order' (p. 354). Indeed, the writer of satire is not necessarily conservative, and may reflect an alternative system of values: 'the traditional code is never the *only* morality' (p. 358). Moreover, Lehmann observes: 'Straight satire, in fact, is itself despotic; it assumes the absolute validity of the satirist's values and is intolerant; it judges without misgiving; it does more than condemn, it excludes' (p. 167). These are actually two sides of the same coin.

Molière's excuse is a typical example: 'If one takes the trouble to examine my comedy [*Tartuffe*] in good faith, he will surely see that my intentions are innocent throughout, and tend in no way to make fun of what men revere. . . . I have used all the art and skill that I could to distinguish clearly the character of the hypocrite from that of the truly devout man' (1669: 444). In fact, 'Molière proposed in *Tartuffe* to unmask an example of religious hypocrisy. Yet the effect of the play has seemed to many people genuinely subversive — with the attack on the hypocrite somehow insidiously, becoming an attack on religion itself' (Elliot: 340). It should be noted that Tartuffe is not necessarily a comic character but, rather, a villainous one (see CHAPTER 6).

Indeed, whether Molière meant it or not, in his own days *Tartuffe* was perceived as a satire on the clergy. Nonetheless, in most of his comedies it is quite clear that his intention was not to correct excesses, such as misanthropy, hypochondria and fear of infidelity, but simply to exploit their inherent ludicrous nature in order to produce *humorous* laughter. His doctors are possibly a liminal case. In contrast to Sypher, who claims that 'there is an undercurrent of satire in most comedy' (p. 240), I suggest that this is not the case. To claim that Plautus in *The Pot of Gold* and Molière in *The Miser*, are criticizing avarice is to say that they are preaching the obvious: the mere use of the word 'avarice' implies a negative value, as established by the communal ethos. Rather, they are exploiting the ludicrous nature of such a psychical deformation. Indeed, Molière was well aware of the power of satire: in his preface to *Tartuffe* he remarks: 'Criticism is taken lightly, but [real] men will not tolerate satire. They are quite willing to be [portrayed as] mean, but they never like to be ridiculed' (1669: 445). In general, while humor is accepted willingly, even by those who are afflicted by a similar comic *hamartia*, the victims of satire might react angrily and even aggressively.

A good example of cinematic satire is Hal Ashby's film *Being There*, starring Peter Sellers.

Aristophanes' *Plutus*

Chremylus' naïve idea is to cure Plutus, the god of wealth, of his blindness. The burlesqued myth reveals that this god had wished to confer wealth only upon the virtuous, but, out of sheer jealousy, Zeus had blinded him in order to prevent his endeavor — with the result being that wealth is granted indiscriminately. The allegoric character Poverty tries to persuade Chremylus that all that is good in the world stems from poverty, but its ideas are ignored. Chremylus thus sets out to correct this unfortunate blunder by curing the god of his blindness, and succeeds. Paradoxically, however, the results are devastating: for example, the wealthy become poor, and the enriched and once virtuous people now cease to bring offerings to the gods, who consequently suffer hunger, including Zeus himself.

This fictional world is initially structured according to an assumedly spontaneous expectation of the synchronic spectator, who probably resented the absurdity embodied in the distribution of wealth, in clear discrepancy with the rich individuals' lack of ethical qualities; and harbored a wish that wealth be distributed in accordance with personal virtues. The narrative seems to lead to the gratification of the spectators' expectations, but ends in increased absurdity. Aristophanes thus exposes the naïvety of the idea that wealth should be distributed on ethical grounds.

Gogol's *The Government Inspector*

The rumor is that the Czar has sent an inspector to the capital of a Russian province. The corrupt officials try to preempt dangerous consequences by bribing Khlestakov, who is believed to be the expected emissary, by all kinds of ludicrous means. These efforts are made in order to cover up the fact that money sent by the Czar had not been used for its intended purposes but been stolen. The visitor exploits the situation and makes promises of promotion for all. All dream about their wished-for futures, especially the governor's wife, who expects her husband to be appointed a general and asked to live in Moscow. Eventually, following their reading a letter by Khlestakov, written after leaving the city, in which he derides their gullibility, the officials face the fact that they have been swindled by the supposed inspector, who is a crook, and discover that the real inspector is only now on his way to the provincial capital.

Nikolai Gogol's narrative ends with the expected punishment of the corrupt local authorities; i.e., in the gratification of the spectators' archetypal expectations. In this sense, this satire of administrative corruption is structurally similar to comedy. It is a satire in aiming a severe critique at the real provincial establishment by attributing ludicrous behavior to its officials, which amounts to an overall image of governmental corruption. Nonetheless, in general, satire best combines with absurdist structures, as in the previous example.

Wilde's *The Importance of Being Earnest*

The narrative is a typical love story in which two men, Algernon and John (Jack), complicate their attempts to conquer the hearts of two girls, Cecily and Gwendolen, by their own lies. *Inter alia*, Algernon pretends to having an invalid friend named Bunbury who lives in the country, and whenever he wants to escape unpleasant social obligations, he "goes Bunburying"; and Jack pretends to having a wastrel brother named Ernest Worthing: while in the country he goes by his proper name, but in London he assumes the name and behaviour of his libertine brother. Nonetheless, both are extremely friendly fellows and extremely serious about Cecily, who is Jack's ward, and Gwendolen, who is Algernon's cousin.

Jack proposes to Gwendolen who loves him because of his (pretended) name Ernest. Lady Bracknell, Gwendolen's mother, questions Jack's social background and finds, to her distress, that he had been abandoned as a baby in a handbag at a railway station. She consequently forbids her daughter from seeing him. Jack's description of his pretty young ward so appeals to Algernon that he is resolved to meet her, which he does, pretending that he is Jack's brother Ernest. Cecily too had imagined herself in love with Jack's younger brother, mainly because of his name Ernest. Both Gwendolen and Cecily insist that *she* is the one engaged to Ernest. When Jack and Algernon reappear, their deceptions are exposed. When the men explain themselves, they are forgiven, and the women agree not to break off the engagements when each man announces his intention to be re-christened.

Lady Bracknell also opposes the engagement of her nephew Algernon to Cecily, but consents when the size of Cecily's trust fund is revealed. Jack then denies his consent until Lady Bracknell agrees to his own marriage to Gwendolen. Miss Prim, disentangles the situation by remembering that in a moment of abstraction she had put a baby in a handbag, which she had left at Victoria Station. Jack produces the very same handbag, revealing that he is the lost baby, the oldest son of Lady Bracknell's late sister, and thus Algernon's elder brother. Lady Bracknell assumes that, being the firstborn son, he must have been named after his father, General Ernest Moncrieff, which is confirmed. Then the two happy couples embrace; and Algernon concludes: 'I've now realized for the first time in my life the vital importance of being earnest.'

The narrative reflects an archetypal structure, typical of comedy: both couples are in love and obstructed by a Victorian mother/aunt — thus engaging the spontaneous expectations of the audience for a happy ending. However, this action is no more than a platform for Algernon's satiric and witty remarks, which reflect Wilde's own viewpoint on the absurdity and hypocrisy involved in the norms of the upper-class typical of Victorian society, epitomized by the opinionated Lady Bracknell. Whereas Algernon remarks are ironic, Lady Bracknell's ones are the object of irony; for example:

> 1) *Algernon*: The amount of women in London who flirt with their own husbands is perfectly scandalous. (p. 257)
>
> 2) *Algernon*: Relations are simply a tedious pack of people, who haven't got the remotest knowledge of how to live, nor the smallest instinct about when to die. (pp. 266–7)
>
> 3) *Lady Bracknell*: Illness of any kind is hardly a thing to be encouraged in others. Health is a primary duty of life. (p. 260)
>
> 4) *Lady Bracknell*: I need hardly tell you that in families of high position strange coincidences are not supposed to occur. (p. 305)

While Algernon is an instance of the buffoon, Lady Bracknell is meant to be his butt. The play-script is an example of what is usually termed 'comedy of manners' but should be more appropriately termed 'satiric drama'.

Synge's *The Playboy of the Western World*

The narrative is set in County Mayo, Ireland, during the early eighteenth century. In running away from his farm, having killed his father by driving a spade into his head, Christy Mahon stumbles into Flaherty's tavern. Rather than condemning his crime, the locals are captivated by his story. Pegeen, Flaherty's daughter and barmaid, falls in love with Christy, to the distress of her betrothed Shawn Keogh. Other women too are attracted to Christy because of his "heroic" story. Widow Quin tries to seduce him at Shawn's request, but fails. After winning a race, he becomes the local hero — with people cheering him as 'the playboy of the western world'.

Christy's father, Old Mahon, who was only wounded, tracks his son to the tavern. When the locals realize that the father is alive, including Pegeen, they abuse Christy as a schemer, a coward and a liar. In order to regain their respect and Pegeen's love, he attacks his father once more; but, believing again that Old Mahon is dead, in place of praising Christy they harshly blame him, and even prepare to hang him for his atrocious crime. Pegeen has "learned" that 'there's a great gap between a gallous story and a dirty deed' (p. 77). However, albeit severely wounded, Old Mahon reappears and saves his son. They reconcile and leave together to wander the world and enjoy telling the story of 'the villainy of Mayo, and the fools there' (p. 80). Pegeen laments betraying and losing Christy.

John M. Synge contrasts the fascination in listening to a story about killing a father to the aversion of a "real" murder of a father. Whereas the former is thoroughly enjoyed, and even cathartic, the latter is thoroughly shocking. This reveals a profound poetic insight. The final reconciliation of father and son, and their decision to exploit the people's fascination (and possible cathartic response) at the narrative, should be understood as a satiric comment on people's unawareness of their own hypocrisy and callousness or, rather, it can be said, of their inhibited drives. The anti-romantic ending of the narrative of love between Christy and Pegeen is absurdist due to frustrating the archetypal expectations of the audience. The final reconciliation of father and son and their triumphant departure possibly exacerbates this sense of absurdity because it is a final gestus of criticism on foolish humanity.

Grotesque drama

It is seldom that a scholar attempts to outline the entire life cycle of a genre from birth to death. However, that is exactly what Erich Segal attempts to do in *The Death of Comedy* (cf. George Steiner's *The Death of Tragedy*). His history commences with the alleged pre-comedian ritual, in Cornford's sense, and Megarian comedy, and ends with his post mortem: 'The drama will have no happy ending. Indeed, it will have no ending at all. . . . The traditional happy ending is no longer possible — because comedy is dead' (p. 452). In other words, what in his view is the main condition for comedy to exist is allegedly unthinkable in the context of the present *weltanschauung*. Perhaps he should just have said: 'Comedy is dead because happy endings are no longer possible.'

However, this untimely obituary ignores several facts: (a) happy endings are not the specific difference of comedy, but are shared by most other genres, including tragedy, as Aristotle himself acknowledges (*Poetics*: XIII, 8); (b) a happy ending or, rather, an archetypal ending, should be seen not as an optimistic statement on the nature of real life, implying that all troubles have ended according to the spectator's expectations, but as a metaphoric statement on the validity of values and beliefs; and (c) comedy continues to thrive not only in theatre productions of classic comedies, but also in newly scripted ones, including cinematic comedy. In fact, what Segal describes, in analyzing playscripts by Jarry, Ionesco and Beckett (pp. 403–52), indicates not the death of comedy but the birth of a new genre, which reflects the advent of a new constellation of structural choices, and whose mood is predominantly grotesque.

Theoretically, Aristotle's qualification concerning the ludicrous in comedy, 'which is not painful or destructive' (*Poetics*: V, 1), actually implies and foreshadows the possibility of treatment of a 'defect or ugliness' that *is* painful or destructive; i.e., the treatment of a serious theme, through laughter devices, which is widely perceived as generating a grotesque mood. However, he ignores the existence of the grotesque mood and, therefore, the possibility of a distinct genre: grotesque drama. In regard to modern grotesque drama, Corrigan correctly remarks: 'make no mistake, this is a special kind of comedy, a grotesque kind of comedy, which makes us laugh with a lump in our throats' (p. 10).

In contrast, Horace implies such a possibility: 'A comic subject is not susceptible of treatment in a tragic style, and similarly the banquet of Thyestes cannot be fitly described in the strains of everyday life or in those that approach the tone [mood] of comedy. Let each of these styles be kept for the role properly allotted to it' (p. 82). In the context of his consistent attempt to promote harmony in every respect, Horace presupposes that there must be harmony between the nature of the subject matter and its treatment on the level of style or, rather, mood: whereas the tragic mood fits extremely serious themes, the comic mood only fits trivial ones. Paradoxically, this argument implies the possibility of intentional disharmony. Such disharmony is, however, certainly not an innovation of modernist drama: it is already found even in ancient Greek drama; e.g., in Aristophanes' *Frogs*, divine Dionysus is depicted as doing in his pants from fear.

In modernist drama the grotesque mood is widely employed in the treatment of certain themes that for centuries were conceived of as exclusively tragic, while reflecting a fundamental change in attitude to the human condition. Therefore, its inclusion in a general theory of fictionality does not contrast Aristotle's insights and constitutes a substantial contribution to a comprehensive theory of fictionality.

Among the essential elements of the grotesque Wolfgang Kayser mentions: 'the mixture of heterogeneous elements, the confusion, the fantastic quality, and even a kind of alienation of the world . . . the abysmal quality, the insecurity, the terror inspired by the disintegration of the world' (pp. 51–2); 'the mixture of the incompatible' (p. 136), and the fusion of '[f]arce and tragedy' (*ibid.*). For him, '*[t]he Grotesque is the estranged world*' (p. 184). He thus concludes that 'the grotesque [is] *an attempt to invoke and subdue the demonic aspects of the world*' (p. 188). The problem is that Kayser's approach conflates the principles of the grotesque with those of the absurd, which, albeit combining well, belong on different structural levels: e.g., '*[t]he grotesque is a play with the absurd*' (p. 187)

In contrast to Kayser, I suggest that a clear distinction should be made between the '*absurd*', which refers to a kind of surface structure, which eventually contrasts the archetypal expectations of the synchronic audience; and the '*grotesque*', which refers to a kind of mood and, *inter alia*, results from the ludicrous treatment of a highly serious and painful theme, which often concerns the spectators' basic orientation in the world. The grotesque mood thus contrasts their sensibilities; i.e., their spontaneous models of harmony in regard to such themes (cf. Horace as above). In contrast to the satiric drama that aims at deriding the blind acceptance of established values, in grotesque drama the deriding treatment through laughter devices aims at undermining the attitudes of the audience to serious themes, for example, the theme of death in both Ionesco's *Exit the King* and Beckett's *Happy Days*. Nonetheless, despite applying to different aspects of the fictional world, the satiric and grotesque principles may complement one another.

The grotesque mood reveals that the either serious or ludicrous associations attached to a certain theme are vital components of the distinct effect of a fictional world on the audience. Moreover, it reveals that, on this level, either agreement or discrepancy is a crucial factor in determining the nature of its mood; i.e., the prism through which a fictional world is perceived. That this factor is made prominent in cases of contrast should not obscure the fact that it also operates in cases of agreement; e.g., tragedy treats serious themes seriously and comedy treats trivial themes lightheartedly. While these genres indicate the existence of archetypal models of harmony in the spectator's mind, it is clear that the grotesque mood contrasts them. The laughter devices in grotesque drama, therefore, are meant to produce a unique effect: 'The result is a mixture of genres and styles. Its grimacing comic effect paralyzes the spectator, who can neither laugh nor cry freely' (Pavis: 166).

Martin Esslin claims that the grotesque mood characterizes what is usually termed the 'Theatre of the Absurd'. He explains the uniqueness of this dramatic style by its tendency to express the inability of all religions, philosophies and ideologies to satisfy the existential need for a meaningful world. Esslin finds support in Camus' and Ionesco's definitions of the 'experience of the absurd'. In *Le Mythe de Sisyphe*, Camus asserts: 'A world that can be explained, even through bad reasons, is a familiar world; but, in a world suddenly deprived of illusions and lights, a person feels alien. [...] This divorce between a person and his own life, between an actor and his set, is essentially the feeling of absurdity' (1942: 18; my trans.). For Ionesco '[a]bsurd is what is devoid of purpose . . . Cut off from its religious, metaphysical and transcendental roots, man is lost; all his actions become senseless, absurd, useless' (quoted by Esslin: xix).

Esslin characterizes this style, which reflects such an absurdist attitude, by its tendency to create allegoric fictional worlds, *promote a grotesque mood*, produce a satiric image of the world, abstain from alternative cognitive systems, encourage the projection of images from the depths of the unconscious, and induce defamiliarization and disorientation in the audience (pp. 290–316). In particular, '[t]he Theatre of the Absurd has renounced arguing *about* the absurdity of the human condition; it merely *presents* it in being — that is, in terms of concrete stage images of the absurdity of existence' (p. xx).

Esslin admits that the experience of the absurd is also achieved by other styles, the so-called 'existentialist theatre' in particular; e.g., Camus' and Jean-Paul Sartre's dramatic works (p. xix); but contends that the specific difference of the Theatre of the Absurd lies in its 'striving for an integration between the subject matter and the form in which it is expressed' (p. xx). There is no point, however, in seeing this style as the only integrative one; it is more sensible to assume that through their structural choices, modal choices in particular, these styles aim at different concluding experiences of absurdity.

Esslin, like Kayser, errs not only in conflating the principles of absurdist structure and grotesque mood, but also in seeing absurdity as the dominant trait of the Theatre of the Absurd. I suggest, in contrast, that it is the grotesque mood that is the dominant trait, and that its combination with absurdist structures constitutes the specific difference of this style; e.g., whereas Sartre's *No Exit* combines a serious mood with an absurdist structure of action, Ionesco's *Rhinoceros* combines a grotesque mood with an absurdist structure of action. In the latter, the grotesque mood undermines the seriousness of Bérenger's "heroic" determination to fight the monstrous metamorphosis. It is the combination of a fictional world's mood and a certain surface structure that not only determines the genre of a fictional world, but also prominently indicates the author's rhetoric intention.

The nature of the style of the Theatre of the Absurd is indeed unique in its combination of peripheral principles in the theatre tradition. Its style can be characterized as follows: (a) the frequent use of the grotesque mood, (b) the propensity to employ mixed stage metaphor and allegoric structure; (c) the tendency to animate set and prop characters in an unprecedented way; (d) the tendency to embody absurdist surface structures that aim at producing cognitive disorientation and thus shocking effects; in general, the grotesque mood does not operate any outlet for tension, i.e., the laughter devices do not aim at producing comic laughter and, in particular, when combined with an absurdist structure, they preclude catharsis; and (e) the proclivity to create artificial overall stage metaphors, which totally differ from the spectators' familiar world.

An artificial metaphoric fictional world is accessible not through the spectator's recognition of familiar qualities, events and experiences, but through its echo of truth in the spectator's mind, under the assumption that it is a sheer figment of the imagination. Such a world can only be explained on metaphorical grounds, because of its utter difference from anything known by the spectator; e.g., García Lorca's *Quimera*, Pinter's *A Slight Ache* and Ionesco's *The Future is in the Eggs* (*L'Avenir est dans les Œufs*). In this sense, myths too are artificial fictional worlds; e.g., Aristophanes' *Plutus*. In the unique structural configuration of the Theatre of the Absurd, including the artificially-metaphoric nature of its worlds, the grotesque mood is its dominant element, which determines its unique generic character.

A commonplace impression is that the Theatre of the Absurd tends to present absurd dialogues that truly epitomize the meaninglessness of the real world. This is a fallacy, because its dialogues are perfectly meaningful, on condition that the spectator knows and applies the relevant rules of reading and interpretation; particularly, the use of mixed stage metaphor on the level of speech interaction (Rozik, 2008b: 223–37).

The grotesque mood conveys an extremely derogatory attitude to highly serious themes regarding the human predicament, as portrayed by serious traditional theatre; e.g., to evil (Jarry's *Ubu Roi*), to death (Ionesco's *Exit the King*), and to the existential expectation for divine epiphany and salvation (e.g., Beckett's *Waiting for Godot*).

A good example of cinematic grotesque drama is Peter Brook's film *Marat/Sade*, based on Peter Weiss' play-script of the same name.

Ghelderode's *The Blind*

Michel de Ghelderode's play-script alludes to Peter Bruegel the Elder's painting *The Blind Leading the Blind*, which in turn is based on Jesus' parable in *Matthew* 15: 4 & *Luke* 6: 39. In the play-script, three blind people, De Witte, De Strop and Den Os, set out on a pilgrimage to Rome, in the expectation of being cured by the Pope. Seven weeks after leaving Brussels, while believing that they are about to enter the Holy City, they are told by Lamprido (the half-blind king of the canals) that they have actually been walking in circles and that they are in danger of drowning in a canal. They do not believe him, and even abuse him; but eventually, as predicted, they march into a canal and drown. The combination of their extremely serious predicament and Ghelderode's ludicrous treatment results in a grotesque mood, which is complemented by the absurdist structure of the narrative. This is a ready-made metaphor for *mentally* blind people in any specific situation and perhaps for humans in general in their existential and blind craving for salvation.

Arrabal's *Guernica*

The bombardment of Guernica, perpetrated upon innocent people, has been seen ever since as one of the most atrocious crimes of the Nazi regime, deserving the most serious mood; e.g., Picasso's *Guernica*. In contrast, Fernando Arrabal's play-script *Guernica*, while preserving the absurd ending (the death of the innocent characters), reveals a grotesque treatment of this extremely serious theme. This mood is achieved through the characterization of Fanchou and Lira as a ludicrous childish and senile couple; e.g., the death of Lira in a toilet against the background of the mythical tree, the *Guernikako arbola* (p. 27), the proud memorial of this ignominious war crime. The same applies to the ridiculous recurrent image of the woman and little girl carrying weapons and ammunition, which probably represents the otherwise glorified war of the Spanish people against oppression. This grotesque characterization intentionally undermines the heroic image associated with the Spanish struggle against Fascism and, possibly, even parodies the melodramatic nature of Picasso's painting.

Ionesco's *Exit the King*

This allegoric play-script deals with the theme of individual death. The whole human being is allegorically represented by three characters, enacted by three actors who enact dying King Bérenger; Queen Marie, who personifies the wishful principle in encouraging illusion; and Queen Marguerite who, in contrast, personifies the reality principle in promoting total awareness of the precarious nature of the human condition and recurrently reminds him of his true condition (Rozik: 2008b: 223–37). King is thus left to choose between illusion and awareness. On the level of the overt narrative, this regal trinity goes through all the stages of dying.

Similarly to the anonymous *Everyman*, neither Queen can accompany the King in his death. They take leave of him before it happens: first Marie — thus metaphorically describing his final renunciation of illusion, and then Marguerite — thus metaphorically describing his acquired ability to face death. Illusion and awareness are integral to his life, but not to his death. Moreover, in contrast to the metaphor of journey that structures *Everyman*, the concept of 'death' embodied in this fictional world is of total cessation. 'Death' means: '[e]verything will be guarded in a memory without recollection' (my trans.; cf. English version: p. 89); i.e., absolute nothingness and oblivion. Death is staged accordingly: King Bérenger ascends his throne, which he (ludicrously) fails to do in his dying moments, but fades away 'into a kind of mist' (p. 93); i.e., disappears into the void. This ending is preceded by the sudden disappearance of the Queens and echoed by the gradual and final devastation and sinking of the palace set, which are additional stage metaphors of the King's collapsing world. *Exit the King* is an absurdist version of the archetypal *Everyman*.

Furthermore, in contrast to Everyman, in *Exit the King* the theme of death is consistently treated by laughter-eliciting devices, such as childish behavior, cowardice and repeated failure in climbing the throne, which create a grotesque mood. It also achieves its grotesque effect by contrasting the lofty connotations of royalty with the actual lowly mode of King Bérenger; for example:

Marguerite (*to the doctor*): They mustn't hear him. Stop him shouting!

King: Hands off the King! I want everyone to know I'm going to die (*He shouts*)

Doctor: Scandalous!

King: I've got to die!

Marguerite: What was once a king is now a pig that's being slaughtered.

Marie: He's just a king. He's just a man.

Doctor: . . . It is your Majesty's duty to die with dignity.

King: Die with dignity? (At the window.) Help! Your king is going to die. (p. 40)

The intuition conveyed by *Exit the King* is that life and death are serious only from a very restricted perspective; and that the excessive seriousness that humans attach to both is ludicrous in itself. In the final moments of King Bérenger, Queen Marguerite concludes: 'It was a lot of fuss about nothing, wasn't it?' (p. 93)

Stand-up comedy

Stand-up comedy is a verbal and thematic genre, meaning that it is not generated by a fictional structure (see CHAPTER 4). It usually comprises a string of witty comments, often interspersed with jokes and unified by an overarching theme — with the transition from theme to theme being based on associative grounds. It is basically episodic. It is performative, in the sense of being performed in front of a live audience by a single person who is generally not an actor, but the author of the text (on 'the relationship between the live and mediatized as competitive, conflictual and antagonist' see Auslander: 184) In this sense, this art is closer to oral storytelling. It is basically satiric because it is meant to put foolish human behavior under a ludicrous light, especially when focusing on current authorities, institutions and ideas; but, it can also be comic in its benevolent approach. Therefore, its laughter can be employed either in a castigating or a humorous capacity.

Spectators may become the butts of witty comments, especially if they annoy the stand-up comic. Occasionally, the comic uses props, music and magic tricks. A performance may make the impression of improvisation, which occasionally it is, but more usually it is a scripted and well-rehearsed text. In contrast, the reaction of the audience is always spontaneous and unpredictable, and can even ruin the show. A good example of a stand-up comic was Lenny Bruce, who was in constant legal trouble for flouting the obscenity laws. Paradoxically, he capitalized on lifting the inhibitions of his prudish spectators. The film *Lenny*, directed by Bob Fosse (1974), with Dustin Hoffmann in the leading role, depicts the tragic end of Lenny Bruce's stand-upist career.

Seinfeld

This series created an artistic situation without precedent. The background for the stand-up comic's remarks is usually provided by live spectators; i.e., the common ground of the artist and the receivers is their shared experiences. In contrast, in this series, both the artist and the audience are fictional. In this sense, the experience of the series' spectator is mediated by a fictional world, while the common ground is basically the same.

In *The Apartment* (season 2, episode 5), Jerry finds an apartment for Elaine to rent at a reasonable price in his building. He immediately regrets the offer, in the fear that she might intrude into his life. Jerry shares the problem with George, who only magnifies his concern. In the meantime, somebody offers a five thousand dollar bonus for the apartment. Although feigning sorrow, Jerry is delighted. To his distress, in front of Elaine, Kramer suggests that Jerry make a friendly gesture and loan her the money needed to meet the new price. Unwillingly, Jerry agrees, in the fear of being perceived as unfriendly; but, after Elaine's departure, he scolds Kramer for ruining his plans. At one point, ironically, Elaine asks Jerry if living that close might upset their friendly relations and, again, Jerry pretends that it will not. Eventually, Kramer breaks the news that a new contender has offered a ten thousand dollar bonus for the apartment. Elaine then gives up, and Jerry is secretly very pleased. This brief description does not reflect the comic episodes intertwined in the comic main line of the action. This sequence is interrupted to show Jerry, as a stand-up comic, commenting on the fictional situation in front of an audience. He wonders why life is not like a rehearsal for the shooting of a cinematic scene: "'Let's take the scene again from the beginning". People, think about what you are saying! At any moment it's possible to stop the game and start over again.' This observation focuses on people who do things in order not to make the wrong impression. Probably, in Seinfeld's view, this habit is characteristic of the spurious decorum of a hypocritical culture, which, instead of improving things, can only complicate them. This episode should thus be seen as a very mild satire.

Satiric drama and grotesque drama share with comedy only their use of laughter devices. Their moods and the expected responses of the audience, however, are completely different, justifying their perception as independent genres, only tangential to comedy. Stand-up comedy does not create fictional worlds, but is inherently verbal and 'thematic' in Frye's terms. Although it often shares the humorous mood with comedy, it is basically a satiric genre.

Commedia dell'Arte 9

Commedia dell'arte was a breed of popular comedy, of Italian origin, which originated in Italy during the sixteenth century, maintained its popularity throughout the seventeenth century and declined in the course of the eighteenth century. The companies were organized in troupes based on family and craft-oriented tradition. These troupes used to play for audiences free of charge and fund their needs by donations (passing the hat). They used to wander throughout Italy and Western Europe. Abroad they were known as 'Italian Comedy'. *Commedia dell'arte* has kept alive the tradition of classical comedy and had a crucial influence on later comedy, especially on the play-scripts of Molière and Goldoni, and through them on western comedy to the present day.

A professional theatre

A commedia dell'arte troupe would play according to a 'scenario', a sketchy script of a performance, which provided basic information on the action: the masks, the succession of scenes, the entrances and exits, the peripeteias and the ending, while the dialogue was left to the actors to improvise (cf. Lea: 130). In fact, improvisation was quite limited and modular in nature: performers made use of well-rehearsed verbal and physical gags, known as *lazzi* (singular: lazzo) (Duchartre: 36–7), which are bits of comic stage business, as well as interpolated stock speeches, episodes and *burle* (singular: *burla*), which is the Italian word for jokes. Stock speeches could be prolonged or cut short to meet any emergency. Even the gestures and stage movements were pre-prepared. The result was, therefore, a composite of stock interactions, stock speeches and dialogues and stock punch-lines, learned by heart, like modules, which the actors skillfully adapted to different narratives (Lea: 23). Possibly, because of this kind of improvisation, the scripting was actually super-fluous. The modular nature of this style also enabled the short-lived inclusion of topical remarks on local scandals and current events, and the rapid adaptation to regional tastes. It is these aspects of the actors' art that made them stage professionals.

The troupes performed not only comedies, but also tragedies, tragicomedies and pastorals. The name '*commedia dell'arte*', therefore, referred to their theatre profession, (like the word 'comedian' in its sense of 'actor'). Their preferred themes were 'obstructed love', 'jealousy', 'adultery' and 'cuckoldry' — with the latter being currently perceived as typical of farce. In many a case the narratives and their fictional structures can be traced to ancient play-scripts, such as lost Greek comedies written around the fourth century BCE and the Roman comedies of Plautus, Terence, some of which were actual translations and adaptations of the former; i.e., these too were stock elements. The *capocomico* (leader) of the troupe was entrusted with adaptation of texts and their interpretation.

A typical narrative would be about two young and naïve lovers (*innamorati*) whose wish to consummate their love in marriage is thwarted by an elderly father, leading the young lovers to ask one or more *zanni* (eccentric servants) for help. Eventually, after complications, the story ends happily, with the marriage of the *innamorati* and clemency for the obstructing character. Frye's theory of comedic structure clearly draws from this model (see CHAPTER 4). There are as many variations of this stock narrative, as there are those that differ wholly from it such as the narrative of Arlecchino becoming mysteriously pregnant and the Punch and Judy scenario.

Commedia dell'arte was characterized by its emphasis on the performing aspects of the 'art' of theatre, comic acting in particular. Little is known about its acting style. Most of the available descriptions are in fact the result of speculation and reconstruction. A scenario was performed by members of the troupe who specialized in specific stock-types, wearing characteristic masks, except for the innamorati and the servetta (serving maid) (Duchartre: 41–9). There was a kind of intimate relation between actor, mask and name of character: 'each actor had his *mask*, his stock-type, the same name every time he played' (Lanson: 382). Such a mask was usually operated by a single actor throughout his life, and often bequeathed to the next generation. Nonetheless, it was occasionally enacted by different actors, even during the same performance. Such masks wandered from narrative to narrative. Characters were also characterized by particular costumes and typical props such as Harlequin's club known, as the 'slapstick' (Duchartre: 29). The spectator was, therefore, capable of identifying the character or, rather, the stock-type, in any new production, without previous presentation; of anticipating its role in the narrative, and even laughing at its first entrance on stage. These masks covered all the face except for the mouth, which had an advantage over the ancient Greek and Roman rigid masks in enabling greater clarity of speech. (cf. drawings of *commedia dell'arte* masks by Claude Gillot, French, early eighteenth century)

The following are examples of such stock-types or, rather, 'masks': *Pantalone*, who was an elderly father or paternal character, usually fulfilling the two functions of blocking the action of the *innamorati* and serving as a ludicrous butt; *Dottore*, who was a learned elderly fellow, usually fulfilling the function of a ludicrous butt and possibly an obstructing father; the *innamorati*, who were a pair of young, handsome, graceful, naïve and helpless lovers (Lea: 102), and usually the victims of the blocking fathers and the beneficiaries of the peripeteia that enabled their eventual happy marriage; and the *zanni*, who were often amoral and witty or boorish servants, usually fulfilling the functions of always promoting the humorous mood (buffoon), often the dramatic irony, and only seldom the advancing of the action.

The troupe was quite regularly composed of around ten to fifteen members: basically, two *vecchi* (old men), *Pantalone* and *Dottore*, four *innamorati* (two male and two female young lovers), two *zanni* (male servants), a *capitano* (boastful captain) and a *servetta* (serving maid). The old people were the blocking and the laughed-at characters. The *zanni* were the laughed-with characters (the buffoons and stupid rustics). The best known *zanni* were Arlecchino (Harlequin), Pedrolinno (Pierrot), Brighella and Pulcinella. Arlecchino, for example, was a rascal, a mixture of stupidity and cunning, dressed in shreds and patches (changed later to a checkered costume), wearing a black half-mask, a hat surmounted by a hare tail, a belt purse, and often a slapstick. The *innamorati* were naïve lovers, seemingly dependent on the trickeries of the *zanni*, who were meant to enable the *innamorati* to consummate their love. The late Jonathan Dubosarsky, an Israeli scholar and translator of post *commedia dell'arte* comedy, once suggested that such a troupe constituted a group of clowns, including the *innamorati*.

'Originally, ... the *masks* [of *commedia dell'arte*] had local and professional traits that particularized them: Pantaloon was a Venetian merchant; the doctor was from Bologne; and, as his name indicates, knew his law; Harlequin, [the naïve and awkward valet] was a peasant from Bergamo, Scaramouche, a Napolitan adventurer; and the Captain also Neapolitan vaguely crossed with Spanish. The latter, although not the great lord he claimed to be, was a rich gentleman' (Lanson: 391). They also spoke their native regional dialects; e.g., Pantalone in Venetian, Dottore in Bolognese and Pulcinella in Napolitan. *Commedia dell'arte* capitalized on the ludicrous potential of dialects (Lea: 123). Only the *innamorati* spoke in the Tuscan dialect, probably due to its being perceived as the literary language of Italy (*ibid.*: 102). The lack of masks, their beauty and the Tuscan language of the latter probably indicated the intention to make them attractive characters.

The "improvised" texts of *commedia dell'arte* were performed in temporary outdoors venues by masked professional actors, as opposed to the written *commedia erudita* (erudite comedy), whose scripted texts were presented indoors by non-masked and amateur actors. The wandering *commedia-dell'arte* troupes would carry with them their basic set, usually a painted backdrop depicting a street and a few houses, the costumes and masks.

The best collection of scenarios is Flaiminio Scala's *Teatro*, 1611, which contains 39 comedies, one tragedy, one tragicomedy, one mixed entertainment, one pastoral and a few fairy tales. There are manuscripts of scenarios in various Italian and other libraries (cf. Lea's Appendix G; pp. 555–74).

A brief history

Although *Commedia dell'arte* flourished in Italy during the Renaissance period, according to Nicoll's highly illuminating theory it reflects an uninterrupted tradition originating in the Dorian mime (pp. 20–134). Indeed, its roots can be traced back to the Dorian mime, the Phlyakes, Menander's comedy, the Fabula Atellana, the Roman comedies of Plautus and Terence, and the Roman mimes. The earliest records of *commedia dell'arte* performances are from 1551.

Nicoll contends that '[m]asks, . . . had been associated with the early Dorian representations, and, although actors might appear without them, masks were used in both the Phliakes and the Atellanae' (p. 91). Cornford distinguishes a group of seven masks which recur in different kinds of ancient folk comedy, with local modifications: the Buffoon, the Doctor, the Cook, the Soldier, the Parasite, the Old Man and the Old Woman (p. 188). If we add the young man and the young woman, these overlap all the dramatis personae of *commedia dell'arte*. The existence of such masks in the folk play-scripts indicates that these were typical functions in motivating the action and promoting the humorous mood. The existence of stock masks indicates an established theatrical tradition. It is highly possible that this kind of improvised art was passed down the Italian generations until the 1500s, when it was revived as a professional theatre.

By the mid-1500s, specific troupes of commedia performers began to coalesce, and by 1568 the Gelosi had become a distinct company, with their own name and logo featuring a jovial two-headed Janus. The Gelosi performed in northern Italy, eschewed patronage and pursued autonomy. Despite some fluctuations, the Gelosi maintained stability.

Commedia dell'arte is notable in that female roles were played by women, as documented as early as the 1560s, In the 1570s, English theatre critics denigrated these troupes because of their female actors. By the end of the 1570s Italian prelates attempted to ban female performers; however, by the end of the century, actresses were standard performers on the Italian stage.

By the early seventeenth century, the *zanni* comedies were moving from improvisational performances to specified and clearly delineated acts and characters. Three books written during the seventeenth century — Cecchini's *Fruti della moderne commedia* (1628), Barbieri's *La supplica* (1634), and Perrucci's *Dell'arte rappresentativa* (1699) — presented firm recommendations concerning performance-practices. As a result, *commedia dell'arte* was reduced to formulaic and stylized acting, far distant from its "improvisational" genesis a century earlier. This comedy dwindled during the eighteenth century as new forms like the *comédie larmoyante* gained popularity in France. Nonetheless, as currently used, the term '*commedia dell'arte*' was coined in the mid-18th century.

In the nineteenth century, in France, George Sand, Frédéric Chopin and other intellectuals, while exploring and discussing ancient forms of theatre, rediscovered this theatre style. Their interest focused on *commedia dell'arte* and, in 1848, they constructed a theatre devoted to performances in its (hypothetical) style. In the twentieth century this style has received a great deal of attention from several theatre practitioners, including Jacques Copeau, Vsevolod Meyerhold and Jacques Lecoq, related to their endeavors to move away from naturalism and rejuvenate the art of theatre.

A specimen scenario: *The Three Cuckolds*

Main characters: Pantalone; Flaminia his wife; Coviello; Cintia his wife; Zanni; Franceschina his wife; and Leandro a young man.

Act I: Coviello and Cintia have a scene of reciprocal jealousy. Coviello discloses his passion to Flaminia, Pantalone's wife, and she reciprocates. She asks him to come to her hidden in a chest of lemons. Coviello asks Zanni to put him in such a chest and deliver it to Flaminnia. Pantalone discloses his love to Franceschina, Zanni's wife, and she reciprocates. Leandro declares his love to Cintia and she reciprocates. She instructs him to disguise himself as a dumb beggar.

Act II: Zanni blames Flaminia for the trick she has played on her husband and praises Franceschina for her honesty. Pantalone is satisfied by Franceschina, and Coviello by Flaminia. Upon Coviello's return Cintia tells him about the poor beggar in the house, while Leandro comes out with a plate of soup. Leandro enjoys the trick. Zanni tells of the beggar hoax to Pantalone and the latter reveals the lemon chest trick. Coviello is told of the beggar hoax. Each betrayed husband shouts 'cuckold' at the others.

Act III: Pantalone wishes to repeat his act with Franceschina and she hides him in a laundry basket. Zanni is suspicious and tries to throw the clothes into the copper and boil them. Coviello tries to repeat his success with Flaminia, and Leandro does the same with Cintia. Zanni returns to hear what is going on in his home and wishes to burn down the house. All the couples rush off to the sounds of the fire alarm. Leandro explains the entire situation and all the couples reunite and rest content. A kind of happy ending.

The scenario notates that antics are performed by Zanni and Franceschina. It also mentions the three trickeries as the number of infidelities: the chest of lemons (Coviello and Flaminia), the beggar (Leandro and Cintia) and the washing basket (Pantalone and Franceschina. These serve to both hide the adulterers and to reveal them. They are laughter devices in themselves. Only Zanni does not join in the game. The farcical nature of the scenario is reflected in its central theme, cuckoldry (for the full scenario see Lea: 582–4).

The heritage of *commedia dell'arte*

Lanson claims that Molière was mostly influenced by *commedia dell'arte*, in which 'the dialogue was governed by a supple, loose plot and by rigid comic types or *masks*' (p. 381). In Molière's time, 'Italian actors had frequently returned to France, and were always appreciated for their vivacity and inventiveness, and for the expressive originality of their *masks*' (*ibid.*). Lanson also claims that, like in *commedia dell'arte*, 'It is not through the plot that Molière's comedy rates high. . . . the plot is only a thread to link comic situations, a framework for witty scenes. It is only a pretext to control the strings of human puppets whose expressive gestures make the comedy' (pp. 388–9).

For Lanson, like in *commedia dell'arte*, Molière's typical character, at least in the comedies that are perceived as his major legacy, 'is powerfully unified by the domination of a passion or vice that destroys or subdues all other likes and dislikes of his soul, and this quality becomes the motivating force of all his thought and action. . . . and the comic springs forth from this resistance, from its partial defeat or his unforeseen compromises' (p. 390). Although this description seems to better fit melodrama than Molière's comedies, in overlooking their common emphasis on the comic mood and laughter devices, the argument is sound. Even the emphasis on either the ludicrous blocking character or the deriding astute servants, with the young lovers being relegated to a secondary role, which is typical of *commedia dell'arte*, is also found in them.

Despite stating this common ground, Lanson qualifies his approach:

> in Molière's comedy, there is an important part that Italian farce does not contain, at lest for the French spectator: the painting of social conditions and relationships. Molière shows us all the classes and relationships . . . that composed French society in his time: peasants, bourgeois, squires, wits, great lords, servants, middle-class women, young and older ladies. A large part of his gift lies in spreading vices and ridiculous qualities through these different classes. (pp. 393–4)

In other words, Lanson claims that in Molière's play-scripts there is a full social representation, which reflects his profound social interest and involvement. Nonetheless, it is doubtful as to whether the claim regarding the elements of social criticism and even satire, which critics usually ascribe to Molière's comedies, should be accepted. Although a few of Molière's comedies feature such socially-oriented elements, his major comedies do not.

Lanson also argues that 'consciously or not, Molière actually followed in the path of French farce, where what is laughable is what shocks the moral judgment and social prejudice of the public' (p. 395). Furthermore, it is through this social interest that 'Molière broke the last bond that attached him to the comedy of the *commedia dell'arte*' (p. 392). In contrast, I venture to say, Molière enriched the tradition of *commedia dell'arte* with his humorous inventiveness. Although he wrote alleged satiric play-scripts, such as *Tartuffe* and *Don Juan*, what characterizes his comedies, rather than social criticism and any intention to improve society, is the exploitation of people's potentially ludicrous nature for the purpose of comic laughter. The claim that he wished to educate people not to be avaricious, hypochondriac or misanthropic, whose foul nature is quite obvious for any spectator, is indeed absurd.

Rather than stressing the rupture of Molière with the tradition of *commedia dell'arte*, it is the view of this study that his comedies reflect a synthesis of this tradition and classic comedy; and constitute a vital link in the historical chain that connects ancient to modernist, including cinematic comedy. Similar considerations apply to Goldoni. Even today, Molière's comedies are enacted in what is believed to have been the style of the *commedia dell'arte*.

Goldoni's *The Servant of Two Masters*

Pantalone had promised his daughter Clarice in marriage to Federigo, who is killed by Florindo. Pantalone then promises her to Dottore's son, Silvio who is actually her lover. Beatrice disguises herself as Federigo (her brother) in order to recover money that Pantalone owes him. The moment Beatrice arrives (as Federigo) Pantalone ignores his promise to Silvio to the disappointment of both his daughter and the young lover. Silvio persistently wishes to fight Federigo (Beatrice) for Clarice. Florindo, Beatrice's lover, also arrives on the scene looking for her. Neither one is aware of the presence of the other in town. The main action revolves around the confusions caused by Truffaldino's decision to serve both Beatrice and Florindo and enjoy the wages of the two masters. For example, Truffaldino (who is illiterate) delivers letters and Pantalone's payment to the wrong masters; he mixes up their trunks and clothing; and invents an additional servant, Pascuale, to excuse his own blunders. Beatrice and Florindo are not aware of sharing the very same servant, who is beaten up by both. Beatrice reveals to Clarice that she is actually Federigo's sister and that she does not wish to marry her. Eventually Pantalone reinstates his promise to Silvio, and Beatrice and Florindo recognize one another and renew their loving bonds. They forgive Truffaldino. There is a triple wedding: Beatrice and Florindo, Clarice and Silvio, and Smeraldina and Trufffaldino. It should be stressed that Truffaldino does not promote the action towards the dénouement, but only confusion and the humorous mood, which is at the heart of this comedy.

Commedia dell'arte should be seen as a crucial link in the historical tradition of comedy: it reflected the previous tradition of theatre, popular farce in particular, and has had a significant influence on subsequent comedy and farce. Its performances were characterized not by improvisation in the regular sense of the term, but by a form of modular creativity, in which stock characters combined with stock plots, stock speeches and stock comic routines as basic building blocks for different narratives, probably making scripting redundant. Even the theoretical emphasis on the art of acting that characterizes this style is misleading: the power of comedy has always been based on the nonverbal aspects of typical comic acting (see CHAPTER 3).

Comedy and Carnival

10

The clear affinity between comedy, in the narrow sense of this study, and carnival has long been noticed. Carnival is mainly characterized by the temporary and socially authorized suspension of certain established values, and includes the parodic treatment of sacred texts and rituals. Its affinity with comedy is substantiated by their shared lighthearted mood, optional comic laughter, and ultimate aim to reaffirm and buttress the prevalent values and beliefs of the synchronic culture.

Nature of carnival

Carnival is a very short episode within the context of an almost year-long extra-carnival established behavior, as sanctioned by a synchronic culture. In this brief period of time people are allowed to behave contrary to their usual observant behavior and to the hegemonic class hierarchy; e.g., servants become temporary masters and vice versa. These principles are not foreign to comedy; e.g., Molière's *The Trickeries of Scapin*.

Mikhail Bakhtin conceives of the 'spirit of carnival' as the expression of folk culture that appears to oppose all that is decent and sacred in serious culture. He characterizes the spirit of carnival as 'the people's second life, organized on the basis of laughter' (p. 8). This alternative life evinces:

> a characteristic logic, the peculiar logic of the "inside out" (à l'envers), of the "turnabout", of a continual shifting from top to bottom, from front to rear, of numerous parodies and travesties, humiliations, profanations, comic crownings and uncrownings. A second life, a second world of folk culture is thus constructed; it is to a certain extent a parody of the extracarnival life, a "world inside out". (p. 11)

By 'parody of extracarnival life' Bakhtin means the temporary reversal of quotidian behavior, of its established values and notions of order; in particular, what is serious is mocked and what is sacred is profaned. The spirit of carnival has been a steady companion of serious culture for millennia, possibly since early humanity.

In the Middle Ages in particular, the serious side of society was consolidated in religious and civic rituals, which 'sanctioned the existing pattern of things and reinforced it' (Bakhtin: 9). In contrast, the carnivalesque ceremonies 'offered a completely different, nonofficial, extraecclesiastical and extrapolitical aspect of the world, of man, and of human relations; they built a second world and a second life outside officialdom, a world in which *all* medieval people participated more or less, in which they lived during a given time of the year' (*ibid.*: 6; my italics).

Seriousness and laughter are thus perceived as two complementary aspects of the same culture. Such duality, however, is by no means symmetrical. I suggest that in this respect the temporal aspect is essential: in clear disproportion, up to 364 days are devoted to seriousness and only one, or a few more, to carnival. Coexistence is precluded because there is an apparent contrast between the necessities of real life and the spirit of carnival. Whereas the former requires the observation of values, the latter promotes a sanctioned-by-tradition relaxation. Paradoxically, this opposition leads to the conjecture that these constitute two mutually dependent sides of the same culture; i.e., that the spirit of carnival reflects a need of the established culture and that a lack of temporal symmetry is in the nature of things.

Why should one need to relax from 'official' life? Although there might appear to be an inherent contradiction between the serious culture and the spirit of carnival, because of the latter's profane nature, I suggest that this contradiction is only apparent. The paradox is settled if we assume that in order to endure official life people have to sacrifice vital energies; meaning that whatever contradicts the synchronic *philanthropon* has to be suppressed. Therefore, since suppression creates both pressure and anxiety, due to their possible eruption under uncontrolled circumstances, such an established 'relaxation' is socially healthy, enjoyable and possibly indispensable.

This function, of safely releasing pressure for the sake of preserving the rule of the established culture, is best described by Welsford's analogy to 'a safety-valve' (p. 216). He invokes a Doctor of Auxterre who explained the vital and sacred function of carnival by means of a secular analogy: 'wine barrels break if their bung-holes are not occasionally opened to let in the air, and the clergy being "nothing but old wine-casks badly put together would certainly burst if the wine of wisdom were allowed to boil by continued devotion to the Divine Service"' (p. 202; cf.

Willeford: 82). In other words, carnival fulfils a cathartic function, which releases the mental pressure generated by obediently and consistently coping with the ethical expectations of society (henceforth: 'functional pressure'), and enables people their healthy return to the routine of life. In Sypher's words, '[t]he irreverence of Carnival disburdens us of our resentment and *purges* our ambivalence so that we can return to our duties as honest men' (p. 222; my italics). I would say that carnival *catharts* the side effects of suppression, correlated tension in particular, of the merely day-to-day living by the rules of society, by means of a brief and well-controlled license.

Bakhtin suggests that the spirit of carnival — by simply opposing seriousness — bears the stamp of freedom: 'As opposed to the official feast, one might say that carnival celebrated temporary liberation from the prevailing truth and from established order; it marked the suspension of all hierarchical rank, privileges, norms, and prohibitions' (p. 10). and the people temporarily 'entered the utopian realm of community, freedom, equality, and abundance' (p. 9). These statements probably constitute an idealized and exaggerated picture of carnival. They reflect Bakhtin's own ideological interest in furthering the idea of an independent secular folk culture, and possibly the idea of the people's superior wisdom. Nonetheless, the fact is that in this 'folk culture', allegedly opposing the established culture, all walks of life, including the ruling class and the clergy, participated. While Christianity permitted carnival, including parody of the ecclesiastic ritual, actual heresy was bitterly persecuted; which indicates that there was an awareness of carnival's healthy function in buttressing the religious foundations of society.

Nonetheless, the spirit of carnival is potentially rebellious and the borderline between a humorous attitude to the establishment and militant criticism aimed at overthrowing the social order could not always be clearly drawn. Similarly to the borderline between comedy and satire, it is often only the difference of intention that counts. Some initially naïve carnivalesque customs became dangerous and had eventually to be prohibited, indicating that carnival freedom was not absolute and that the permit was granted only within certain limits, possibly as long as it served the establishment. There could be no absolute freedom in carnival, because medieval society could not allow the jeopardizing of serious life and faith. Despite Bakhtin's enthusiast praise, the underlying principle remains the same: a temporary and officially-limited freedom for the sake of catharsis of functional pressure and anxiety, whose aim is the conformist reaffirmation of established rules of behavior. In this sense, the carnivals of Rio de Janeiro and Venice, for example, are probably corrupt specimens, in being created for the purpose of being watched by others. True carnival is not a kind of theatre — all are involved in its practice (cf. Bakhtin: 7).

In the following sections I illustrate the nature of carnivalesque practices through several of its main manifestations: the Feast of Fools, the parody of sacred texts (e.g., the *purim-shpil*), the *purim-rabbi*, and the mask and disguise. The ultimate aim is to draw some conclusions regarding the existence of carnivalesque elements in comedy.

The Feast of Fools

'Feast of Fools' is used here in a wide sense that applies to a variety of traditions such as the Feast of Fools, Feast of the Ass, the Mock King, the Abbot of Unreason, the Prince of Fools, the Patriarch, Bishop or Pope of Fools, the Boy Bishop and the Lord of Misrule, which are all communal manifestations of the spirit of carnival (cf. Bakhtin: 5). All of them revolve around the inversion of the established rules of normative behavior and of the social hierarchy for a limited period of time, often but not always for a single day. For example, the Lord of Misrule presides over twelve days from Christmas to 6 January.

Welsford traces the roots of the Lord of Misrule to ancient Rome, where these 'must be sought among the old pre-Christian customs, more particularly the Kalends and Saturnalia of pagan Rome' (p. 199). He alludes to Lucian who, in his *Saturnalia*, 'has drawn a vivid picture of the "Liberties of December", that merry festival when the winter darkness was lightened by the restoration of the golden reign of Saturn, and for a short while masters and slaves changed places, laws lost their force, and a mock-king ruled over a topsy-turvy world. The same freedom prevailed at the New Year festival of the Kalends, when people exchanged presents, masqueraded, played the fool and gave reign to their appetites, with the laudable object of ensuring prosperity and plenty for the next twelve months' (Welsford: 199).

Early Christianity, determined to uproot this Pagan custom, waged a ceaseless war upon the Kalends during the first centuries of the Christian era, perceiving it

> as a form of devil-worship leading to inevitable damnation. But in spite of all her efforts, the old pagan rites not only survived as rustic amusements, they actually penetrated into the interior of the churches and at length gave rise to that famous clerical Saturnalia in which mighty

persons were humbled, sacred things profaned, laws relaxed and ethical ideals reversed, under the leadership of a Patriarch, Pope, or Bishop of Fools. (Welsford: 199)

In the twelfth century, 'Joannes Belethus, who was rector of theology at Paris, informs us that the priests, deacons, subdeacons and choir children each have their special days of rejoicing after Christmas, and that the festival of the subdeacons which is held on the Circumcision or on Epiphany or the Octave of the Epiphany is called the Feast of Fools' (*ibid.*: 199–200). This custom was forbidden in 1438 by the Pragmatic Sanction of Charles VII and gradually declined, although its traces are found as late as the seventeenth century (*ibid.*: 201).

Such feasts were professedly of an anti-ritual character. Glynne Wickham contends that '[c]lerics could involve themselves in dramatic parodies of sacred rituals like the Feast of the Ass or the Boy Bishop, just as easily as artisans of city guilds could devote themselves to the re-enactment of the Crucifixion or the Last Judgment' (p. 4). The functions of the high clergy were usurped by the 'despised subdeacons', and '[e]ven the Mass was burlesqued. Censing was done with pudding and sausages' (Welsford: 200; cf. Bakhtin: 7). Thus, the Feast of Fools was an inversion of the social hierarchy for the sake of inversion of values, and ultimately for the sake of catharsis and eventual reaffirmation of synchronic values.

Although folly does lend a rational dimension to anti-ritual, there is no antagonism between such limited mockery and faith. Welsford's most fitting analogy to a 'safety-valve' is meant to describe both the functional pressure produced by constant devotion, and the cathartic function of carnival in general. This analogy aptly applies to the Feast of Fools. Welsford stresses: 'Circumstances, as we have seen, drove the vicars and subdeacons to emphasize the idea of folly as a *safety-valve*, a permitted form of relief and relaxation' (p. 216; cf. Nicoll: 19).

The spirit of the Feast of Fools often transcends the limits of time and space set for its expression. 'Clowns and fools . . . were the constant, accredited representatives of the carnival spirit in everyday life out of carnival season. . . . they were not actors playing their parts on a stage, as did the comic actors of a later period, impersonating Harlequin, Hanswurst, etc., but remained fools and clowns always and wherever they made their appearance' (Bakhtin: 8).

Parody of sacred texts — the *purim-shpil*

The object of carnivalesque parody can be a ritual text, such as a prayer, a hymn, or a ritual narrative, and even an entire ritual. Welsford maintains that 'even the Mass was burlesqued' (p. 200). The Mass should be seen as a complex act/action, performed by means of a set of verbal or other texts, whose intended effect is to dispose God to bestow His grace on its performers. As a complex macro-semiotic act, the Mass satisfies the definition of 'text' and the requirements of a potential object of parody (see CHAPTER 3).

Judaism possesses a vast literature that parodies rituals and ritual texts such as the Passover '*Seder*' and the requiem (*Kaddish*). Jewish parody is known to have originated in Spain during the twelfth century, and continued after the expulsion of the Jews in 1492 (Rozik, 1992). From the very beginning, literary parody established an umbilical bond with the holiday of Purim, which celebrates the salvation of the Jews from extermination in the Persian empire, several centuries before the Christian era, as related in the Book of Esther. Most Jewish literary parodies on sacred texts were written for this occasion, and this link has been consolidated in subsequent centuries. The creation of such parodies is explained by the typical atmosphere of the holiday, which allows an exceptional disregard of certain religious rules. This could not have been possible unless the rabbinical authorities had given their blessing to a day of established misrule.

These parodies were usually written in Hebrew and occasionally in Aramaic before they began to be written in Yiddish. For all these languages, a distinction should be made between parodies of actual texts such as prayers, and parodies of the styles of sacred books such as the Bible (Hebrew) and the Talmud (Aramaic) (Shmerok: 49–50). The latter are usually confined to the humorous imitation of formal and stylistic elements, while dealing with a trivial subject such as feasting and carousing. Perhaps the most extreme case is the parody of the *Kaddish* (requiem), a prayer of utmost sacredness, composed in the fifteenth century in Aramaic (Davidson: 31).

In all these parodies there is no hint of an intention to undermine seriousness and faith (*ibid.*: 19). On the contrary, they indicate a clear intention to circumscribe the experience to within the limits of the Purim holiday and to the release of the functional pressure accumulated during the year due to strict observance of religious rules, under the strict surveillance of the religious authorities. In this sense, this type of parody reflects the carnivalesque duality of Purim: whereas the sacred texts were definite sources of functional pressure, their parodic treatment had no aim beyond catharsis itself.

The use of theatrical parody on the *Purim* holiday became consolidated in Ashkenaz (Germany) in the seventeenth century. By then Yiddish was already acknowledged as one of the cultural languages of Judaism. In fact, the Yiddish term '*purim-shpil*' originally applied to all humorous literary texts written especially for *Purim*, usually in Yiddish, and only later on was it restricted to theatrical works. Yiddish was thus attached to the basic triangular relationship — carnivalesque permissiveness, parody and theatre — to become the hallmark of Purim. Subsequently, theatrical parody spread throughout Eastern Europe and eventually, following the major waves of emigration at the end of the nineteenth and beginning of the twentieth century, reached the New World and Israel, where it is still being performed in the present day. In Israel, Hebrew was restored to theatrical parody, the original language of both source-texts and parody.

Most theatrical *purim-shpils* are parodies of the Book of Esther, and reflect humorous treatment on two levels: a) the entire narrative of the book and b) short parodic texts inserted into the main narrative. The latter are interspersed in between the text for being relevant to the various situations in the Biblical action such as prayers, legal discussions in the style of the Talmud, and the matrimonial contract; e.g., the parody of this contract at the royal wedding in the *Ahashverosh shpil*, based on the narrative of the Book of Esther.

In these play-scripts the parodic intent is evident, for they were predominantly produced for an audience extremely familiar with all the source-texts in their original serious guise. The Book of Esther itself is read twice in the synagogue — during the serious services of the eve and the following morning of Purim, before the performance of the parodic play during the festive meal (Shmerok: 86). The mere contiguity of the serious reading and the parodic performance emphasizes the symbiotic relationship between the sacred text and its parody. Moreover, the audience of the *purim-shpil* also included women and children, — thus reflecting the permissive atmosphere of the holiday.

The parodic treatment of the Book of Esther could have been created in literary form, similar to the source. The use of the theatre medium is probably best explained by the two-fold injunction against theatre and parody in ordinary life, and the parallel lifting of these prohibitions at Purim. The use of Yiddish should be explained on similar grounds, in being conceived as a non-sacred language. However, these liberties do not herald the development of a secular culture in Judaism. They only indicate, by mere contrast to the strict rule of religion throughout the year, the cathartic function of *Purim*. It is the sacredness of the Book of Esther that explains the complementary ritual function of its parody, in the context of a religious establishment that zealously safeguards its authority.

The *purim-rabbi*

Although the custom of the *purim-rabbi* is the Jewish equivalent of the Mock King or the Abbot of Misrule, it is of more recent origin. This tradition began and developed in the Jewish communities of Central and Eastern Europe alongside the *purim-shpil*. Its geographical distribution overlaps that of Central and East European Jewry. Although the similarity between the *purim-rabbi* and the carnivalesque fool is quite evident, it is difficult to establish direct influence. While the Christian custom seems to have disappeared completely by the end of the seventeenth century, the Jewish custom was only then emerging.

Contemporary examples still exist today, albeit confined to a few Orthodox communities, particularly in the United States and Israel. Their methodological advantage lies in that, in contrast to the feast of fools and similar Christian customs, it allows access to exiting texts created within this tradition, in addition to descriptions of performances by scholars who have actually witnessed them; and even to actual performances.

It is characteristic of this custom to appoint a *yeshiva* student as a mock rabbi, with the blessing of the head of the school, for a single day — with the second day of Purim, called '*Shoshan-Purim*', being the typical one in most communities. The custom, which includes several phases, culminates in the delivery of a parodic sermon by the *purim-rabbi*, which aims at enhancing the holiday cheer.

This sermon is usually performed in the synagogue in front of a male audience of teachers and students, including the head of the *yeshiva*, who is the object of the mocking imitation, and in contrast to the *purim-shpil* that used to be performed at home in front of a mixed audience, including women and children. A male audience is necessary because of their extreme familiarity with the parodied texts, especially their proficiency in the languages — Hebrew, Aramaic and Yiddish — involved in the mocking of the sacred texts. Furthermore, all of them live under the direct administrative, moral and religious authority of their rabbi who, within their social system, is the chief source of functional pressure. This explains the cathartic function of the mock-sermon.

Initially, the elected student is dressed in the garments of a rabbi, including the typical black silk gown and *shtraiml* (fur-hat) worn by Orthodox Jews on holidays. He is also given a beard in addition to his long side-locks. He is then appointed as "rabbi" in a ceremony that is a parody of the real one, and ratified by a *ktav rabbanut* (rabbinical credential) that is too a parodic version of the original. This document usually specifies his future earnings; for example, in one of the extant texts the newly appointed "rabbi" is promised 'the noises of the doors revolving on their hinges, the echo of the tune of a *shoffar* (ritual horn), chicken's milk, and in addition to his income: the twilight of crepuscule, the shades of the walls of a *succa* (the cubicle built for the Feast of Tabernacles), and the morning cloud.' All these are promised on condition that his teachings are devoid of any trace of truth. Subsequently, the *purim-rabbi* and his entourage enter the *yeshiva* precinct, taking the habitual place of the real rabbi, while the latter withdraws to the students' place, and praying with the community. Eventually, the mock-rabbi engages in imitation of the real rabbi at prayer, particularly his voice inflection, facial expression and bodily gestures, while delivering the mock sermon, which often includes humorous insinuations aimed at the school establishment, at the head of the *yeshiva* in particular.

The mock-sermon parodies its model in the way of reasoning, ample quotation from the Holy Scriptures, mixture of languages, and constant allusions to actuality. An excerpt from one such text reads as follows:

> Is it the case that Ha'man [the villain of the Book of Esther] was a righteous man? Yes, he was a righteous man. We learn that from Abraham, who wanted to kill only one Jewish soul [the binding of Isaac] and was called righteous; Ha'man, who wanted to annihilate all the Jews, is he not entitled to be called righteous? And, since he was a righteous man, why was he hanged? The learned Rabbi *Kozban* [in Hebrew: deceiver], Rabbi *Shakran* [in Hebrew: liar] and Rabbi *Barozovi Falakar* [in Yiddish: nickname for a rude person] were divided on this issue. Rabbi *Kozban* says: Ha'man was handsome and he was hanged for the sake of ornament, as a beautiful picture is hanged on the wall. Rabbi *Shakran* says: Ha'man was a miser and he hanged himself for less than a penny. And Rabbi *Barozovi Falakar* says: he was found wet in the morning and was hanged under the sun to dry out. (my translation)

One of the sources refers to the criticism leveled at a *purim-rabbi* who, although having excelled in his imitation of the rabbi, was found to have been too serious, breaching thereby the conditions of his mock appointment. The student excused himself by revealing that all the sources on which he had based his line of argumentation were of his own invention. The excuse was accepted, since in his own way he had succeeded in fooling his learned audience.

The *purim-rabbi* enjoys the typical license allowed to the Fool. Some sources indicate that the mock-rabbi is permitted to say whatever he wishes, including barbed criticism and satire. In this sense, this custom harbors a potentially subversive element that might overpower its cathartic function. The paradox resides in that its benefit to the social structure in releasing functional pressure depends on its ability to put the authorities in a humorous, and possibly satiric perspective. However, the more proficient the performer is, the more dangerous the custom becomes, and the more the borderline between healthy humor and derogatory satire is blurred. This basic duality may explain the persistent and consistent objections to the custom found in various accounts. Indeed, in some communities the *purim-rabbi* so extremely breached the rules of the game that the custom was banned.

This temporary "usurpation" of authority reflects the carnivalesque nature of this custom. Its underlying principle is usually referred to by the expression '*nahafokh hu*', which means 'the opposite is the case', found already in the Book of Esther (9, 1). In this sense too the *purim-rabbi* exhibits a ritual reversal of the social and cultural system, which is usually reflected in the interchange of roles in meaningful pairs, such as man-woman, master-servant and, in the case of the *purim-rabbi*, teacher-student, aiming at catharsis of the psychological pressure in the characteristic spirit of Purim.

Mask and disguise

Carnival shares the use of masks with some styles of comedy, including Classical comedy and *commedia dell'arte*. However, this is not necessarily an indication of a shared function. In principle, device and function are mutually independent, in the sense that the same device (e.g., the mask) can fulfil different functions, and the same function can be fulfilled by different devices. As a device, a mask covers the face, presents the image of a face other than that of its wearer, and conveys the message that the wearer is temporarily not representing himself. On this level, this device is indeed shared by carnival and theatre. Beyond this, their functions in these domains substantially differ (cf. Rozik, 2002: 211–15):

By wearing a mask the carnival reveler implicitly claims to be other than him/herself and, therefore, entitled to display behavior that is consistent with the mask. In terms of psychoanalysis, the mask enables the projection of an image of a desired, a non-realized and, in some cases, even a suppressed aspect of its wearer. By concealing his/her own identity the mask bestows on the reveler momentary freedom, within the temporal boundaries of carnival. It is this freedom that makes possible the expression of what is not actualized. Thus, paradoxically, the mask, rather than concealing often reveals these hidden aspects of the "true" self.

To be more precise, during carnival, more than in ordinary life, the reveler displays the inherent duality of the real and the potential. The freedom of carnival lies in giving the individual the opportunity to experience the potential as real, in the context of an atmosphere of social permit, in which everybody joins the game. This social permit consists in allowing revelation in the guise of concealment. It is an '*authorized* transgression' (Eco: 6). Moreover, it is this freedom that enables the cathartic function of carnival. In this sense, within serious life, carnival is a permit to play for a limited period, since 'an everlasting carnival does not work' (*ibid.*).

It is because of such a disclosure of the relegated and/or suppressed contents of the psyche that the carnival revelers, without necessarily being aware, probably have to dissociate themselves from their masks. They have to conceal the fact that they are both revealing hidden aspects of themselves and protecting themselves from the scrutiny of others when the carnival is over. In most cases, the carnival reveler is not aware of this duality.

In contrast, in wearing a mask, an actor, while enacting a character other than himself, embodies the basic theatrical duality performer/character. 'Acting' means inscribing an image of a fictional or a real human being on the actor's real body. While reference is made to a character, the actor — mind and body — retains his own identity. At any given moment, the audience knows, albeit not constantly aware, that both the actor and the image of a character are simultaneously "present" on stage, the former as producing the description and the latter as the description of a fictional entity. Only thus can the audience's final applause to the actor be understood. Whereas the actor is always real, the character is always a figment of the imagination, which has to be evoked in the mind of the spectator by its enacted description. This duality indicates the textual nature of the theatre performance

In principle, make-up is a kind of mask, and several theatrical styles have adopted this device. Nonetheless, the duality actor/character has proved to be preserved even when the actor appears in his bare face, as typical of modern theatre. Therefore, the use of a mask in the theatre is not only non-essential, but even superfluous. However, when used, it basically indicates this duality. Acting emphasizes the juxtaposition of the mask on a face.

Additional advantages to the use of mask in theatre are: first, it serves as a screen for the projection of the spectator's imagination; second, it can be used by different actors to enact the same characters even during the same performance; and third, it stresses certain traits such as gender, age, social class, economic status and even state of mind. *Commedia dell'arte* also employed masks for stock-types that migrated from narrative to narrative, despite occasional change of actors. Their main disadvantages are: they divert expression from the face to the body, and may hinder vocal communication. The half-mask of *commedia dell'arte* partly solves this problem.

Stage costume can be seen as an expanded mask for the entire body, without implying 'disguise', which only characterizes the carnivalesque costume. The actor is neither disguising the fact that he is enacting a character, nor pretending that he is the character.

Costume too fulfils functions of characterization, such as gender, age, status, mood, style, season, part of the day and, in some cases, profession, cultural period and nationality. However, there is a fundamental difference between mask and costume. Whereas a mask is an unusual attachment to the face, clearly distinguished from it, a costume is a usual addition to the body. Whereas wearing a mask on stage does not necessarily enact the use of a mask in the fictional world, wearing a garment always enacts the use of a fictional garment. Therefore, unlike the mask, the use of costume does not necessarily serve to indicate theatrical acting. Moreover, disguise is used in theatre only in actual carnivalesque scenes; e.g., the ball in Shakespeare's *Romeo and Juliet*. Comedy employs disguise in cases of intentional trickery; e.g., Viola in Shakespeare's *Twelfth Night* and Beatrice in Goldoni's *The Servant of Two Masters*.

Carnivalesque elements in comedy

In general, despite fundamental differences, comedy and carnival are performative in nature, but differ in that comedy actors perform descriptions of characters by imprinting images on their own bodies, while carnival revelers perform their anti-ritual behavior *through* their own real minds and bodies. It should be stressed that carnival is not a textual phenomenon and does not reflect fictional structures. Nonetheless, they do have in common, with no qualifications, the comic mood and ulti-mate cathartic effect, which presupposes that both are fuelled by anxiety, and aim at reaffirming the synchronic *philanthropon*. They also share the possible use of episodic laughter devices for the purpose of cathartic effect. In addition, the infiltration of carnivalesque elements into drama is quite widespread. Following are several examples:

(A) *The Fool*: The comic servant is occasionally a fool in the carniva-lesque sense of making humorous and witty remarks on serious fictional situations from the viewpoint of extra-established life; e.g., the gracioso in Calderón's *Life is a Dream* and the Fool in Shakespeare's *King Lear*:

> *Fool*: If thou wert my fool, nuncle, I'd have thee beaten for being old before thy time.
> *Lear*: How's that?
> *Fool*: Thou shouldst not have been old till thou hadst been wise. (I, v, 33–36)

Such a comment cannot be understood unless this fool is granted the very same license accorded to the fool during carnival. In his wit the fool often fulfils the function of 'eiron' as defined in this study (see CHAPTER 6). Furthermore, King and Fool should be seen as a dialectic unity, which is personified and enacted by two actors: Fool is permitted to say what the King does not permit himself even to think. Indeed, the Fool is an anti-King, as shown by the floppy crown on his head.

(B) *The inversion of social hierarchy*: Whereas in serious drama it is the interactive characters that fulfil the function of either advancing or blocking the action, e.g., in cases of conflict, in comedy it is often the shameless servant who runs the show; e.g., Palaestrio in Plautus' *The Swaggering Soldier* and Scapin in Molière's *The Trickeries of Scapin*. Such an inversion of roles and even the eventual restoration of the estab-lished hierarchy are carnivalesque in nature. It is noteworthy that the inversion of social roles is possible not only in lighthearted but also in serious fictional worlds; e.g., in Strindberg's *Miss Julia*, it is Jean, her liveried footman, who brings about the suicide of Julia. The question is, therefore, whether the inversion of roles is done either in the serious or the humorous mood typical of comedy. It is only the latter that is carni-valesque in nature.

(C) *The mask*: In ancient Greek comedy the comic mask assisted in depicting the ludicrous nature of the comic character. It added an image of physical deformity to its usual mental deformity — with the former being a metaphor of the latter; e.g., the mask of Pantalone. The metaphoric principle also applies to the real physical traits of comic actors in all styles of comedy. Physical ugliness and beauty, even of the bare face, often fulfil such metaphoric function.

(D) *Parody*: This device is employed as a possible means of comic drama; e.g., the parody of the myth of Hercules' birth from Zeus and Alcmena, in Plautus' *Amphitryon*, and the parody of the first *stasimon* in Sophocles' *Antigone* by Guard in Ionesco's *Exit the King* (see CHAPTER 3).

In particular, *commedia dell'arte* materializes most of these carniva-lesque principles. In addition, as suggested above, carnival and comedy share the lighthearted attitude to human nature that is at the heart of the comedic metaphor. (see CHAPTER 9).

Molière's *The Trickeries of Scapin*

While Géronte and Argante are away on business, Géronte's son Leandre falls in love with Zerbinette, a Gypsy girl, and Argante's son Octave falls in love with Hyacinte, a girl living with her mother in extreme poverty. Octave asks his servant Scapin to defend him and Leandre against the possible fury of their fathers. Indeed, upon their return Géronte and Argante are furious and adamantly oppose the weddings. Scapin tells Argante that money is needed for canceling the wedding with Hyacinte, and tells Géronte that money is needed to release his son who has been kidnapped by Turks;. and, if he does not pay the ransom, Leandre will be taken away to Algier. Scapin receives the moneys. He also warns Géronte that Zerbinette's brother is about to arrive and beat him up, and persuades him to hide in a sack. The servant then impersonates the brother and repeatedly slaps the sack. Géronte discovers the trick. Without noticing that it is Géronte who is listening, Zerbinette rejoices in the trick and derides the old man, while describing him as a miser and a villain. Eventually, through *deus ex machina*, Géronte discovers that Hyacinte is his own daughter, who was thought to have drowned; and Argante too recognizes Zerbinette as his own daughter, who had been abducted when she was four years old. Both fathers then bless the marriages of their children. Scapin, for fear of punishment, arrives in the final scene with his head bandaged, pretending that he is dying and telling that a stonemason's hammer had fallen on his head. Initially,

Géronte is prepared to pardon him only on condition that he dies; but eventually forgives him in order not to spoil the joyous day. Although Scapin momentarily runs the show, reflecting thereby the carnivalesque nature of the narrative, he does not promote the dénouement of the action, and even complicates it. He mainly promotes the *humorous mood*. He inverts the social hierarchy only for a while and for cathartic purposes.

The anonymous *Maître Pierre Pathelin* too can be seen as reflecting a carnivalesque structure in bestowing final victory on a character that is no less fraudulent than the others, but lower in the class hierarchy. This is probably no more than a comic variation on the typical comic poetic justice (see CHAPTER 11).

The Trickeries of Scapin on stage

The Jerusalem Khan Theatre first staged Molière's *Les Fourberies de Scapin* (under the title *The Scams of Scapin*) on 19th December 2009, in the Hebrew translation by Nathan Alterman, and directed by Udi ben Moshe. It is currently being performed by the Khan Theatre throughout Israel, to great acclaim by both critics and audiences. It was named

9 Dance in the style of *commedia dell'arte*, in the Khan Theatre *The Miser*.
Photo: Gadi Dagon. Courtesy of the Jerusalem Khan Theatre.

171

10 Scapin's eyes, in the Khan Theatre *The Trickeries of Scapin.*
Photo: Gadi Dagon. Courtesy of the Jerusalem Khan Theatre.

11 Scapin slaps Géronte in the sack, in the Khan Theatre
The Trickeries of Scapin.
Photo: Gadi Dagon. Courtesy of the Jerusalem Khan Theatre.

'Comedy of the Year', for 2009, by the Israeli Theatre Academy. The performance starts with the entire troupe singing a non-scripted song, led by Scapin. To the sound of a cheerful tune, the song introduces the play by its name, the author Jean-Baptiste Poquelin, known as Molière, and the actors in their roles. The singing reflects a playful mood and straightforward address to the audience. The song is then repeated before the interval and again at the end of the performance. This framing device proclaims the lighthearted and playful mood of the performance — thus creating the appropriate atmosphere for the detached attitude of the audience and their possible laughter. The audience received the initial song with loud applause.

In general, the production closely follows the original play-script, and the acting is in the spirit of *commedia dell'arte* or, rather, what is currently thought to have been the acting style of *commedia dell'arte*.

In place of the script's expectation for the spectator to imagine some parts of the action, based on the evocative power of words, the director has interspersed several mimed scenes among the dialogues.

Vitali Friedland interprets Scapin as a typical zanni, with a touch of Harlequin. His eyes betray a brain that is constantly concocting trickeries. He is the buffoon who runs the show. He manipulates the old fathers, Argante and Géronte, into giving him large sums of money under the pretext of saving their sons, while actually seeking to help the sons in their endeavors. He achieves his ends through a mixture of feigned empathy and threatening trickeries. When beating Géronte who is hidden in a sack, he impersonates Zerbinette's brother, including his foreign accent, and enacts a "dialogue" between the bully and himself, pretending that he is both protecting his master and being overpowered by the ruffian. Like Harlequin, he also uses an electronic slapstick that amplifies the sound of the beating, which he exchanges for larger and larger ones in the course of the scene.

The beating is not a necessary element of the action, but reflects the sheer revenge of a servant against his oppressive master. Similarly, when Scapin is threatened by Leandre, for allegedly having betrayed him, and the servant is forced to reveal previous trickeries, he takes his revenge by kicking Leandre and even demanding that he kisses his shoe, when the young master is most in need of his help. This duality of cunning helper and cruel retaliator also characterizes some of the zanni. Flattery, manipulation, disguise, impersonation and violence are the tools of Scapin's trade.

Erez Shafrir enacts Silvester as a minor buffoon, an assistant to Scapin's trickeries, through impersonating Hyacinte's ailing mother; the

12 Sylvester in Turkish disguise, in the Khan Theatre
The Trickeries of Scapin.
Photo: Gadi Dagon. Courtesy of the Jerusalem Khan Theatre.

bully who allegedly threatens Argante; the Gypsy who supposedly receives money for releasing Zerbinette; and the Turkish waiter, who serves Turkish coffee and allegedly kidnaps Leandre — all of which are the fabrications of Scapin's mind. In his various disguises, Silvester's impersonations are hilarious, and are warmly applauded.

The fathers too are enacted in the spirit of *commedia dell'arte*, following the model of Pantalone or, rather, of the *senex iratus* (irascible old man). Arie Tcherner enacts a Parkinson-afflicted old Argante and Yehoyachim Friedlander a stiff and cold Géronte. These flaws are physical metaphors of their mental flaws. These parsimonious old men create the impression that, for them, money is far more important than their own sons. When asked to give money in order to save their sons, they hardly part from it, offering any excuse to avoid the transactions. Argante and Géronte produce parallel routines of such mental impediments, with the latter constantly reiterating the same question 'Que

Comedy and Carnival

13 Care for Hyacinte's mother, in the Khan Theatre
The Trickeries of Scapin.
Photo: Gadi Dagon. Courtesy of the Jerusalem Khan Theatre.

diable allait-il faire dans cette galère?' (What the hell was he doing in that galley?). Against the background of his avarice, these questions lend an ironic innuendo to Géronte's care for his son.

The young lovers are modern versions of the *innamorati*, devised in the spirit of *commedia dell'arte*. Octave (Yoav Hyman) and Leadre (Udi Rotschild) are young, handsome, naïve, helpless, and deeply afraid of their fathers. Scapin improvises a rehearsal for the future confrontation of Octave with his father, in which Scapin impersonates a furious Argante; and Octave, rather than standing up for his rights, faints. Naïveté and helplessness are not in the girls' nature: in place of Molière's mere innuendos of sexual relations, Hyacinte (Shimrit Lustig) initiates an embrace with Octave that ends on the floor in clear indication of sex; while the coquette Zerbinette (Nili Rogel) lures Leandre in a kind of display that recalls a *femme fatale*, which suits her gypsy upbringing. Her gypsy behavior is epitomized in her vulgar derision of Géronte, while unwittingly revealing to him the trickeries played on him by Scapin (III, iii — the wrong confidant: see CHAPTER: 3). Hyacinte's mimed concern for the health of her mother verges on parody of melodrama due to sheer exaggeration.

175

14 "Wounded" Scapin on a wheelchair, in the Khan Theatre
The Trickeries of Scapin.
Photo: Gadi Dagon. Courtesy of the Jerusalem Khan Theatre.

The ending too is *deus ex machina*, in the spirit of *commedia dell'arte*. Scapin does not manage to bring about the fathers' consent to their sons' weddings (his trickeries are revealed by the furious and derided Géronte at the end of the sack-beating scene). It is Silvestre and Leandre who reveal that Argante and Géronte are the true fathers of Zerbinette and Hyacinte respectively, thus making the latter suitable wives for their sons. Scapin's final trickery — entering the stage on a wheelchair, pretending to have been injured by a stonemason's hammer, bleeding and dying — is nonetheless crowned with success: Argante persuades Géronte to pardon him in order not to spoil the joy of the day and the prospective weddings.

This Khan production, like the original play-script, maintains the basic structure of the typical troupe of *commedia dell'arte*: two old men, two young couples, two zanni and a servetta (Hyacinte's mother's nurse).

Carnival and comedy share several essential features such as light-hearted mood, optional cathartic laughter and the ultimate aim to reaffirm and buttress the prevalent values and beliefs of the synchronic culture. In addition, although these are essentially different phenomena, comedy adopts some carnivalesque devices. Furthermore, it is sensible to conjecture that carnival and comedy inherently complement a culture that produces functional pressure — with carnivalesque breaks probably originating at the very beginnings of human history.

Comedy and Joke-Telling

The ultimate aim of telling a joke, which is a brief narrative, is to produce laughter. It thus shares this aim with comedy, farce in particular. For in joke-telling too, laughter is employed as a cathartic mechanism. Moreover, similarly to comedy, joke-telling is performative in the sense of being performed in front of an audience, even if it is a single listener. Nonetheless, there is at least one obvious difference between them: whereas theatre comedy is an iconic art, joke-telling is a verbal art, subspecies oral storytelling. The joke-teller may engage in enacting a short dialogue or in an individual reaction of a character comprised in a joke, reflecting its character, but this is done in the guise of storytelling in which enactment is usually confined to inflection of the voice and facial mimicry. The joke-teller is definitely not an actor.

On such grounds, I adopt the distinction between wit and joke. Whereas a witticism is a kind of verbal remark, the joke is a kind of narrative, usually of very short scope. For example, the following Jewish joke:

> Yankel returns home to find his best friend making love to his wife.
> He is astonished, and asks: 'Yosel, I must; but you?'

These two sentences describe a full narrative that can be developed into an entire scene of a comedy. The first sentence of the joke, which describes the initial situation, is extremely serious, and prone to produce anxiety in the listener; probably due to its realizing a suppressed fear: each listener may harbor in his mind the anxiety of being betrayed by a spouse and, even worse, by a best friend. On this level of utter seriousness, Yankel's possible reactions are quite restricted — with all of them being in the domain of harsh punishment of his wife, his best friend, or both. He might even kill one of them, or both. Instead, to the listener's possible surprise, Yankel's reaction is ludicrous. His question presupposes that making love to his wife is a matter of obligation or, rather, a penalty of matrimony; and indicates that he is angry neither at his wife, nor at his friend. He is only astonished by his friend for doing what he is not obligated to do. His question thus transmutes the narrative from a dead-serious story to a humorous one. Therefore, the sudden transition from such a pregnant situation to a humorous dénouement is prone to produce laughter. It is a joke because a situation that deserves concern is shown to only deserve laughter.

Does the listener laugh at Yankel or with him? This depends on the interpretation of the character by the joke-teller: whether he enacts the question as articulated by a naïve character or an ironic one. In both cases, the joke is funny.

I am aware that 'when a joke is dissected, it abruptly ceases to be funny, which is disconcerting to say the least' (Styan, 1968: 39). However, this dissection is carried out here not in order to explain to a listener why he should laugh, but to understand the mechanism of eliciting laughter.

Another example of a Jewish joke:

> The bridegroom was most disagreeably surprised when the bride was introduced to him, and drew the broker [*schadchen*, match maker] to one side and whispered his remonstrances: "Why have you brought me here?" he asked reproachfully, "She is ugly and old, she squints, and has bad teeth and bleary eyes . . . " — "You needn't lower your voice", interrupted the broker, "she's deaf as well." (Freud, 1989: 74–5)

The very serious and embarrassing situation is dissolved in a humorous punch-line, whose main function is to mark the sudden and even surprising transition from a serious to a humorous mood — thus potentially producing comic laughter.

In contrast, a witticism is a kind of remark; e.g., 'A wife is like an umbrella — sooner or later one takes a cab' (*ibid.*: 132). A dramatic example: in *The Importance of Being Earnest* Algernon's remark *that* '[g]irls never marry the men they flirt with. Girls don't think it right' (p. 253). This is a sharp and concise remark that is put in the mouth of a character, with no necessary narrative implications. In other words, in a dramatic context, witticisms are fundamentally episodic: they can be added or subtracted at will. These remarks may reflect either a character's humorous or satiric intent, depending on the object of derision.

Freud's theory of jokes

For Freud, there is no difference between laughter elicited by a comedy, a joke or a witticism: 'Freud's thesis is simple and straightforward: Laughter occurs when repressing energy is freed from its static function of keeping something forbidden under repression and away from consciousness' (Grotjahn: 270). Furthermore, 'laughter arises if a quota of psychical energy which has earlier been used for the cathexis of particular psychical paths has become unusable, so that it can find *free discharge*' (Freud, 1989: 180; my emphasis). 'Cathexis' is employed here in the sense of concentrating mental energy in inhibiting a forbidden drive. This is an explanation of laughter in terms of 'expenditure of energy' (see CHAPTER 2). Still, its cathartic function is not ignored: 'free discharge' should thus be seen as synonymous with 'catharsis'. In other words, in Freud's view, laughter occurs when a joke or a comic situation lifts an inhibition of a forbidden drive — thus releasing the physical energy invested in the inhibition. He adds: 'it is . . . plausible to suppose that *this yield of pleasure corresponds to the psychical expenditure [of energy] that is saved*' (*ibid.*: 145).

This explanation in energetic terms is possibly equivalent to the Aristotelian notion of 'catharsis', which is usually perceived as a source of pleasure in itself. However, Freud suggests that the actual source of pleasure is not the mere release of tension involved in keeping an inhibition, but in that the lifting of an inhibition enables access to sources of pleasure that 'have been rendered inaccessible by those inhibitions;' (1989: 160); e.g., the gratification of an aggressive wish, which could not have been achieved unless by its straightforward gratification (cf. *ibid.*: 143).

Freud's explanation is deficient in a crucial respect: the mere lifting of an inhibition cannot explain the release of energy. It is more sensible to assume that the lifting of an inhibition produces additional tension, and that this accumulated tension is released by means of a peripeteia (in the case of the joke too) from a serious to a humorous mood (see CHAPTER 2).

In this context, Freud's distinction between innocent and tendentious jokes is to the point (*ibid.*: 107). Whereas the aim of an innocent joke lies in producing comic laughter, a tendentious joke has a purpose beyond laughter (cf. *ibid.*: 114). Accordingly, tendentious jokes are subdivided according to their additional purposes, such as being (a) 'hostile', i.e., 'serving the purpose of aggressiveness, satire, or defence'; (b) 'obscene', i.e., 'serving the purpose of [sexual] exposure' (*ibid.*: 115); and (c) 'cynical', i.e., serving the purpose of, for example, attacking 'religious dogmas and even the belief in God' (*ibid.*: 136). A paradigmatic example of an hostile joke is the one that conveys a sense of rebellion against an authority (*ibid.*: 125), either by explicitly naming the victim or hinting at such.

The explanation of the pleasure derived from the tendentious joke as the surrogate gratification of an inhibited drive opens the way to an improved explanation of the innocent joke, which has no purpose such as aggression beyond laughter but sheer catharsis, which, as suggested above, presupposes anxiety (see CHAPTER 4). The lifting of an inhibition undoubtedly produces anxiety in the spectator/listener, which is released by the innocent joke; i.e., in Freud's terms, 'the value of the censorship' is reduced 'to zero' (*ibid.*: 229).

Nevertheless, there is a cathartic effect too in the telling of a tendentious joke, in also gratifying an inhibited aggressive drive, in particular if the joke-teller and the listener are dependent on the object of derision, such as a high-ranking personality: e.g., the following joke: A citizen brought a book as a gift to the mayor of Haifa who was considered illiterate. The mayor's response was: 'No, thanks, I already have one.' His discontent citizens enjoyed the joke tremendously, because of deriding the Mayor's ignorance, and kept telling and spreading it. Nonetheless, the causes of catharsis are different: whereas the innocent joke is a benevolent play with ludicrous elements, a tendentious joke aims actual aggression at its real object through deriding means. There is something merciless in the latter.

Freud's distinction between the intentions underlying innocent and tendentious jokes also applies to the difference between comic laughter, which characterizes comedy (see CHAPTER 2), and satiric laughter, which characterizes satiric drama (see CHAPTER 8).

Grotjahn's theory of wit

Grotjahn offers a vivid description of the process whereby an aggressive intent is disguised as a witticism, in the terms of an analogy to a 'a train in a mountain tunnel', thus making it acceptable to consciousness.

> A *witticism* starts with an aggressive tendency or intent — an insult-like, shocking thought. This has to be repressed and disappears into the unconscious like a train into a mountain tunnel. The wit work begins there in the darkness of the unconscious, like the dream work; it disguises the latent aggressive thought skillfully. It combines the

disguised aggression with playful pleasure, repressed since childhood and waiting for a chance to be satisfied. After this *wit* work is accomplished, the *witticism* reappears at the other end of the tunnel and sees the daylight of consciousness and conscience again. By now it has become acceptable, and the energy originally activated to keep the hostility under repression is freed into laughter. The repressed energy is no longer needed; the shock of freedom of thought and freedom from repression is enjoyed and leads to laughter. (pp. 270–1; my italics)

Moreover, '[t]he disguise must go far enough to avoid guilt; it must not go so far that the thrill of aggression is lost' (p. 271). In other words, essentially, wit is a veiled form of aggression: 'The wit as a person is closely related to the sadist' (*ibid.*).

However, the person who generates a witty remark is not necessarily the one who laughs. In order to satisfy his hostile intent he should probably even refrain from laughing. Freud is correct in contending that the intention is to hurt a second person through producing laughter in a third person (Freud, 1989: 122). I would suggest that the disguise aims not only at beguiling consciousness, but also at precluding a possible aggressive response from the victim. After all, 'it was only a joke.' It should be noted that this process is meant to apply to wit, and occasionally to tendentious joke-telling, but by no means to innocent joke-telling, due to the latter abstaining from aggressive intent in nature.

Seemingly, Freud's contentions are corroborated by open aggression on stage; e.g., when Scapin' pitilessly hits Géronte hidden in the sack in *The Trickeries of Scapin* (III, ii). However, in fact, no harm is inflicted on Géronte, only derision. However, since Geronte is a fictional entity and not a real individual, such an event, which is farcical in nature, is done within the boundaries of the lighthearted mood of comedy. It momentarily lifts the inhibitions upon open aggression, produces additional anxiety, and allows its release by hinting at the humorous intention of the scene. Indeed, comedy operates within the permissive atmosphere granted by the audience, by their merely experiencing it in a communal context. In such a case too, we laugh *at* Géronte, *with* Scapin. We should add that *The Trickeries of Scapin* is a metaphoric representation of aggression toward parental oppression, which is tabooed. However, when transferred to an oppressed servant and done in the comic mood, it becomes rational and enables both the pleasing release of tension and lack of guilt feelings.

If the psychoanalytic explanation of the joke is sound, it implies that any instance of a tendentious joke reveals the existence of a shameful or suppressed drive and their inhibition in both the joke-teller and the listener. Similarly, even an innocent joke may reveal the existence of such a drive and an inhibition. In this sense, both may serve to bridge the gap between the conscious and the unconscious. Perhaps this is what Grotjahn has in mind in claiming that '[t]he analytic study of laughter is a study of creative communication between the unconscious and the conscious, leading to the experience of happiness in fulfilling one's potentialities. This is man's challenge, his destiny and the meaning of human life' (p. 270). In general, Freud's approach leads to the conclusion that jokes play a significant role in the homeostasis of the psyche. They touch highly serious chords that potentially both produce extreme anxiety and dissolve it into laughter. 'The best jokes are not only compatible with the most solemn intention, but are likely to be the best jokes for that reason' (Styan, 1968: 46).

Bentley's approach

Following Freud, Bentley distinguishes between 'two kinds of jokes: the harmless and the purposive. Only the purposive or tendentious joke . . . [has] enough violence in it to be useful in farce. . . . The harmless joke is rooted in sympathy, the purposive joke in scorn' (p. 311). It should be noted that the terms 'purposive' and 'harmless' correspond to 'tendentious' and 'innocent' in Strachey's translation of Freud's *Jokes and their Relation to the Unconscious*. Indeed, Bentley believes that violence is the hallmark of farce (p. 219). In contrast, as suggested above, a distinction should be made between the aggressiveness of satiric drama and the violence of farce — with the latter not evincing a derogatory intention to a personality, institution or idea in the real world (see CHAPTER 7).

Bentley also suggests a distinction between two types of comedy 'by recourse to the old distinction between wit and humor' (p. 311), which, in his view, corresponds to the distinction between farce and comedy respectively:

The two kinds of comedy would seem to have two different ends in view. In the logic of the first is a shock effect in the shape of a revelation of what is horrible. This kind of play seems to drive inward toward the forbidding truth. Its "happy ending" is purely ironical [absurd]. In the logic of the second kind of comedy is an effect of enchantment in the shape of realization of our fondest hopes — that is, our hopes for love and happiness. (p. 313)

Furthermore, 'the art of farce is but joking turned theatrical — joking fully articulated as theatrical characters and scenes' (p. 234). However, first, Bentley does not distinguish clearly between wit and joke; and second, again, the distinction between purposeful (tendentious) joke and harmless (innocent) joke better suits the difference between satire and comedy, including farce, respectively, as defined in this study.

Bentley also addresses the question of the joke work or, rather, the wit work, which he views as germane to farce:

> How does the sense of humor go to work? Its aim is to gratify some of the forbidden wishes. But what is repressed is repressed. We cannot get at it. Our anxiety and guilt are taking care of that. Only, there are tricks of eluding anxiety and guilt, and the commonest, the least artificial, is the sense of humor. The mildly amusing preliminaries of a joke allay our fears, lower our resistance. The gratification of the forbidden wish is then slipped upon us as a surprise. Before our guilt and anxiety have time to go into action, the forbidden pleasure has been had. A source of pleasure far deeper than those directly available has been tapped. Inhibitions are momentarily lifted, repressed thoughts are admitted into consciousness, and we experience that feeling of power and pleasure, generally called elation. (p. 230)

Bentley thus presupposes that, like wit, farce produces pleasure by gratifying forbidden wishes through a kind of trick that circumvents consciousness. It should be noted that wit can also be innocent. I would say, first, that farce is not tendentious; and second, that farce enables the confrontation with forbidden wishes, probably the crudest ones, not in order to satisfy them but to release tension, albeit temporarily, through a reversal of moods, with no hostile intention in regard to the real world.

Bentley definitely endorses the cathartic nature of laughter: 'Why do we laugh at jokes? . . . The intellectual content is not the essence. What counts is the experience which we call "getting" the joke or "seeing the point." This experience is a kind of shock, but, whereas shocks in general are unpleasant, this one opens a sluicegate somewhere and brings a sudden spurt or gush of pleasure' (pp. 229–30; cf. Welsford's 'safety valve': 202 & 216). For Freud, 'jokes are fundamentally cathartic: a release, not a stimulant' (Bentley: 229). The catharsis of a joke is like tragic catharsis, which 'is not only an excitement but a release from excitement. It will not burst the boiler with its steam because it is precisely the safety valve' (*ibid.*: 223). However, like Freud, Bentley fails to address the crucial role of anxiety in the cathartic process. Therefore, the psychical energy saved in the lifting of an inhibition cannot explain catharsis unless it is assumed that such lifting produces additional anxiety and that there is a sudden and abrupt transition from the serious to the humorous mood.

It follows that a joke must be divided into two parts: one that produces/augments anxiety and the second that releases it, which are mediated by such a peripeteia; e.g., the above joke on a man's best friend making love to his wife illustrates this dual structure: 'Yosel, I must; but you?'

A cathartic approach

Initially, a joke or a witticism positions the listener in a position of disorientation or, rather, of object of irony: the role of the initial part is to introduce a shameful or suppressed theme, which triggers serious expectations and correlated anxiety; e.g., the theme of marital infidelity. In contrast, the role of the final part, usually a punch line, is to reveal the humorous intention, following a sudden change of moods. The appropriate reception of a joke or a witticism thus depends on the perception of this change, even if unconsciously. The increased anxiety is then released through comic laughter and thoroughly enjoyed. A listener who does not understand a joke usually asks for an explanation, which indicates that disorientation persists. A series of jokes may profit from both the previous arousal of anxiety and the previous release of the additional anxiety. Indeed, in entering a humorous mood, even poor jokes elicit laughter.

Actual catharsis indicates that the power of a joke depends on its own ability to increase anxiety; i.e., on the lifting of an inhibition of a suppressed or shameful drive. Similarly to comedy and farce, listeners to a joke are sensitive to different inhibitions. Therefore, people of different genders and different ages react to different inhibitions; e.g., toddlers laugh at jokes referring to wee-wee, married people laugh at jokes about mothers-in-law, and old men laugh at jokes about impotence. Laughter is also culture-dependent: 'It is . . . notorious that a "sense of humour" is an unreliable quality, and what will seem laughable to an English audience will not necessarily seem so to a Scottish.' (Styan, 1968: 39) Indeed, different cultures impose different inhibitions.

Elements of joke/wit in comedy

Despite nuances and qualifications, the psychoanalytic approach is the only one that opens the way to a sensible explanation of the psychical mechanism that is triggered by a joke or witticism. While the innocent joke/witticism and comedy share the intention to produce laughter with no ulterior purpose; the tendentious joke/witticism and satiric drama share the intention to deride and humiliate a real object. Nonetheless, the dramatic use of elements that characterize jokes and witticisms are not restricted to this common ground. The following are several examples:

(A) A playwright can put either a joke or a witticism in the mouth of a character, which requires special attention, especially if it offers an interpretation of a situation or another character from an ironic view-point; e.g., a fool. Typically, the spectator laughs with the fool and at the butt, if the latter reflects a naïve viewpoint. In both cases, however, it is the nature of the comment on a character or fictional situation that reveals the nature of the wit/joke; e.g., the witticisms in Wilde's *The Importance of Being Earnest.*

In regard to the tendentious joke/witticism, if the psychoanalytic description of the psychical mechanism is sound, the questions are: who lifts the inhibition, who is the butt and who laughs? It is sensible to assume that it is the wit/joke-teller character (the first person) that lifts the inhibition in the spectator (the third person), who laughs; while the butt character (the second person) is not always aware of the aggressive intention.

(B) A joke/witticism, like any unit that is meant to elicit laughter, is episodic, and must reflect the said dual structure: it should commence as a serious description, which augments static anxiety, and end with its sudden release. Indeed, in understanding a joke, there is an initial phase of disorientation that may produce anxiety, until the receiver perceives that he has been lured into an erroneous state of mind, and that the intention was to pull his leg either playfully or aggressively. As such it can become part of a fictional world.

Third, a joke can be the basic pattern/structure underlying a comic or satiric fictional world; e.g., the anonymous *Pierre Pathelin.*

Anonymous *Maître Pierre Pathelin*

Maître Pathelin, a dishonest and penniless lawyer, tricks Maître Guillaume, a mean cloth merchant, into selling him fabric for his wife.

The shrewd merchant boasts of having fooled the lawyer in price, but, when it comes to paying for it, the latter pretends mental insanity. In the meantime, a shepherd and wool seller fools the merchant by eating the sheep already paid for by the latter, under the pretext of having been exploited. The merchant then sues the shepherd who hires Maître Pathelin to represent him in court. The shrewd lawyer advises him to answer 'baa' (like a sheep) to any of the judge's questions. The judge then becomes impatient and dismisses the trial. When Maître Pathelin demands his fee, however, the shepherd replies with the very same 'baa'.

Both the shrewd characters, the lawyer and the merchant, are outwitted by the astute shepherd who is shrewder than both. There is symmetry between the two parts of the narrative, and a double inversion of power relations — with the representative of the lower class eventually gaining the upper hand. The astute shepherd is relatively justified by the merchant's avarice and the lawyer's shrewdness. The shepherd reverses the situation by fooling the lawyer using the very same means by which the lawyer had fooled the merchant and the judge.

This play-script could be seen as generated by a comedic fictional structure, based on the principle of 'proportion': Lighthearted transgressions lead to light punishments (see CHAPTER 5). Nonetheless, it is better explained as reflecting the structure of a joke: the shrewd character is eventually outwitted by its own trick. A measure of poetic justice is thus achieved.

Sigmund Freud's significant contribution to a theory of joke/witticism lies in turning the attention of scholars to the unconscious repercussions of joke-telling and wit, and their implications for comedy, the role of lifting inhibitions in particular. Indeed, joke-telling and listening involve all the levels of the psyche. This contribution helps in elucidating the affinities between the innocent joke and comedy, and between the tendentious joke and satire. In particular, while telling an innocent joke aims initially at increasing anxiety, and eventually at producing comic laughter, telling a tendentious joke aims at eventually producing aggressive laughter. Although the mechanism of producing laughter is the same, its underlying intentions and purposes are different.

The Comic Vision   **12**

During the twentieth century scholars went to great lengths to elevate comedy from its traditional inferior status vis-à-vis tragedy. Such a derogative attitude was first recorded by Aristotle: 'Comedy has had no history, because it was not at first treated seriously. It was late before the Archon granted a comic chorus to a poet; the performers were till then voluntary. Comedy had already taken definite shape when comic poets, distinctively so called, are heard of' (*Poetics*: V, 2). This attitude remained the lot of comedy for millennia.

In challenging this tradition, in *The New Art of Making Comedies in This Age* (my trans.), 1609, Lope repeatedly declares that in writing comedies he deliberately ignores the rules of the *Poetics* (e.g., 1965: 5; p. 64). As noted above, the use of 'comedy' for his play-scripts is more often than not unjustified (Introduction). Cornford's theory of ritual origin was probably the first modernist attempt to bestow a dignified ancestry upon comedy by claiming that it had originated in ritual (Introduction). Furthermore, twentieth-century scholars took up the challenge to upgrade the status of comedy by searching for what Corrigan terms the 'comic view of life' or the 'comic spirit' (p. 3) and Weitz terms the comic 'vision of life' (p. 36), which assumedly contrasts that of tragedy, while enjoying the same status, probably under the influence of modernism and the advent of grotesque styles.

The notion of 'comic vision' should be seen neither as a thematic component of a fictional world nor as what is usually termed its 'message'; but as a basic cognitive attitude toward the world that is embodied in the nature of comedy. It should be noted that the term 'comic vision' is seldom used by the following theories, and it is used here for all the arguments in favor of the above-mentioned 'comic view of life'. In the following sections I suggest a critical review of prominent perceptions in regard to the alleged essential 'comic vision' of comedy.

The Comic Vision

Langer's 'feeling and form'

In *Feeling and Form*, Susanne Langer attempts to establish the 'organic form' of comedy under the assumption that it is a specific kind of *feeling* that determines the *form* of a genre: 'Drama . . . always exhibits such form; it does so by . . . composing its elements into a rhythmic single structure' (1967: 326). Accordingly, she suggests that '[t]he pure sense of life is the underlying feeling of comedy, developed in countless different ways' (*ibid.*: 327; cf. p. 331). In contrast, '[t]ragedy has a different basic feeling, and therefore a different form' (*ibid.*: 331). This basic feeling is epitomized by the 'foreknowledge of death', which determines its form (*ibid.*: 333). Comedy's 'pure sense of life' is thus contrasted to tragedy's 'knowledge of death'. In other words, these crucial differences in their forms reflect these different basic feelings.

This is an odd contrast, however, because, first, in tragedy death is only one possible ending. There are additional kinds of sad endings such as self-punishment, defeat and ostracism. As Aristotle himself observes, there are tragedies that end even in reconciliation; e.g., Euripides' *Hippolytus*. He thus implies that, despite the usual perception, it is not the kind of ending that characterizes tragedy but its serious/sublime mood (cf. *Poetics*: XIII, 7–8; see CHAPTER 2). In contrast, comedies always conclude in archetypal, including happy endings, because of the dominant role of the humorous mood.

Langer also claims that '[t]ragedy is the image of Fate, as comedy is of Fortune' (1967: 333); and '[d]estiny viewed in this way, as a future shaped essentially in advance and only incidentally by chance happenings, is Fate; and Fate is the "virtual future" created in tragedy' (*ibid.*). Accordingly, '[d]estiny in the guise of Fortune is the fabric of comedy; it is developed by comic action, which is the upset and recovery of the protagonist's equilibrium, his contest with the world and his triumph by wit, luck, personal power, or even humorous, or ironical, or philosophical acceptance of mischance' (*ibid.*: 331). Consequently, '[t]heir basic structures are different; comedy is essentially contingent, episodic and ethnic; it expresses the continuous balance of sheer vitality that belongs to society and is exemplified briefly in each individual; tragedy is a fulfillment, and its form therefore is closed, final and passional' (*ibid.*: 333–4).

In contrast, I claim that both these views — that only the sense of 'fate' shapes tragedy and that only the sense of fortune shapes comedy — are fallacies. In place of structural considerations, they bestow the role of generating generic forms on thematic specifications, which are meant to characterize either all tragedies or all comedies. For example, even in Sophocles' *Oedipus the King* the theme of 'fate', albeit prominent, is subordinated to the theme of hubris. Furthermore, most known tragedies do not even relate to this theme or underlying feeling. Similar considerations apply to fortune in comedy. It follows that these feelings cannot determine the 'organic forms' of either tragedy or comedy. It is the overall structure of a fictional world, including mood, and thematic specification that convey a basic attitude to the world.

Langer also contends that 'the comic rhythm is that of vital continuity ... The comic hero plays against obstacles presented either by nature ... or by society; that is, his fight is with obstacles and enemies, which his strength, wisdom, virtue, or other assets let him overcome' (1967: 335). Moreover, 'comedy abstracts, and reincarnates for our perception, the motion and rhythm of living' (*ibid.*: 344). However, first, there are serious play-scripts in which the "hero" also struggles against 'obstacles and enemies' and prevails, and which are entitled to be labeled tragedies on modal grounds; e.g., Corneille's *Le Cid*; and, second, not all comedies focus on such a kind of hero. The question is, therefore, who is the comic hero in Langer's eyes? It is neither the ludicrous character suggested by Aristotle nor the obstructing character suggested by Frye — with these two functions being combined, for example, in the main characters in comedies by Molière. It is not the young lovers of the *commedia dell'arte* either: they do not struggle for anything. Langer sees the epitome of the comic character in the buffoon:

> what the buffoon really is: the indomitable living creature fending for itself, tumbling and stumbling (as the clown physically illustrates) from one situation to another, getting into scrape after scrape and getting out again, with or without a thrashing, He is the personified élan vital [the creative and demanding life forces]. . . . He is neither a good man nor a bad one, but is genuinely amoral, — now triumphant, now worsted and rueful, but in his ruefulness and dismay he is funny, because his energy is really unimpaired and each failure prepares the situation for a new fantastic move. (*ibid.*: 342)

This too is an odd thesis: first, not all comedies feature a buffoon; and second, not all buffoons struggle against 'obstacles and enemies' and prevail; e.g., in Goldoni's *The Servant of Two Masters*, Truffaldino only entangles the situation and is eventually beaten by both his masters. In fact, in contrast to its nature, Langer attributes to the buffoon the extremely serious role of epitomizing the vision of comedy. The buffoon is neither in charge of promoting the goals of interactive characters, nor in charge of epitomizing the meaning of a comedy, but only in charge of the humorous mood. Only seldom can the interactive functions be attributed to the buffoon.

It is true that comedy eventually restores 'a lost balance' and implies 'a new future (Langer, 1967: 335). This is implied by the archetypal ending for all its characters, which is not the sole prerogative of comedy but occurs in some tragedies too. In fact, the main problem in Langer's approach lies in that, in order to characterize comedy, it exclusively focuses on the structure of the action while ignoring the comic mood.

Langer perceives tragedy as 'a mature art form, that has not arisen in all parts of the world, not even in all great civilizations', due to requiring 'a sense of individuality which some religions and some cultures — even high cultures — do not generate'. (*ibid.*: 334) The erroneous implication of this contention is that comedy is not a mature art form. In contrast to tragedy, Langer views comedy as 'an art form that arises naturally wherever people are gathered to celebrate life' (*ibid.*: 331). Although this is true for many a comedy, it does not apply to all of them, e.g., the anonymous *Pierre Pathelin*. In addition, it is not at all clear exactly what 'celebration of life' means. In principle, it is possible that a tragedy too may occasionally convey such an underlying feeling.

Langer's attempt to determine the underlying feeling that is conveyed by all forms of comedy is commendable in itself. In opposing it to tragedy's underlying feeling it positions both on the same level as dramatic genres that deserve equal status and prestige, which is essentially appropriate: just as there are excellent comedies, there are also poor tragedies. Considerations of value, therefore, should not apply when trying to determine the nature of a genre.

Sypher's 'double view'

In 'The Meanings of Comedy', Sypher follows the lead of Kierkegaard who, 'like Kafka, finds that "the comical is present in every stage of life, for wherever there is life there is contradiction, and wherever there is contradiction the comical is present"' (p. 196). He adds: '*We have . . . been forced to admit that the absurd is more than ever inherent in human existence: that is, the irrational, the inexplicable, the surprising, the nonsensical — in other words, the comic*' (p. 195; my italics). Sypher thereby conflates the principles of the 'comic', the 'absurd' and the 'grotesque', which together allegedly epitomize the nature of life: 'After all, comedy, not tragedy, admits the disorderly into the realm of art; the grotesque depends upon an irrational focus. Ours is a century of disorder and rationalism' (p. 201). 'This sense of having to live amid the irrational, the ludicrous, the disgusting, or the perilous has been dramatized by the existentialists' (p. 197). Furthermore, 'the comic perception comes only when we take a double view — that is, a human view — of ourselves, a perspective by incongruity' (p. 255). By 'double view' he would seem to mean a simultaneous and ambivalent serious and comic attitude to life, which is the hallmark of the grotesque (cf. pp. 237 & 242). Whereas Kayser conflates the 'grotesque' and the 'absurd', which are principles on different structural levels (see CHAPTER 8); Sypher conflates the 'comic' and the 'grotesque', which are two different moods. Albeit employing similar laughter devices, comedy and grotesque drama aim at different impacts on the spectator (see CHAPTER 8).

Sypher's view that irrationality or, rather, absurdity, is equivalent to the comic or, rather, the mood of comedy, ignores that there is also serious absurdity, as otherwise how should the prophesies in Sophocles' *Oedipus the King* be categorized to the effect that Oedipus is meant to kill his own father and marry his own mother; and Theseus' wish in Euripides' *Hippolytus* to the effect that his own son will be killed by the request of his father, not to mention Poseidon's eagerness in realizing this wish?

Sypher is consistent with his own view in concluding that

> if the sense of contradiction and absurdity is a cause of comedy, then Hamlet is a profoundly comic character. He encounters what Kierkegaard calls either/or choices, the extremes that cannot be mediated but only transcended. This is, the comic hero and the saint accept the irreconcilables in man's existence. Both find themselves face to face with the Inexplicable and the Absurd. (p. 237)

However, it is this consistency that reveals Sypher's theoretical mistake: to see Hamlet as a case of absurdity is acceptable, but to see him as a comic character is inherently absurd. Sypher could have found a better example for a comic character. Hamlet could be seen as a grotesque character, but never as a comic one. Indeed, Sypher ignores the existence of tragic absurdity. He is clearly dealing not with comedy, but with grotesque drama.

Scott's 'whole truth'

In 'The Bias of Comedy and the Narrow Escape into Faith', Nathan A. Scott follows Aldous Huxley's essay 'Tragedy and the Whole Truth', and concludes that, in contrast to Aristotle, 'the art of comedy is not an art that is dedicated to the ludicrous, but is rather an art that is dedicated to the telling of the Whole Truth' (p. 95). He thus supports Langer's contention that '[r]eal comedy sets up in the audience a sense of general exhilaration, because it presents the very image of "livingness"' (quoted by Scott: 102; Langer, 1967: 344). In other words, '[t]he major purpose of the comedian . . . is to remind us of how deeply rooted we are in all the tangible things of this world' (Scott: 102). Comedy thus 'brings joy because it reminds us again how inescapable our humanity is, how established and permanent and indestructible it really is' (*ibid.*: 103).

Does Scott imply that tragedy is not dedicated to the telling of the whole truth, or that both tragedy and comedy are dedicated to the same purpose? His approach raises a basic question in regard to what is the nature of truth in drama. I have suggested elsewhere that on the level of relation between the fictional world and the spectator, all genres reflect a rhetoric structure (Rozik, 2009: 162–72). Following Aristotle's *Rhetoric*, this structure is enthymematic in nature. In contrast to syllogism, which is a form of logical deduction, an enthymeme presupposes that its premises are not necessarily true but, rather, are held to be true by the objects of persuasion (pp. 74–7). The enthymematic process of persuasion aims at demonstrating that a pre-determined conclusion "logically" follows from the axioms accepted by a certain audience. It thus aims not at truth but at an experience of truth. It should be borne in mind that the rhetoric aim is to persuade the spectator to experience and adopt an overall fictional metaphor, which also establishes its specific truth conditions and is subordinated to the rhetoric intent. The enthymematic principle explains why politicians, while being able to persuade people who share their own axioms to accept the "truth" of their conclusions, cannot persuade others who adhere to different axioms.

The 'enthymematic' principle also explains how the values of a particular audience, including valued beliefs, for all surface structures and genres, provide the common ground for the fictional experience to take off, whether the intention is to reaffirm their validity or not. In contrast to Hegel's presupposition of a metaphysical 'substance of ethical life' (e.g., p. 1196), it is the ethical system of a particular cultural community, the *'philanthropon'* in the sense of what is held to be true and valid by them, that constitutes such a common ground. In theatre, the 'sacred cows' of a community are always tested under extreme fictional circumstances, whether they are finally reaffirmed or confuted. Probing held values under such conditions produces tension, a euphemism for fear, and explains how even reaffirmation of held values can be seen as a change in a psychical state of affairs: *from initial uncertainty — with life constantly providing disproving reasons — to eventual certainty*.

Typically, comedy is archetypal in the sense of gratifying the expectations of synchronic spectators, based on what is held to be true by them. In this sense, it is basically conservative. Therefore, in contrast to Scott, the thesis that comedy is characterized by conveying the 'whole truth' is unsustainable. Furthermore, in principle, the notion of 'truth' presupposes that there is a solid criterion for it. In contrast, what is held to be true and its reaffirmation do not presuppose such a criterion. To which concept of 'reality', therefore, does Scott subscribe?

It is more sensible to suggest that both archetypal tragedy and archetypal comedy are biased images of life, depending on the modal prism of the author. These biases, which converge on the receiver's perception of the real world, are basically symmetric: toward extreme seriousness and extreme lightheartedness. The humorous mood neither negates nor reaffirms the tragic mood. In their linear form of combination, they can coexist even in the same fictional world, without upsetting the spectator's view of that world (see CHAPTER 1). In fact, the two moods are complementary perspectives on life — with the gaps between these perspectives and reality rather supporting the metaphoric nature of the tragic and comic fictional worlds, on the grounds of the inherent difference between these worlds and the receiver's world. Genre thus depends on the overall metaphor that an author wishes to offer for the spectator to experience. Otherwise, how can Scott consider the clown, in the guise of Charlie Chaplin, as the epitome of the 'comic rhythm of action' (Scott: 91); and Falstaff 'the original prototype of the existentialist man' (*ibid.*: 105), without invoking the notion of 'metaphor'?

The historical fact is that biased tragedy and comedy tend to appear and thrive together as two opposed and symmetric departures from what the spectator believes things really are. Such biases can be abolished, as shown by naturalistic drama; but at the cost of blurring the metaphoric gap and meaning.

In fact, Scott deals with satiric and grotesque fictional worlds. These genres often question the validity of established systems of values and, therefore, they may give the impression of promoting improved values, which deserve the status of genuine truth, whether they preach return to traditional values or adoption of innovative ones. However, the fact is that in all cases such fictional worlds are pre-structured to achieve a pre-determined experience that precludes any possibility of disclosing the 'whole truth'.

Bentley's 'enduring life'

Bentley asserts that '[t]he plain man goes wrong only if he assumes that comedy has nothing to do with pain at all' (p. 299). He observes: 'We conventionally consider comedy a gay and light-hearted form of art, . . . I am proposing instead, to regard misery as the basis of comedy and gaiety as an ever-recurring transcendence. Seen in this way, comedy, like tragedy, is a way of trying to cope with despair, mental suffering, guilt, and anxiety. But not the same way' (p. 301). Moreover, '[t]he comic dramatist's starting point is misery; the joy at his destination is a superb and thrilling transcendence. . . . Comedy is indirect, ironical. It says fun when it means misery. And when it lets the misery show, it is able to transcend it in joy' (p. 302). 'The comic sense tries to cope with the daily, hourly, inescapable difficulty of being. For if everyday life has an under-current or cross-current of the tragic, the main current is material for comedy' (p. 306). '[Comedic] tone says: life is fun. The undertone suggests that life is a catastrophe' (p. 312). Stott supports this insight by stating that 'laughter is the close cousin of pain' (p 146). Bentley concludes that 'tragedy and comedy have the same heuristic intent: self knowledge' (p. 309), albeit by different means.

In an attempt to integrate Bentley's and Langer's approaches, Corrigan sums up this trend in the theory of comedy in claiming that '[t]he constant in comedy is the comic view of life or the *comic spirit*: the sense that no matter how many times man is knocked down he somehow manages to pull himself up and keep on going. Thus, while tragedy is a celebration of man's capacity to aspire and suffer, comedy celebrates his capacity *to endure*' (p. 3; my italics).

Weitz echoes Bentley's approach in stating that '[a] happy ending seems generally to recompense the preceding obstacles and misfortunes in a "*vision of life*" which might tell us, for example, that perseverance is rewarded, that true contentment is somehow earned, or that things come right in the end. . . . a *vision of life* in which selfishness, corruption, hypocrisy or downright evil are sure to lose out in the end' (p. 36; my italics). Weitz too seems to have ignored the metaphoric and cathartic meanings of archetypal endings.

Basically, Bentley's view of comedy are variations on the previous approaches, and deserve a similar critique.

Vision vs. mood

Do the above approaches deal with actual comedies and tragedies or theoretical ones? These over-abstract formulas are probably deductive in nature, characterized by deriving features of comedy from abstract ideas, which defies any inductive approach; i.e., the analysis of actual comedies and generalization of findings. I would contend that the above-reviewed theories do not and cannot demonstrate their contentions. Furthermore, the extreme diversity of kinds and styles of what is usually termed 'comedy' precludes any possibility of reflecting a common vision. Although such theories apply to comedy together with the tangential genres, including satiric drama and grotesque drama, as suggested in this study, at most each of these genres could have been characterized as reflecting a unique vision, but not as offering a vision common to all.

Nonetheless, all the theories that promote the idea of an alleged comic vision are cognitive in nature. Even in the domain of comedy proper, the contention that all comedies convey a single cognitive perspective on the world contradicts the theoretical assumption that fictionality is a mode of thinking potentially capable of conveying different and even contradictory thoughts (Rozik, 2009). In general, it is not the role of comedy to tell the spectators how the world is or should be. The fact that the ultimate effect of a certain fictional world depends on what is held to be true or valid by the synchronic spectator corroborates this conclusion: usually, all genres are pre-structured and aim not at truth but at an experience of truth (Rozik, 2009: 162–72).

Rather than conveying a single perception of the world, comedies presuppose such perceptions, which are culture-dependent. Indeed, comedies have been written in different periods for different audiences with different perspectives on life. This principle holds true even for the same fictional world that may produce different effects in diachronic audiences; e.g., whereas the ending of *George Dandin* was probably perceived by Molière's contemporaries as an appropriate punishment for Dandin's class pretensions, it might be perceived as sheer absurdity by a modern audience.

In contrast to the above-mentioned theories, because of their complete preference for archetypal fictional worlds, comedies are pre-structured to reaffirm held values and views, and only aim at the catharsis of functional pressure. As defined above, 'functional pressure' is the anxiety produced by living by the rules and inhibitions of a synchronic culture. Therefore, it is the intention of comedy to momentarily suspend the effects of sources of pressure, only in order to impose them anew, with increased vigor. In this sense, comedy functions similarly to the various customs of carnival (see CHAPTER 10) and joke-telling (see CHAPTER 11).

Therefore, the common denominator of comedy is not the 'comic vision', but the comic mood (see CHAPTER 1), which is occasionally manifested in comic laughter (see CHAPTER 2). In principle, vision and mood not only pertain to different structural levels, ironic and modal respectively, but also belong in two different levels of experience. Whereas the comic vision, at least in the approaches surveyed above, is cognitive, i.e., a particular view on the nature of the world, which is meant to permeate all the fictional worlds within the domain of comedy; the comic mood is a kind of prism, which conditions the spectator's perception of the world, and which only fulfils a *momentary* cathartic function in the economy of the psyche. It is not the intention of comedy to promote the adoption of the comic mood as a mode of behavior in real life. The humorous mood implies not the abolition of established values, but the insight that their validity can occasionally be ignored in order to eventually reinstate seriousness. In its cathartic intent, it is as effective as carnival. The comic mood of comedy implies that there is an aspect of seriousness that undermines itself, if it is assumed that extreme anxiety, due to inhibitions, can unexpectedly erupt forcefully and in the wrong circumstances. Therefore, any culture based on inhibitions, and all human cultures are thus, must operate cathartic mechanisms in order to ensure their sound operation.

The humorous mood is a crucial component of the deep structure of the comedic fictional world, mainly of its overall metaphoric nature and rhetoric mechanism, thus revealing an author's overall intent. Therefore, for example, it is indeed possible that the comic mood, which is the fundamental specific difference of comedy, also conveys, albeit momentarily, an attitude to life that is inherently lighthearted, i.e., benevolent, tolerant and compassionate, while aiming at the catharsis of harmful anxiety. In contrast, satire conveys a basic attitude to life that is inherently severe; i.e., judgmental, intolerant and merciless, while usually precluding catharsis. However, none of these attitudes is equivalent to the allegedly shared vision.

✦

The Comic Vision

The conjecture that comedy conveys a unique vision, which is cognitive in nature, and shared by all the kinds of comedy in the current wide sense, does not stand to reason, even for comedy in the narrow sense of this study. Whereas vision and mood are categories on different structural levels (ironic and modal), only the humorous mood and its cathartic functions amount to a common trait of comedy proper. The trend that attempted the vindication of comedy on the grounds of a shared vision was, however, merely a fleeting fashion, and one which has provided no real insight into the nature of comedy.

Comedy in Different Media 13

Although this study focuses on comedy in theatre, this is not its only possible medium. Throughout more than two millennia, Aristotle's *Poetics* has inspired a vast body of studies on the principles that structure fictional worlds. Although most of these have been devoted to tragedies and comedies, including their possible performances on stage, by now it is quite evident that they can be generated by other media as well, cinema in particular, without affecting the fictional principles that structure them.

The notion of 'fictional world' should be understood as *reflecting the spontaneous (and originally preverbal) capacity of the brain to think through creating complex images of characters and their actions* (see CHAPTER 4). I thus suggest a fundamental distinction between arts that are capable of generating descriptions of such worlds and those that are not. The common denominator of all the arts that can describe fictional worlds, particularly comedies, is the imagistic nature of their medium/language; i.e., their being grafted upon the spontaneous ability of the human brain to produce mental images and employ them as units of a particular form of thinking. Obviously, only figurative arts, not abstract arts, are capable of generating descriptions of fictional worlds. In some cases this divide applies within a single art, such as the distinction between abstract and figurative painting/drawing, and between abstract and figurative ballet.

A fictional/imagistic text thus combines a fictional world, which is generated by poetic, aesthetic and rhetoric rules, and a describing text, which is generated by semiotic rules. Moreover, imagistic media and fictional worlds are mutually independent in the sense that the same medium can describe different fictional worlds and the same fictional world can be described by different media. Nonetheless, despite mutual independence, the semiotic and poetic components complement one another. This two-fold structure of the fictional-text, generated by two complementary systems, is shared by literary texts, which generate fictional worlds through the mutual complementation of the fictional system and language; i.e., through the ability of words to evoke images.

In speaking of the 'same fictional world' reference is made to the same characters that evince the same motives and perform the same actions, which reflect the same fictional structure, create the same overall metaphor, and indicate the same rhetoric intent. Nonetheless, even the translation of a fictional text from one medium to another is usually mediated by a creative interpretation; which is conditioned by the personality of the translating artist and the culture of the synchronic receivers. Although the effect of a medium cannot be ignored, I conjecture that in regard to the spectator's fictional experience it is marginal.

Most of the arts that generate descriptions of fictional worlds belong in the imagistic/iconic system, which consists of the following media: theatre, opera, figurative ballet, mime (pantomime), audio drama, painting/drawing, sculpture, strip cartoon, animation, puppet theatre, photo-novel, silent movie, cinema and TV drama. Additions to this list and combined texts are possible.

Unfortunately, traditional definitions of 'iconicity' do not consider its crucial imagistic element. I have suggested elsewhere that *'iconicity' should be redefined in terms of imagistic thinking and communication*, thus connecting iconic media to the natural faculty of the brain to produce images and employ them in thinking procedures. I support this definition through recent findings in neuroscience (Rozik, 2008a: 21–33).

The imagistic roots of iconicity

In *Philosophy in a New Key*, Susanne Langer claims that images are 'our readiest instruments for abstracting concepts from the tumbling stream of actual impressions. They make our primitive abstractions for us, they are our spontaneous embodiments of general ideas' (1976: 145). Furthermore, images are 'just as capable of [syntactic] *articulation*, i.e., of complex combination as words' (*ibid.*: 93). It follows that the image is the basic unit of this mode of thinking, which is thus anchored in perception, the 'raw material' of mental imagistic representation. In her view, 'thinking' presupposes two main conditions: representation of things in the mind and their manipulation *in absentia* (in the absence of stimuli); i.e., thinking takes place when such representations are disconnected from actual experience. This definition of thinking equally suits verbal and imagistic representation and thinking.

Conceiving of images as fundamental units of thought is amply supported by recent findings in neuroscience. In *Descartes' Error,* Antonio R. Damasio asserts that having a mind means 'the ability to display images internally and to order those images in a process called thought' (p. 89). Moreover, whatever is not 'imageable', including words and mathematical symbols, cannot be known and, therefore, cannot be manipulated by thought (p. 107). In *Image and Brain,* on the grounds of digital methodology, Stephen M. Kosslyn contends that '[i]magery [in the sense of mental representation] is a basic form of cognition, and plays a central role in many human activities — ranging from navigation to memory to creative problem solving' (1995, 1). He distinguishes between 'propositional' and 'depictive' representations, with the latter being stored in the brain spatially, like the objects they represent: 'Depictive representations convey meaning via their resemblance to an object, with parts of the representation corresponding to parts of the object' (*ibid.*: 5). 'Depictive' representation is thus synonymous with 'imagistic' representation.

Damasio distinguishes between 'perceptual images' (e.g., running your fingers over a smooth metal surface); 'recalled images', which occur when one conjures up a remembrance of things; and images 'recalled from plans of the future [that] are constructions of your organism's brain' (pp. 96–7). The latter should be conceived of as images that have been disconnected from actual experience and become units of thought. Such images are not exact reproductions of objects, qualities or acts, but a combination of faint reproduction and interpretation, 'a newly reconstructed version of the original' (p. 100).

Kosslyn characterizes thinking as hinging on two properties: 'First, information must be *represented* internally; and second, [...] information must be manipulated in order to draw inferences and conclusions' (1996: 959). He reconfirms thereby Langer's definition of 'thinking' in general, and thinking by means of images in particular.

The definition of 'iconicity' on the grounds of imagistic thinking poses two problems: first, spontaneous mental images are figments of the imagination, i.e., non-material entities, which cannot be communicated. They thus require a material carrier to enable the communication of their signifying function. I suggest, therefore, that the 'iconic unit' is an image imprinted on matter. In Saussurian terms, the imprinted image and the imprinted matter together constitute the signifier of the iconic unit (cf. Saussure: 99); e.g., the image of a smile as imprinted on the face of an actor.

Second, in contrast to words, spontaneous mental images carry diffuse signifieds. In particular, they do not determine clear boundaries between core sense and associative peripheries, often personal in nature, making interpersonal communication problematic. I suggest, therefore, that in order to become an established cultural medium, iconicity requires the mediation of a language, which is the main repository of relatively controlled abstractions in any culture. Assumedly, mediation is spontaneous because a brain conditioned by a language naturally assigns signifieds to iconic units, according to the words that conventionally categorize their models; e.g., the signified of the word 'smile' to the imprinted image of a smile. It is precisely in this sense that an imprinted image of an object and the verbal sentences used to describe it are equivalent in different systems of signification. This implies that understanding an iconic text presupposes linguistic competence.

An image thus becomes a cultural unit of representation and communication, which can be used as a unit of thinking and description of thoughts, under two conditions: imprinting on matter and mediation of language. Moreover, according to speech act theory, speech acts are equivalent to nonverbal acts and, therefore, for example, an image of a verbal promise can be imprinted on an actor's voice, face and body, and mediated by the word 'promise'.

The definition of 'iconicity' in terms of 'imagistic thinking' does not contradict the traditional semiotic definition of 'iconicity' in terms of 'motivation through similarity' to real models (Peirce: 2.2.47 & 2.274–308), because the notion of 'image' implies 'similarity' to these models; e.g., between an image of a smile and a real smile. In this context, 'motivation' means that an iconic text can be read without learning the medium. In addition, the new definition of 'iconicity' in imagistic terms (a) *connects the iconic unit to the natural faculty of the brain to produce images and employ them as units of thinking*; and (b) *expands the set of its models to images created in the mind.*

In this sense, iconic media, including theatre, are nonverbal by definition. The imprinting and language mediation of these images enables the generation of iconic texts, which are descriptions of fictional worlds, comedies in particular, and which are as univocal as verbal descriptions are.

In contrast to literature, iconic media afford a particularly suitable method for describing fictional worlds in conveying the spontaneously created images of such worlds in the mind through the imprinting of these images on matter. Nonetheless, language too should be perceived as an imagistic medium, in communicating images by the evocative power of words. Whatever the medium, the analysis of an imagistic/

iconic text aims at grasping the nature of a fictional thought embodied in it (Rozik, 2009).

Limitations and compensations

The principle of 'iconicity', as defined in this study, bestows homogeneity not only on each iconic medium, but also on the entire set of iconic media — thus enabling their combination in a single description of a fictional world, without impairing the reading, interpreting and experiencing capacities of the spectator, and even the translation from one medium to another. Nonetheless, this homogeneity does not blur the evident differences between them, the limitations that characterize each iconic medium in particular. Furthermore, whereas a fictional world requires the ability of an iconic medium to fully describe it, each medium compensates its limitations through medium conventions. The following paragraphs focus on several specific traits of different iconic media and their typical limitations and compensations, which in their specific configurations characterize each medium.

(A) *Similar vs. dissimilar imprinting matter:* An iconic description of a fictional interaction presupposes materiality, due to being a macro-image imprinted on matter. Although all iconic media imprint their images on matter, each medium is characterized by the particular nature of its imprinting matter. A basic distinction should be made between iconic arts that use matters different from those of their models, which highlight their signifying and communicative functions, e.g., painting, sculpture and puppet theatre; and those that expand the principle of 'similarity' to the material level, which adds a dimension of similarity to their real models, e.g., theatre, figurative ballet and cinema, which imprint images of human beings on real actors, images of garments on real fabric, and images of light on real light. This similarity, however, does not hinder their signifying and communicative functions. On this level there is no need for medium conventions.

(B) *Temporal vs. atemporal media:* A description of a fictional interaction presupposes temporality, because of its basic similarity to real interaction. While some iconic media exhibit the ability to produce a sense of passing time, which adds a dimension of similarity to their descriptions, e.g., theatre, puppet theatre and cinema, other iconic media lack it; e.g., painting, sculpture and still photography.

It might be difficult to see how a single figurative painting or sculpture can describe an entire fictional world, which is a complex of characters and their interactions deployed on the time axis. However, such a work can allude to and evoke a source-text that features its full description, including its time dimension, which presupposes its knowledge by the audience. On such intertextual grounds, a single picture or sculpture functions as a prism through which an entire narrative is perceived, while possibly offering an alternative interpretation.

A single-frame iconic art can also overcome its handicap through a series of discrete frames that convey a sense of elapsing time through the conventional alignment of single images in the typical order of a specific verbal culture (from left to right in English or the opposite in Semitic cultures), creating thereby a sequence that spatializes the temporal nature of the fictional world.

(c) *Dynamic vs. static media*: A description of a fictional interaction presupposes dynamism, because of its basic similarity to real interaction. 'Iconic dynamism' means here the generation of continuous sequences of images, separated and reconnected by transitional and neutral positions of expressive organs, which create the semblance of fluidity typical of real human behavior. Whereas some iconic media exhibit this ability, e.g., theatre, opera and cinema, other iconic media lack it; e.g., strip cartoon and photo-novel — with the two latter resulting in a series of discrete static images.

This limitation is overcome by animation: static pictures or inert puppets can create the illusion of a dynamic medium by projecting sequences of them at a certain speed through a mechanical device. In fact, cinema too decomposes dynamic acting in front of a camera into discrete static frames, and screens them by a mechanical device that recreates the impression of a dynamic medium.

(d) *Spatial vs. non-spatial media*: The iconic description of a fictional interaction presupposes specific locations; which imply three-dimensional space and a certain measure of continuity between particular places. Whereas three-dimensional media add an aspect of similarity to real models, e.g., opera, figurative ballet and sculpture, two-dimensional arts do not; e.g., painting, still photography and cinema.

Two-dimensional arts, such as painting and drawing, enable the description of fictional three-dimensional space by means of various conventions such as foreshortening and perspective. Still photography and cinema are perspectival in nature: they project a spatial object (e.g., the actors in front of the camera) onto a two-dimensional surface (paper or screen). Audio drama, which lacks the ability to represent space, overcomes this limitation by sound effects that can evoke a three-dimensional space such as the sounds of a passing train, a market place or a concert hall.

(E) *Speechful vs. speechless media*: The iconic description of a fictional interaction presupposes speech, which is a fundamental form of real or fictional interaction. A distinction should be made between iconic media that articulate speech, such as theatre, opera and audio drama, and those that do not such as photo-novel, figurative ballet and silent movie. Whereas the former create an additional aspect of similarity to real models, the latter do not. Moreover, whereas the former articulate images of speech by actors that imprint them on their vocal organs, the latter employ various conventions for overcoming this handicap; e.g., speech balloons, printed speech and voice-over.

(F) *Prosaic vs. stylized media*: A description of a fictional interaction presupposes that, like its real models, a fictional world is 'prosaic', in the sense of not being stylized to an extreme degree. In contrast, there are iconic media that aim at producing an enhanced aesthetic effect in the receivers through the addition of music, singing and/or dancing such as opera and figurative dance.

Music, singing and dancing should be seen as stage conventions, fulfilling a stylizing function because in their own worlds characters do not sing and/or dance to music under similar circumstances; e.g., in opera stage monologues become arias, dialogues — duets, and choruses — choral songs.

(G) *Recording/reproducing media*: There are iconic arts that, in addition to the description of a fictional interaction, record or reproduce such texts. A recording or a reproduction does not impinge on the iconic nature of the recorded text, but preserves its semiotic nature. If the recorded object is iconic it should be read as an iconic text, and if its verbal as a verbal text. Therefore, recording or reproduction can be employed for any kind of iconic text; e.g., moving photography in cinematic drama and reproduction in pictorial arts. I have suggested elsewhere that cinema is the recording of the description of a fictional world generated by the theatre medium (Rozik, 2005a). In other words, it records the acting of actors, according to the rules of theatrical acting, in front of a camera. Since film recording is restricted to the visual aspects of acting, it is compensated by the parallel recording of voice (the sound track).

From the viewpoint of the receiver the method of recording/reproduction is immaterial, because the iconic description of a fictional interaction exists already in the recorded/reproduced object. In principle, for example in cinema, such a recording is an indexical phenomenon, in being the traces left by its iconic object on two mechanical devices; e.g., film and sound track. Similar considerations apply to the reproduction of a pictorial work.

Although iconic conventions partly or totally cancel the principle of 'motivation through similarity', which defines them as such, they are nonetheless images imprinted on matter, as otherwise their perception by the receiver would be precluded.

Representative examples

On the grounds of their shared iconicity and particular limitations and compensations, each medium evinces a particular configuration of them. On such grounds, two major distinctions emerge: (a) between dramatic and pictorial iconic media; and (b) between straightforward iconic media (dramatic and pictorial) and recording/reproducing ones — with the latter presupposing the former. For reasons of efficiency, I suggest three main prototypes as representing three groups of fictional/iconic arts: theatre as the prototype of the dramatic media; painting/drawing as the prototype of the pictorial media; and cinema as the prototype of the recording/reproducing media.

(A) *The dramatic group*: 'Dramatic' is used here in the original sense of representation of a narrative by enacted action (Introduction). The theatre prototype is characterized by the imprinting of images of fictional interaction on similar matters; e.g., images of human characters on live actors, images of costume on real fabric and images of light on real light. It is also a temporal, dynamic, three-dimensional and speechful medium. Its aesthetic effects are achieved not only on the level of the poetic structure of a fictional world, but also on visual and aural grounds. In this sense, opera and figurative ballet are texts generated by the theatre medium, while differing in their additional stylization by music, singing and dancing respectively. Audio drama and mime too are generated by the theatre medium, while differing from theatre in their lack of spatial and aural dimensions respectively, and compensation by particular conventions.

(B) *The pictorial group*: The painting/drawing prototype is characterized by imprinting its images on matters dissimilar to their models. It is also an atemporal, static, two-dimensional and speechless medium. Its aesthetic effects are achieved not only on the level of the poetic structure of a fictional world, but also on visual grounds. Similar considerations apply to sculpture, which only differs by its three-dimensional nature. The strip-cartoon medium overcomes the temporal and dynamic limitations of the single-frame cartoon by spatialization of time. This medium also overcomes speechlessness by various conventions such as speech-balloons and conventional hand gestures. Thoughts are represented by thought-balloons. The animated cartoon overcomes the static nature of the strip cartoon by the mechanical projection of static frames in a way that creates the impression of a dynamic medium; and overcomes speechlessness by live or recorded voice-over. Puppet theatre should be seen as a combination of animated sculptures and voice-over.

(c) *The recording/reproducing group*: The cinematic prototype is characterized by the dual recording (visual and aural) of its dramatic object, such as theatre, opera and figurative ballet, through photography and sound track. As recording devices these are indifferent to the nature of their objects, whether fictional or real. Similar considerations apply to the reproduction of a static art work such as a painting, a drawing and a sculpture.

The following examples relate to the descriptions of Shakespeare's *Twelfth Night* in different imagistic/iconic media, which illustrate the above-suggested groupings. These descriptions should be seen as translations from the stage production in the medium of theatre, which reflects the intention of the play-script, to other media, under the assumption that each translation is mediated by a creative interpretation.

Twelfth Night in the dramatic group

Basically, the theatrical nature of the production of a play-script does not need illustration, in being written for the stage. In this context, however, the intention is to show that even in the context of the same medium each new production is mediated by a unique interpretation, which reflects not only the viewpoint of the diachronic director, but also the new perceptions and expectations of the synchronic audience. For example, in the production of *Twelfth Night* at the Windham Theatre, London, director Michael Grandage perceived the mistaken identities of the characters as indicating not the blurred borderline between the sexes, but their comic potential. The emphasis on the comic mood was manifested in the prominence of the trickery played on Malvolio, and especially in the choice of Derek Jacobi for this role. This interpretive approach, which marginalized the romantic action, was probably influenced by the play-script being written in the carnivalesque spirit of twelfth night, which explains Viola's disguise, the mistaken genders, the comic rebellion of the servants against Olivia's steward, and the central

15 Feste, Olivia and Sebastian, in the Khan Theatre *Twelfth Night*.
Photo: Yael Ilan. Courtesy of the Jerusalem Khan Theatre.

function of Feste, the fool, as the representative of the spirit of carnival in this fictional world (see CHAPTER 10).

The comic mood also prevailed in the Jerusalem Khan Theatre production of *Twelfth Night*, directed by Udi Ben-Moshe (2011), by stressing the comic potential of Sir Toby Belch and Sir Andrew Ague-cheek and the trickery on Malvolio. In contrast, Feste is interpreted as a rather mature, wise and sad fool.

In the context of the dramatic group it is worth mentioning the opera version of *Twelfth Night*, libretto by Joseph Papp and music by David Amram, New York, at the Summer Musical Theater; the ballet version, choreography by Boris Eifman, at the Academy of Ballet, Saint Petersburg; and the radio version of *Twelfth Night* by Radio 3, BBC.

Twelfth Night in the pictorial group

As I have claimed above, a single picture can describe an entire fictional world, under two conditions: (a) that it maintains an inter-textual rela-tion with a source-text that describes the entire fictional world in all its dimensions; and (b) that it provides an alternative interpretation of the entire fictional world (Rozik, 2007). These conditions are met by Walter Howel Deverell's painting *Twelfth Night*, which relates to act II, scene iv in Shakespeare's play-script (see internet).

In the original play-script, this scene confronts two themes: love and death. Gloomy Orsino asks Feste to console his spirit by music, and the fool sings, first, 'What is love' and, then, 'Come away. Come away, death'. Whereas the former laments the cruel nature of love, the latter echoes the Duke's deeply frustrated love.

The fool thus reflects the non-expressed contents of his master's mind through the romantic theme of the umbilical bond between unreciprocated love and death (see CHAPTER 10). Indeed, in the source-text, the absurdity of love is conveyed by the typical image of a chain of unrequited love: Viola loves Orsino, who loves Olivia, who loves no one. The situation seems to worsen when Olivia falls in love with Cesario (Viola) and is reciprocated by Sebastian. Despite complication, this leads toward the final harmonious disentanglement: when Viola reveals her true gender, the marriage of Olivia and Sebastian becomes satisfactory, and Orsino can reciprocate Viola's love. Orsino's thoughts of death are then conquered by true love.

In contrast to the play-script, which focuses on two main characters, Viola and Malvolio, the painting suggests a different focal point: Orsino.

16 Sad Orsino, in the Khan Theatre *Twelfth Night*.
Photo: Yael Ilan. Courtesy of the Jerusalem Khan Theatre.

He sits at the apex of a triangular group, flanked by Viola and Feste. Viola, in male attire, conveys a deep sense of love, yearning and dependency; and Feste, in his fool's attire, conveys a sense of judicious serenity. These are reflected in their facial expressions and bodily postures. While Viola adds a romantic touch, Feste adds a touch of Silenus' wisdom. The entire group, in the forefront of the picture, ignores (sits with their backs to) the crowd behind, who are probably celebrating and enjoying the merry atmosphere of twelfth night, against the background of a pastoral landscape, which represents Illyria. Orsino's disregard of the revelers emphasizes his gloom. Comic Malvolio is absent. It can be conjectured that Deverell views this fictional world as revolving around the basic human contrast between love and death.

In the context of the pictorial group it is worth mentioning Oscar Zarate's cartoon version of *Twelfth Night*; Maria Muat's animated version of *Twelfth Night*; and Vit Horejs' puppet theatre version of *Twelfth Night*, by the Czech-American Marionette Theatre. It can be argued that these are mere illustrations of the play-script; but even the simple attribution of alternative facial traits should be seen as reflecting a creative interpretation of the fictional world. In particular, this applies to Horejs' production, which is definitely in the spirit of farce.

Twelfth Night in the recording and reproducing group

The cinematic version of *Twelfth Night*, directed by Trevor Nunn, was produced especially for this medium. The film was shot in Cornwall, which enacts the landscape of Illyria. The costumes indicate that the action takes place during the nineteenth century. This location and period add to the fictional action not only the metaphoric connotations of the unbridgeable class gap (Malvolio's narrative), typical of the period, but also the romantic aura usually attributed to it (Orsino and Viola's narrative).

The acting is essentially realistic, theatrical and even melodramatic in nature: for example, the additional scenes dedicated to the sinking of the ship in a storm, the extreme sadness of Orsino, and the final encounter between the brothers. The serious mood even permeates the comic scenes of trickery, which are themselves almost serious in mood. The dialogic action follows the play-script, except for Feste's prologue.

Nunn adds a filmed introduction to the original action. Before the depiction of the storm and actual sinking of the ship, Viola and Sebastian perform a comic song, disguised as oriental women, to the applause of the voyagers. At the end, they take off their veils to reveal their moustaches. As the laughter increases, they then remove the moustaches to reveal that (allegedly) both are women. This scene is the key to Nunn's interpretation of the play-script in focusing on the equivocal and shifting differences between the sexes, which are simply a matter of appearances. This motif is cleary manifested in Viola's attempts to hide her femininity when disguising herself as Cesario: cutting her hair, flattening her bosom, affixing a moustache, wearing masculine garments, and adopting manly skills such as billiards and fencing.

In Nunn's interpretation, the main character is Feste, enacted by Ben Kingsley. He already witnesses Viola's arrival on the beach at Illyria and her first attempts to disguise herself as Cesario, including the gesture of throwing away her gold necklace, a symbol of femininity. After the happy ending, the film ends with Feste leaving Olivia's palace, with the guitar on his back, like a wandering troubadour. Nunn bestows upon this character a kind of omniscience, which is reflected not only in his songs of love and death, but also in his returning the necklace to Viola, when she reveals her true gender. It is possible that Feste is made to transcend the traditional role of fool, but is also possible that he is made to realize its full potential in Shakespeare's play-script.

In the context of the recording/reproducing media, it is worth mentioning the recorded audio casette of *Twelfth Night* by Radio 3, BBC, 2006, and the reproductions of Deverell's painting *Twelfth Night.*

The theatre medium is not the only possible medium of comedy. In addition to literature, whose imagistic nature was suggested above, all iconic media can generate descriptions of comedic fictional worlds. In order to substantiate this claim, 'iconicity' has been redefined here in terms of 'imagistic thinking'; i.e., as being grafted upon the spontaneous ability of the human brain to produce mental images imprinted on matter and mediated by language, and to employ them as the basic units of the particular mode of fictional thinking,

Reception of Comedy

14

The theatre experience results not only from the nature of the enacted fictional world on stage, but also from its interaction with the spectator, whose contribution to the generation of fictional meaning is no less crucial than that of the descriptive text. For all genres, the spectator is expected to provide indispensable competences, such as accurate framing, theatre medium literacy, associative capacity, interpretive ability, and psychical mechanisms, of which the latter are biologically determined and culturally conditioned. Without these competences and mechanisms no description of a fictional world can generate meaning. A description of a fictional world should thus be seen as a set of cues for the spectator to activate these capacities.

Because of the communal nature of the theatre experience, comedy in particular, a theatre fictional world also embodies the fundamental authorial expectation that a synchronic audience react in unison. The structural control of a theatre-text on its audience is, therefore, much tighter than that by any other fictional art, including literature. In theatre, such a fictional world thus tends to address a fairly wide and shallow common denominator of a synchronic audience, even if it also features additional strata for the more sophisticated spectators.

The assumption of a homogeneous group of spectators is usually termed 'unity of audience'. Taking into account the common values of a synchronic audience is the necessary condition for a comedy to be seen as a meaningful text (see CHAPTER 5). The fact that what is perceived as humorous in one culture may not be thus in another culture corroborates this condition. Authors of comedies probably create descriptions of fictional worlds under the assumption that all the members of such a cultural community are capable of framing, reading, interpreting and experiencing such texts as expected and, in general, of complementing them from their own associative resources or, rather 'cultural baggage', which includes familiarity with the tradition of comedy.

'Unity of audience' rests not only on such a shared cultural baggage, but also on a deeper common denominator: their shared inborn psychical mechanisms of response that, albeit culturally-conditioned, also explain their expected homogeneous response. As suggested above, inhibitions and taboos are culturally-dependent. Every cultural group, including western culture, evinces some kind of unity, as otherwise the comedic experience would be unconceivable.

In addressing the role of the spectator, I suggest *a basic distinction between 'real' and 'implied' spectator*. While the former is usually restricted in various respects, *the latter assumedly possesses all the expected competences for complementing a description of a fictional world and the psychical mechanisms for experiencing it as expected*. I also suggest that *there is an implied dialogue between an implied author and an implied spectator*, which reflects an authorial intuition of the expected real dialogue between real director and real spectator.

Real vs. implied spectator

Following Wolfgang Iser, 'implied spectator' means here the set of cultural competences and psychical mechanisms presupposed in the spectator for a description of a fictional world to make sense (cf. Iser: 34; Marinis: 163–4; & Kaynar). Whereas the real spectator may reveal various handicaps, such as deficient knowledge of the theatre medium, interpretive limitations, incomplete cultural baggage, and psychical biases and inhibitions, *the implied spectator is totally and adequately equipped by definition*, which makes it an integral partner in the process of generating fictional meaning.

It is the real spectator, however, who actually experiences a comedic fictional world. I suggest, therefore, that *the implied spectator is a theoretical construct that reveals an authorial speculation in regard to the real synchronic spectator, and that the success of a comedic fictional world mostly depends on the degree of correspondence between conjecture and reality*. Moreover, since interpretations and experiences of real spectators take place even if they fail to meet authorial expectations, *the analysis of a comedy should focus not on whether the expected contributions are realized or not, but on the nature of the contributions that are expected from the implied spectator*. In this sense the implied spectator is a necessary theoretical assumption in the interpretation of a comedy. Only reception analysis, with all its typical limitations, should be conducted on the grounds of real experiences.

Not only is the notion of 'implied spectator' a construct, but so too is the notion of 'real spectator', possibly influenced by crude generalizations about a social group, usually fostered by journalistic sociology. Rather than the experience of an alleged 'real spectator', the personal experience of the trained scholar should be preferred, as it can serve as a corrective for unfounded generalizations and conclusions.

A comedy usually prescribes not only what is required for generating its meaning but also features restrictive clues 'to prevent a theoretically infinite proliferation of readings' (Marinis: 168). In contrast to Iser's contention, the pre-structured nature of a fictional world reveals that it is not the implied spectator that opens it up to multiple interpretations, but the real one (cf. Iser: 37).

In particular, in interpreting a play-script there is no point in taking into account whatever association may occur in the implied spectator's mind, especially in regard to inter-textual associations. The latter are relevant only if the source-text is known or, rather, is supposed to be known by the real spectator, in order to complement a text as expected by its author. If not, these associations are superfluous. An association must be necessary in the sense that without it the hermeneutic interpretation of a fictional world is impaired. Segal, who follows the linear order of reading a play-script, reveals his own vast familiarity with a comedy's cultural background and provides highly interesting associations. Nonetheless, some of them cannot be integrated into the interpretation. It is the task of the implied spectator to distinguish between what should be retained and what should be ignored.

Implied spectator and reception

The implied spectator of comedy confronts a highly complex text that requires additional inputs, further organization and final integration into a complex unity in order to generate its meaning. This spectator is expected to read and gather scattered pieces of information from the various parts of a text, and bestow order upon them; as well as to complement the description of a comedic fictional world through (a) framing, reading and interpreting abilities, (b) evoking associations from a shared cultural baggage, and (c) activating psychical mechanisms of experience.

(A) *Framing, reading and interpretative abilities*: The implied spectator is supposed to be proficient in adequately framing a theatrical event. Erving Goffman postulates that framing is a precondition for making sense of any event and, by implication, of any experience of a fictional text. Framing logically precedes reading and interpretation, because of determining the rules to be applied (p. 21). In particular, whatever the medium, a fictional world is meant to be appropriately framed as a 'comedy' prior to its reading and interpretation (cf. Rozik, 2008a: 164–6). Weitz suggests that framing is a crucial activity: '*as part of reading comedy effectively means knowing to take it as comedy*' (p. 34). He expands in analyzing examples of initial dialogues in comedies, which already signal to the spectators that they are about to watch a comedy (pp. 26–35). As suggested above, the mere creation of a comic atmosphere increases laughter (see CHAPTER 2). Adverts, programs and reviews, even by merely labeling a production as 'comedy', also fulfil the function of genre markers.

The implied spectator is also supposed to be proficient in reading theatre texts. In particular, this spectator should approach a theatre text according to the rules of its medium. It is the performance of a comedy on stage that is considered such a text. In contrast, the play-script should be perceived as a verbal notation of only the verbal components of a performance-text, written for the purpose of its performance. The notion of 'reading' ('decoding' in traditional terms) should be understood here in a wide sense that applies to all verbal and nonverbal media; i.e., in Ferdinand de Saussure's terms, to the inference of the signified layer from the signifier layer (cf. Rozik, 2002: 166–8). *Reading a comedy thus presupposes medium literacy*.

The implied spectator is also assumed to be proficient in the interpretation of a comedic performance-text beyond reading. This spectator is expected to transmute a multitude of partial clues communicated on the axis of time, first into motif clusters and finally into a complex, atemporal and unified whole unit of meaning. (cf. Rozik, 2002: 168–71)

Interpretation also presupposes the ability to contextualize what has been read. Several kinds of contextualization can be discerned: (a) *intra-textual*: perceiving each expression in the context of the verbal and nonverbal associations evoked by a motif within a comedic performance-text, e.g., the motif of 'stinginess' in Plautus' *The Pot of Gold*; (b) *inter-textual*: perceiving a comedic narrative in the context of associations evoked by explicit or implicit reference to other comedies, canonic in particular, including source play-scripts and previous performances of it, e.g., the relation between Molière's *Amphitryon* and Plautus' *Amphitryon*; and (c) *extra-textual*: perceiving a comedy in the context of associations evoked by explicit or implicit reference to the actual political and socio-cultural context. Although this is typical of satire, e.g., Hal Ashby's film *Being There*, it is often relevant to comedy as well. Associations activated by single words or figures of speech, such as symbols and metaphors, are also extra-textual in nature. Such contextu-alizations can be either conscious or not. In other words, the appropriate interpretation of a comedy presupposes an audience that shares a cultural baggage.

(B) *Evoking associations from a shared cultural baggage*: In inter-preting a comedy, the implied spectator is expected to complement what is not and/or cannot be articulated in the text; i.e., to provide associa-tions from its "own" resources, which are meant to complement the description of a fictional world. The necessity for such associations can hardly be 'verified' in a scientific sense, and their validity is supported only by considerations of fullness and coherence. 'Cultural baggage' means familiarity with culturally-established contexts; of particular importance being the 'theatrical baggage', which *inter alia* includes knowledge of comedic play-scripts, previous performances of them, and earlier productions of the performed comedy by directors and actors.

'Cultural baggage' encompasses not only information, but also a vast periphery of sensory and emotive connotations. The notion 'connotation' indiscriminately applies to both verbal and nonverbal associations — with the latter being crucial for both partial metaphors and symbols and the metaphoric nature of an entire fictional world.

Within the framework of the cultural baggage, the ethical system on which the implied spectator's sense of orientation in the world rests is of outstanding importance, due to the rhetoric/enthymematic intent embodied in the description of a fictional world, which presupposes the values of a synchronic audience. In particular, in regard to comedy, the cultural baggage also includes prejudices and stereotypes; e.g., Molière's *The School for Wives*, which presupposes that the exposure of the betrayed husband to social ridicule is typical of the synchronic culture. Weitz contends that the playwright writes also for the future spectator (p. 94). However, he ignores the fact that a dated play-script can make sense to a diachronic audience only through the mediation of a creative interpretation, which takes into account different terms of reference and a different synchronic system of values. Even a translation from language to language, not to mention from medium to medium, fulfills such a function.

(C) *Activating psychical mechanisms of experience*: A central claim of this study is that the deep structure of the fictional world reflects the psychical mechanisms of response of the implied spectator; i.e., its tendency to react according to its culturally-conditioned wishes and anxieties; i.e., to its archetypal expectations. Comedies should be seen, therefore, as not only mirroring such patterns of response, grafted upon

216

innate psychical mechanisms, but also as pre-structured to manipulate these mechanisms toward an expected cognitive and emotional effect. It is on these mechanisms that the pre-structured rhetoric impact relies. A comedy thus constitutes a complex set of clues by which to activate these mechanisms. *Although psychical mechanisms operate different values and inhibitions in different cultures, the psychical patterns of response are assumedly the same across cultures.* These mechanisms are:

(1) *Catharsis*: This psychical mechanism is presupposed by comedy on two levels: comic laughter, which is optional, and holistic catharsis (see CHAPTER 4). It is the intention of comedy to increase anxiety and to release it at its peak. From the viewpoint of the spectator's experience, as suggested above, comedy presupposes the existence of a single cathartic mechanism that can serve as an outlet for augmented anxiety and that can be activated by either ludicrous episodes (comic laughter) or the entire archetypal fictional world (holistic catharsis) (see CHAPTER 4). The existence of this mechanism also explains the shocking effect when the activation of the cathartic mechanism is intentionally prevented, which is typical not of comedy, but of satiric drama.

These two kinds of catharsis presuppose that a comedy increases anxiety, which is grafted upon the pre-existing diffuse anxiety produced by daily life lived according to established rules of behavior and inhibitions. Comedy typically increases anxiety by lifting the inhibitions characteristic of a synchronic culture (Freud 1989: 70–143), and confronting the spectator with their stage embodiments. The implied spectator is thus perceived as a combination of permitted and inhibited (shameful/suppressed) drives.

An inhibition is lifted when something shameful or suppressed is made explicit by verbal or imagistic representation; e.g., as a drive of a character. In contrast to Freud, I contend that the lifting of an inhibition does not release anxiety but increases it, which is a precondition for both comic laughter and holistic catharsis. In other words, the lifting of inhibitions is a serious matter and not cathartic in itself.

Comedy is built upon the spectators' fear of failure, which may disclose them as stupid and/or clumsy. Any drive that might produce such a ludicrous failure is consequently inhibited. Comic laughter happens when a lifted inhibition is made to be perceived as causing a foolish failure (see CHAPTER 2). Since what is perceived as stupid or clumsy is culturally-dependent, the understanding of comedy presupposes knowledge of the synchronic models of harmony in the spectators minds. In other words, anxiety is produced by the mere prospect of ludicrous failure, and cathartic laughter is produced by the intuition that the embodiment of ludicrous failure reflects comic intent. As suggested above, the conditions of comic laughter are: failure, foolishness, anxiety, lack of pity, and sudden change of mood (see CHAPTER 2).

Holistic catharsis happens when a peripeteia brings about the realization of the spectator's archetypal expectations, against the background of the anxiety that the action may frustrate them (see CHAPTER 4). In order to achieve this purpose, the fictional action must promote the possibility of an undesired ending in order to increase the level of anxiety that ensures its powerful release and concomitant pleasure.

Spectators employ psychical energy to inhibit behaviors that might be perceived as ridiculous, and comedy enables confrontation with characters that intentionally and freely embody stupidity and/or clumsiness — thus lifting such inhibitions. It is this process that both increases anxiety and enables its powerful and extremely pleasant discharge. The principle of 'catharsis' thus explains why comedy taps and mines shameful and suppressed contents of the psyche, in order to transmute them into possible sources of pleasure. Catharsis does not operate in order to abolish inhibitions, but to afford people momentary relief in order to reestablish the validity of these inhibitions and to enable the proper function of their psyches.

This is also the reason why comedic characters are such personified/metaphoric embodiments of drives and actions that can be perceived as stupid or clumsy. Since the lighthearted mood usually permeates an entire fictional world, the rhetoric intention is to convey an overall metaphor of harmony and to persuade the audience to accept this lighthearted perspective on the world, even if only for the moment.

(2) *Dramatic irony*: Comedy also bestows dramatic irony on the spectator. The real spectator in real life is inherently deprived of an ironic perspective, which is only accorded to God (see CHAPTER 3). The implied spectator, in contrast, is given a superior knowledge and understanding of the worlds of the characters, a detached attitude and freedom of judgment, which the characters lack — thus providing an additional source of possible pleasure. The implied spectator is also given the right to perceive the fictional world in the terms of its own culture, which often differ from those of the characters. Comedy thus bestows on the implied spectator a basic sense of superiority that is probably also a pre-condition for laughter. By the very same authority, authors may deny dramatic irony to the implied spectator, which thus becomes the object of fictional irony, by deliberately and consistently precluding the means that ensure this spectator's superiority. This option, however, is not typical of comedy, which substantiates the archetypal structure of the fictional world.

Dramatic irony presupposes the psychical ability of the spectator to gather all the pieces of information wherever they appear, reorganize them in clusters of motifs, including characters, and apply them to the perception of a character and its whole world. It also assumes the spectator's ability to grasp metonyms of ethical systems scattered in the comedic text, especially those provided by functional characters or interacting characters in functional situations, process them accordingly, apply them to the fictional world, and give preference to the ironic viewpoint.

(3) *Models of harmony*: The ultimate gratification of the implied spectator's expectations depends on its operating, first, spontaneous expectations that are biologically-determined and culturally-conditioned, which in this study are termed 'archetypal expectations'. These have a structural function because they project themselves onto an entire fictional world until they are finally gratified or frustrated. And second, such expectations presuppose the existence of models of harmony in the spectator's mind; in particular models of proportion between the ethical nature of a motive and its final success or failure.

It might appear that the existence of models of harmony in the implied spectator's psyche leads to the conclusion that the spectator assesses the characters according to his own personal experience. Indeed, it is widely assumed that the spectator is the standard of all genres. However, although this is true with regard to the synchronic values of a certain culture, personal experience does not affect models of harmony, which are archetypal in nature; i.e., prior to and affecting experience. I conjecture, for example, that the archetypal expectation that two young people will consummate their love and that the old man's desire should be frustrated is also shared by elderly spectators. It is in this sense that a psychical model is the standard of a comedic fictional world; and that the implied spectator operates this standard.

An absurdist situation, such as the initial success of an ethically negative or ludicrous character, naturally produces archetypal expectations for its eventual failure; or the suffering of a positive character naturally produces archetypal expectations for its eventual success. Such expectations presuppose that the human psyche has the faculty to spontaneously develop both wishful and fearful expectations for either final harmony or absurdity respectively. It is the two-fold experience of concomitant fearful and wishful thinking that underlies the spectator's experience of suspense.

Comedy presupposes the implied spectator's archetypal need for its ethos to prevail, which is tantamount to the archetypal need for a harmonious metaphor of the world. Without such an assumption the final harmonious accord of comedy could not make sense. This fundamental expectation explains not only comedy's predilection for archetypal endings, but also for *deus ex machina* (see CHAPTER 5).

(4) *Multiple identification*: If a fictional world is the expression of the single psyche of an author through a multiple world of characters and their actions, it follows that each character is a personification of a partial agency or drive in his/her psyche. Since personification is a specific kind of metaphor whose source of referential associations is the human domain, it also follows that the entire fictional world is built upon a metaphoric infrastructure; i.e., is a complex metaphor of the author's psychical state of affairs.

Such 'multiple-personification' thus implies that the fictional world is a self-referential expression of the playwright. Assumedly, in the process of reception an interchange of referents takes place, through which the implied spectator becomes the referent of the comedic text, merely by adopting the fictional world as an expression of itself. Consequently, this spectator cannot identify solely with a single character, usually a positive one, but must do so with the entire fictional world; i.e., there is multiple-identification with all the interactive characters of a fictional world, including the virtuous, the depraved, the buffoonish and the ludicrous.

The buffoon and the boor are thus not foreign to the psyche, but the personifications of both desired and dreaded qualities and drives. At most, it is possible to speak of positive and negative identification. The principle of 'multiple identification' is advantageous in an additional sense: it explains both the appeal of ludicrous characters *at* which the spectator tends to laugh, and the anxiety in confronting them. Similar considerations apply to buffoonish characters *with* which the spectator tends to laugh. The implication is that the implied spectator is endowed with a psychical mechanism of multiple-identification.

(5) *Detachment*: In many a case *the implied spectator is expected to neutralize involvement and exercise a detached or, rather, defamiliarized attitude in order for its cognitive faculties to take over.* Bertolt Brecht made a substantial contribution to the understanding and operation of this mechanism, which is epitomized in his *'verfremdungseffekt'* (defamiliarization effect), widely employed in modernist and post-modernist criticism (Willett: various; cf. Rozik, 2005b). This mechanism is highly relevant to comic acting, which is detached in nature, and probably underlies the lack of pity that characterizes comic laughter. It may also explain the role of laughter devices in satiric and grotesque drama.

(6) *Knowledge*: Some theories of comedy promote the view that comedy aims at contributing to the self-knowledge of the spectator. A distinction should be made, however, between the authors' knowledge of the human condition, which enables them to manipulate the spectators, and what they intend to impart to the audience in the form of self-knowledge. This study suggests that it is the aim of the comic experience not to improve self-knowledge, but merely to reaffirm the *philanthropon* and to produce catharsis — with both being experienced as pleasure — thus facilitating life within the context of severe inhibitions. In order to succeed, comedy must take the psyche of the spectator into account, as a crucial factor in the comedic experience.

(7) *Fictional thinking*: In generating comedic meaning, there exists a deeper level of cooperation between author and implied spectator: the faculty of the human imagination to spontaneously create and think through fictional worlds. As I have suggested elsewhere, this mode of thinking is of preverbal origin, and also characterizes dreams, daydreams and children's imaginative play (Rozik, 2008b: 269–85). *Fictional worlds, comedies in particular, would have been meaningless were it not for embodying this shared innate and culturally-conditioned thinking mechanism of the human psyche.*

Most of the theoretical tradition about comedy and the comedic practice (playwrighting and directing) indicates a knowledge of psychical mechanisms that is more technological than scientific. Such knowledge relates to the manner through which a certain comedy can produce a certain effect without a full understanding of the psychical mechanisms that predispose such a response. For example, it is taken for granted that comedy produces comic laughter, but its psychological mechanism and its function in the economy of the psyche are not that clear. Even holistic catharsis, which under certain conditions activates a pre-existing psychical mechanism, is not fully understood. It follows that in order to trigger a specific response in the implied spectator it is not necessary to be equipped with a proven scientific theory, but to operate on the grounds of practical experience, in particular, the knowledge of previous successful attempts. In principle, there is nothing wrong with such a technology, and practical intuitions are often verified by scientific means *a posteriori*; e.g., catharsis (Kreitler). Nonetheless, there is every reason for exploring deeper explanations of the implied spectator's involvement in experiencing a fictional world. The psychoanalytic school, Freud in particular, has contributed some fundamental intuitions in this respect; e.g., the crucial role of the lifting of inhibitions, and the anxieties elicited by this, in producing laughter.

The perception of suffering

It is widely accepted that tragedy is a fictional narrative of suffering (cf. Bradley: 70). It is less acknowledged that also comedy, and even farce often feature suffering characters; e.g., Molière's *George Dandin*. Indeed, fictional *suffering can be a powerful factor in the implied spectator's involvement*, depending on several factors: (a) the ethical or aesthetic nature of a character, (b) its role in the action; and (c) the locus of the suffering at either the entanglement or the dénouement.

(a) Whereas the suffering of a negative or ludicrous blocking character is perceived as harmonious, the suffering of a positive blocked character is perceived as disharmonious. (b) Whereas the suffering of a positive character contrasts the implied spectator's archetypal models of and expectations for harmony, i.e., such a contrast is absurd; the suffering of a negative character is harmonious with and gratifies the spectator's expectations. The notion of 'harmony' also applies to a character that is afflicted by a serious or a comic *hamartia*, while its flaws are balanced by failure, similarly to monolithic characters; e.g., the parallel frustrations of both brothers for their opposing excesses in Terence's *The Brothers*. These balancing structures also apply to other kinds of complex characters in both serious and comedic fictional worlds. And (c) Whereas at the entanglement the suffering of a positive character and the happiness of a negative character are disharmonious and expected to change, the final reversal gratifies the archetypal expectations and is perceived as a final accord of harmony. Conversely, whereas at the entanglement the suffering of a negative character or the happiness of a positive character is harmonious and expected to persist, the final reversal frustrates the implied spectator's archetypal expectations; i.e., the ending is absurd.

Such denouements are also perceived as conclusive value statements on these ethical or aesthetic characterizations; i.e., as concluding metaphors of harmony or disharmony (absurdity).

Holistic experience

The implied spectator is expected to "experience" a fictional world through framing, reading, interpretation, associative complementation and psychical identification or detachment; and to perceive the entire narrative complex as a rhetoric macro-speech act. Indeed, a description of a fictional world is an authorial act that embeds a macro-metaphor and indicates a macro-intention (e.g., reaffirmation of held values) and, at least, one macro-purpose (e.g., pleasure through catharsis) — with the author being the performer and the implied spectator its object. While authors of comedies express themselves through metaphoric fictional worlds, which are thus self-referential, *in the process of experiencing them, on the author/spectator axis, the implied spectator is expected to take over the function of referent* (see CHAPTER 4 and Rozik, 2009: 122–3).

The description of a whole fictional world thus aims at evoking an overall macro-image of such a metaphoric world in the "mind" of the implied spectator and "affecting" it in a specific cognitive and emotional manner. This explains the tendency to see in the concluding scenes of a comedy a potentially true metaphoric statement on the spectator's own actual or possible psychical state of affairs. The rhetoric structure of a fictional world aims at an experience of truth, which is achieved by bringing the implied spectator's own beliefs and presuppositions to a pre-designed conclusion in what only appears to be a logical process. The conclusion is that *watching a comedy is a holistic experience.*

Dialogue of author and spectator

The 'implied author' too is a theoretical construct that explains vital aspects in the process of generating fictional meaning. *Whereas the implied spectator is characterized by its expected complementation in order for a description of a fictional world to make sense, the implied author is characterized by its various choices embodied in such a description.* It is assumed, therefore, that *a pre-structured implied dialogue between an implied author and an implied spectator, and their mutual complementation, takes place.* This implied dialogue between these constructs is vital for the fictional meaning to emerge.

The implied spectator of a particular fictional world should be seen as reflecting a real director's intuition of a prospective real spectator. The actual effect of a performance-text thus hinges on the ability of a real director to capture the nature of the real spectator through the nature of the implied spectator, although a full correlation between them is probably seldom achieved. *Real spectators are actually partial implied spectators.* A real author might not possess the correct perception of prospective real spectators, and thus expect competences and mechanisms that they do not possess. Accordingly, while real spectators might feel that they have understood a fictional world, such a feeling may be groundless.

Not only are real spectators limited in their reading and interpretive capacities, but also in their abilities to understand and report their own reactions to fictional worlds, due to involving unconscious layers of their psyches. Their inability to explain their own experiences does not necessarily impinge on their reactions, but does make the results of empirical research based on their reports highly problematic. Similarly, real authors' explanations are usually of restricted value, due to their partial awareness of the reasons of their own decisions and theoretical handicaps. Indeed, their explanations are usually couched in current and short-lived theories of theatre and fictionality. In contrast, an analysis of the implied dialogue between an implied author and an implied spectator rests on firmer grounds by definition. Therefore, only this symbiotic process can explain the implied holistic experience.

The clear advantage in including both the implied director and the implied spectator in the analysis of a comedy, however, should not conceal the fact that the actual dialogue obtains between real author and real spectator. After all, it is the latter's experience that is the object of the description of a fictional world.

The textual fallacy

The generation of comedic fictional meaning depends absolutely on the implied spectator's mental complementation of the text. *The traditional assumption that all is in the text, i.e., that the contribution of the spectator may not be taken into account, is a methodological mistake that can be termed the 'textual fallacy';* e.g., E. R. Dodds claims that 'it is an essential critical principle that *what is not mentioned in the play does not exist*' (p. 180). *The general assumption that both the implied and real spectators are passive participants is ungrounded too.*

The contribution of the implied spectator to the generation of comedic meaning is vital, and, therefore, the fundamental distinction between real and implied spectator is of major importance: whereas the former might be limited in various respects, the latter is a theoretical construct that is fully qualified to complement the text by definition. The actual meaning of a comedic fictional world emerges from the implied dialogue between implied author and implied spectator.

Conclusions

There is a current reluctance to define 'comedy' (cf. Stott: 7). However, if the notion of 'comedy' is applied to all the genres that are currently considered under 'comedy', because of operating laughter-eliciting devices, such a resistance is even sensible. It should be borne in mind that, in general, a definition seldom explains anything, comedy in particular. It does no more than positioning a set of things/phenomena within the notional network of a culture, by stating a term on a higher level of abstraction and its specific difference in regard to other terms that are also categorized by the same abstract term. Therefore, if 'definition' is understood in this sense, the definition of 'comedy', in the narrow sense of this study, is viable and quite simple. In any medium, comedy is a kind of fictional world (abstract term), whose specific differences are: archetypal fictional structure, lowly mode, predominant comic mood and optional comic laughter (cf. Pavis' definition in CHAPTER 7). For the differentiation of comedy from other fictional genres these features indeed suffice. Nonetheless, even a sound definition of comedy should not prevent additional efforts to understand the nature of this genre.

Whereas every choice that a person makes in real life eliminates other possible courses of events, a fictional world is capable of exploring such potentialities. This is particularly conspicuous in regard to the experience of embodied suppressed drives and lifted inhibitions in comedy. The basic question that underlies comedy is: what happens if inhibitions on foolish and/or clumsy behavior are abolished? In this sense, a comic character is the inverse replica of the spectator: it embodies exactly what the latter does not allow himself to be or do. Therefore, the realization of inhibited drives in characters constitutes an opportunity for the spectator to experience the possible consequences of disregarding inhibitions. It is in this sense that for the spectator the comedic experience is a kind of thought experiment, and theatre or cinema a kind of thinking laboratory. This principle equally applies to all other genres, according to their own natures.

Furthermore, the metaphoric nature of the fictional experience switches the spectators' minds into the (suppressed) imagistic/

Conclusions

metaphoric/symbolic pre-verbal mode of thinking, which offers them the opportunity to face even shameful and suppressed contents of their psyches under the safe conditions of a communal experience; i.e., of social approval (Rozik, 2009).

A fictional world, a comedy in particular, thus constitutes the arena of confrontation between the spectators and their own psyches. The amorphous psyche of the spectator and the form-imposing nature of the fictional world are two sides of the same coin: being and description.

Cited Theoretical Works

Aristotle (1951) *The Poetics.* In S. H. Butcher (ed. and trans.), *Aristotle's Theory of Poetry and Fine Arts.* New York: Dover.

Aristotle (1987) *The Poetics.* In S. Halliwell (trans.), *The Poetics of Aristotle.* Chapel Hill: The University of North Carolina Press.

—— (1977) *Politics.* Trans. H. Rackham. Cambridge, Mass.: Harvard University Press & London: Heinemann.

—— (1982) *The Nicomachean Ethics.* Trans. H. Rackham. Cambridge, Mass.: Harvard University Press.

—— (1991) *The Art of Rhetoric.* Trans. H. C. Lawson-Tancred. London: Penguin Books.

Auslander, Philip (2008) *Liveness.* New York: Routledge.

Austin, J. L. (1980). *How to Do Things with Words.* London: Oxford University Press.

Bakhtin, Mikhail (1984) *Rabelais and his World.* Trans. H. Iswolsky. Bloomington: Indiana University Press.

Bentley, Eric (1967) *The Life of the Drama.* New York: Atheneum.

Bergson, Henri (1956) *Laughter.* In Wylie Sypher (ed.), *Comedy.* Garden City, New York: Doubleday; 61–190.

Bradley, A. C. (1965) 'Hegel's Theory of Tragedy'. In *Oxford Lectures on Poetry.* London: Macmillan; 69–95.

Brecht, Bertolt (1987) 'A Short Organum for the Theatre'. In J. Willett (ed. & trans.), *Brecht on Theatre.* New York: Hill and Wang & London: Methuen; 179–205.

Butcher, S. H. (ed. and trans.) (1951) *Aristotle's Theory of Poetry and Fine Art.* New York: Dover.

Camus, Albert (1942) *Le Mythe de Sisyphe.* Paris : Gallimard.

Castelvetro, Lodovico (1965) *Poetics.* In B. H. Clark (ed.), *European Theories of the Drama.* New York: Crown; 48–51.

Clark, Barrett H. (1965) *European Theories of the Drama.* New York: Crown.

Cooper, Lane (1924) *The Aristotelian Theory of Comedy.* Oxford: Blackwell.

Corneille, Pierre (1964) 'Les Trois Discours sur le Poème Dramatique'. In R. Mantero (ed.), *Corneille Critique.* Paris: Buchet/Chastel; 167–260.

Cornford, Francis M. (1914) *The Origin of Attic Comedy.* London: Edward Arnold.

Corrigan, Robert W. (1965) *Comedy: Meaning and Form*. Scranton, Penn.: Chandler.

—— (1965) 'Aristophanic Comedy: The Conscience of a Conservative'. In Corrigan; 353–62.

Damasio, Antonio R. (1994) *Descartes' Error*. New York: Grosset/Putnam.

Davidson, Israel (1907) *Parody in Jewish Literature*. New York: Columbia University Press.

Dijk, Teun A. van (1977) *Text and Context*. London & New York: Longman.

Dodds, E. R. (1988) 'On Misunderstanding the *Oedipus Rex*'. In Erich Segal (ed.), *Oxford Readings in Greek Tragedy*. Oxford University Press; 177–188.

Duchartre, Pierre L. (1966) *The Italian Comedy*. Trans. R. T. Weaver. New York: Dover.

Dryden, John (1965) 'An Essay of Dramatick Poesie'. In B. H. Clark (ed.) *European Theories of the Drama*. New York: Crown; 130–147.

Eco, Umberto (1984) 'The Frames of Comic Freedom'. In U. Eco, V.V. Ivanov and M. Rector (eds.), *Carnival*. Berlin, New York, Amsterdam: Mouton; 1–9.

Elliot, R. C. (1965) 'The Satirist and Society'. In Corrigan; 327–42.

Esslin, Martin (1961) *The Theatre of the Absurd*. Garden City, New York: Doubleday.

Franz, M. L. von (1969) 'The Process of Individuation'. In Carl G. Jung, *Man and his Symbols*. Garden City, New York: Doubleday; 158–269.

Freud, Sigmund (1989) *Jokes and their Relation to the Unconscious*. Trans. J. Strachey. New York & London: Norton.

—— (1990) 'Creative Writers and Day-dreaming'. Trans. J. Strachey. In *Art and Literature*. London: Penguin; 129–41.

Frye, Northrop (1957) *Anatomy of Criticism*. Princeton, New Jersey: Princeton University Press.

Goffman, Erving (1975) *Frame Analysis*. Harmondsworth, Middlesex: Penguin.

Greimas, Algirdas J. (1983) *Structural Semantics: An Attempt at a Method*. Lincoln: University of Nebraska Press.

Grotjahn, Martin (1965) 'Beyond Laughter'. In Corrigan: 270–5.

Hazlitt, William (1901) *Lectures on the English Comic Writers*. Garden City, N.Y.: Doubleday.

Hegel, G. W. F. (1975) *Aesthetics*. Trans. T. M. Knox. Oxford: Clarendon Press.

Holinshed (1973). In Kenneth Muir (ed.) (1973) Shakespeare, *Macbeth*. The Arden Shakespeare; 164–181.

Horace (1972) *On the Art of Poetry*. Trans. T. S. Dorsh. Harmondsworth, Middlesex: Penguin.

Iser, Wolfgang (1991) *The Act of Reading — A Theory of Aesthetic Response*. The Johns Hopkins University Press. Baltimore and London.

Janko, Richard (1984) *Aristotle on Comedy — Towards a Reconstruction of Poetics II*. London: Duckworth.

Jekels, Ludwig (1965) 'On the Psychology of Comedy'. In Corrigan; 263–9.

Jung, Carl G. (1969) *Man and his Symbols*. Garden City, New York: Doubleday.

Kaynar, Gad (1997) 'The Actor as Performer of the Implied Spectator's Role'. *Theatre Research International*, 22, 1; 49–62.

Kayser, Wolfgang (1966) *The Grotesque in Art and Literature*. Trans. U. Weisstein. New York, Toronto: Indiana University Press & McGraw-Hill.

Knox, Bernard (1966) *Oedipus at Thebes — Sophocles' Tragic Hero and his Time*. New Haven and London: Yale University Press.

——— (1979) 'European Comedy'. In *Word and Action: Essays on the Ancient Theatre*. Baltimore: John Hopkins University Press; 250–74.

Kosslyn, Stephen M. (1995) *Image and Brain*. Cambridge, Mass.: MIT Press.

——— (1996) 'Introduction'. In M. S. Gazzaniga (ed.), *The Cognitive Neurosciences*. Cambridge, Mass.: MIT Press; 959–961.

Kreitler, Shulamit and Kreitler Hans (1972) *Psychology of the Arts*. Durham, N.C.: Duke University Press.

Krook, Dorothea (1969) *Elements of Tragedy*. New Haven & London: Yale University Press.

Langer, Susanne K. (1976) *Philosophy in a New Key*. Cambridge, Mass.: Harvard University Press.

——— (1967) *Feeling and Form*. London: Routledge & Kegan Paul.

Lanson, Gustave (1965) 'Molière and Farce'. In Corrigan; 378–96.

Lea, K. M. (1962) *Italian Popular Comedy*. New York: Russell & Russell.

Lehmann, Benjamin (1965) 'Comedy and Laughter'. In Corrigan; 163–78.

Lope de Vega Carpio (1965) 'The New Art of Writing Plays in this Age'. In Barrett H. Clark (ed.), *European Theories of the Drama*. New York: Crown; 63–67.

Marinis, Marco de (1993) *The Semiotics of Performance*. Trans. Á. O'Healy. Bloomington and Indianapolis. Indiana University Press.

Molière (1965) 'Preface to *Tartuffe*'. In Corrigan; 443–7.

Murray, Gilbert (1927) 'Excursus on the Ritual Forms Preserved in Greek Tragedy'. In J. E. Harrison, *Themis — A Study of the Social Origins of Greek Religion*. Cambridge University Press; 341–63.

Nelson, T. G. A. (1990) *Comedy; An Introduction to Comedy in Literature, Drama and Cinema*. Oxford University Press.

Nicoll, Allardyce (1965) *The Development of the Theatre*. London: Harrap.

Olson, Elder (1968) *The Theory of Comedy*. Bloomington and London: Indiana University Press.

Pavis, Patrice (1996). *Dictionary of the Theatre — Terms, Concepts and Analysis*. Trans. Ch. Shantz. University of Toronto Press.

Peirce, Charles S. (1965–6) *Collected Papers*. In Ch. Hartshorne and P. Weiss (eds.). Cambridge, Mass.: Harvard University Press.

Pickard-Cambridge, Arthur W. (1927) *Dithyramb, Tragedy and Comedy*. Oxford: Clarendon Press.

Potts, L. J. (1965) 'The Subject Matter of Comedy'. In Corrigan; 198–213.

Propp, Vladimir I. (1968) *Morphology of the Folktale*. Trans. L. Scott. University of Texas Press.

Rozik, Eli (2001) 'The Chorus: Matrix of Theatrical Conventions'. *Maske und Kothurn*, Year 45, 3–4; 119–136.

—— (2002) *The Roots of Theatre — Rethinking Ritual and other Theories of Origin*. Iowa City: University of Iowa Press.

—— (2005a) 'Back to "Cinema is Filmed Theatre"'. *Semiotica*, 157, 1–4.

—— (2005b) 'Defamiliarization in Theatre: A Rhetoric Device'. *Assaph — Studies in the Theatre*, C, 19–20; 69–82.

—— (2007) 'Medium Translations between Fictional Arts'. In J. Arvidson, M. Askander, J. Bruhn & H. Führer (eds.), *Changing Borders — Contemporary Positions in Intermediality*. Lund: Intermedia Studies Press; 395–415.

—— (2008a) *Generating Theatre Meaning — A Theory and Methodology of Performance Analysis*. Brighton, Portland, Toronto: Sussex Academic Press.

—— (2008b) *Metaphoric Thinking — A Study of Nonverbal Metaphor in the Arts and its Archaic Roots*. Tel Aviv: Tel Aviv University, The Faculty of the Arts.

—— (2009) *Fictional Thinking — Poetics and Rhetoric of Fictional Creativity in Theatre*. Brighton, Portland, Toronto: Sussex Academic Press.

Saussure, Ferdinand de (1972) *Cours de Linguistique Générale*. Paris: Payot.

Schopenhauer, Arthur (1987) *The World as Will and Idea*. Excerpted from J. Morreal (ed.), *The Philosophy of Laughter and Humor*. Albany: SUNY; 51–64.

Scott, Nathan A. Jr. (1965) 'The Bias of Comedy and the Narrow Escape into Faith'. In Corrigan; 81–115.

Segal, Erich (2001) *The Death of Comedy*. Cambridge, Mass. & London: Harvard University Press

Sedgewick, G. G. (1948) *Of Irony, Especially in Drama*. Toronto: University of Toronto Press.

Cited Theoretical Works

Shmerok, Chone (1979) *Biblical Plays in Yidish, 1750–1967.* Jerusalem, Israeli Academy of Science (Hebrew).

Souriau, Étienne (1950) *Les Deux Cent Mille Situations Dramatiques.* Paris: Flammarion.

Stott, Andrew (2005) *Comedy.* New York & London: Routledge.

Styan, J. L. (1967) *The Elements of Drama.* Cambridge University Press.

—— (1968) *The Dark Comedy.* Cambridge University Press.

Sypher, Wylie (1956) 'The Meanings of Comedy'. In *Comedy.* Garden City, N.Y.: Doubleday; 193–255.

Urian, Dan (1990) The Miser *in Theatre.* Hakibbutz Hameukhad (Hebrew).

Vega Carpio, Lope de, see Lope.

Vince, Ronald W. (1984) *Ancient and Medieval Theatre.* Westport, Connecticut and London: Greenwood Press.

Weitz, Eric (2009) *The Cambridge Introduction to Comedy.* Cambridge University Press.

Welsford, Enid (1968) *The Fool.* London: Faber & Faber.

Wickham, Glynne (1974) *The Medieval Theatre.* London: Weidenfeld and Nicholson.

Willett, J. (ed. and trans.) (1987) *Brecht on Theatre.* London, Methuen.

Willeford, William (1977) *The Fool and His Sceptre.* London: Arnold.

Wilshire, Bruce (1982) *Role Playing and Identity — The Limits of Theatre as Metaphor.* Bloomington: Indiana University Press.

Analyzed and Cited
Play-Scripts

Aeschylus (1972) *The Libation Bearers*. Trans. R. Lattimore. In D. Grene and R. Lattimore (eds.), *Greek Tragedies*, Vol. 2. The University of Chicago Press.

—— (1968) *The Eumenides*. Trans. R. Lattimore. In D. Grene and R. Lattimore (eds.), *Greek Tragedies*, Vol. 3. The University of Chicago Press.

—— *The Oresteia*: see Aeschylus, *Agamemnon*, *The Libations Bearers* and *The Eumenides*.

Alarcón y Mendoza, Juan Ruiz de (first published 1634), *La Verdad Sospechosa*.

Anonymus (1962) *Everyman*. In S. Barnet, M. Berman & W. Burto (eds.), *The Genius of the Early English Theatre*. New York and Toronto: Mentor.

Anonymus (2006) *Maître Pierre Pathelin*. http://duke.edu/~pstewart/pathelin.htm

Aristophanes (1974) *The Frogs*. Trans. D. Barrett. In *The Wasps, etc.* London: Penguin.

—— (2001) *Plutus*. Trans. A. H. Sommerstein. Warminster, Wiltshire: Aris & Phillips.

—— (1982) *Clouds*. Trans. A. H. Sommerstein. Warminster, Wiltshire: Aris & Phillips.

—— (1983) *Wasps*. Trans. A. H. Sommerstein. Warminster, Wiltshire: Aris & Phillips.

—— (1973) *Acharnians*. Trans. A. H. Sommerstein. Harmondsworth, Middlesex: Penguin.

—— (1973) *Lysistrata*. Trans. A. H. Sommerstein. Harmondsworth, Middlesex: Penguin.

Arrabal, Fernando (1976) *Guernica*. Trans. B. Wright. In *Plays*, Vol. 2. London: John Calder.

—— (1976) *Picnic in the Battlefield*. Trans. B. Wright. In *Plays*, Vol. 2. London: John Calder.

—— (1976) *The Car Cemetery.* Trans. B. Wright. In *Plays*, Vol. 1. London: John Calder.

Barca, Calderón de la, see Calderón.

Beckett, Samuel (1970) *Happy Days.* London: Faber and Faber.

—— (1970) *Waiting for Godot.* London: Faber.

Büchner, Georg (1991) *Woyzeck.* Trans. J. Mackendrick. London: Methuen.

Calderón de la Barca (1959) *El Alcalde de Zalamea.* Zaragoza: Ebro.

—— (1959) *Life is a Dream.* Trans. R. Campbell. In Eric Bentley (ed.), *The Classic Theatre, Six Spanish Plays*, Vol. III. New York: Doubleday. Spanish: *La Vida es Sueño.* In J. Martel & H. Alpern (eds.), *Diez Comedias del Siglo de Oro.* New York, Evanston and London: Harper & Row.

Castro, Guillen de (1968) *Las Mocedades del Cid.* In J. Martel & H. Alpern, *Diez Comedias del Siglo de Oro.* New York, Evanston and London: Harper & Row.

Congreve, William (1966) *The Way of the World.* London: Dent & New York: Dutton.

Corneille, Pierre (n.d.) *Le Cid.* In Maurice Rat (ed.), *Théâtre Complet de Corneille*, Vol. I. Paris: Garnier Frères.

—— (n.d.) *Oedipe.* In Maurice Rat (ed.), *Théâtre Complet de Corneille*, Vol. III. Paris: Garnier Frères.

—— (n.d.) *Le Manteur.* In Maurice Rat (ed.), *Théâtre Complet de Corneille*, Vol. II. Paris: Garnier Frères.

Dürrenmatt, Friedrich (1981) *The Visit.* Trans. P. Bowles. New York: Grove.

Euripides (1968) *Hippolytus.* Trans. D. Grene. In D. Grene and R. Lattimore (eds.), *Greek Tragedies*, Vol. 1. The University of Chicago Press.

—— (1968) *The Bacchae.* Trans. W. Arrowsmith. In D. Grene and R. Lattimore (eds.), *Greek Tragedies*, Vol. 3. The University of Chicago Press.

—— (1997) *Ion.* Trans. K. H. Lee. Warminster, Wiltshire: Aris & Phillips.

Everyman, see Anonymous.

Feydeau, Georges (2002) *A Flea in Her Ear* (*La Puce à l'Oreille*). London: Methuen.

Friel, Brian (1990) *Dancing at Lughnasa.* London, Boston: Faber & Faber.

García Lorca, Federico (1969) *Yerma.* Trans. J. Graham Lujan and R. L. O'Connel. In *Three Tragedies.* Harmondsworth, Middlesex: Penguin.

—— (1967) *Quimera.* En *Obras Completas.* Madrid: Aguilar.

Ghelderode, Michel de (1950) *Les Aveugles.* In *Théâtre.* [Paris]: Gallimard.

Gogol, Nikolai (1980) *The Government Inspector.* Trans. M. Ehre & F. Gottschalk. In *Gogol, Plays and Selected Writings.* Evanston: Northwestern University Press.

Goldoni, Carlo (1959) *The Servant of Two Masters*. Trans. E. J. Dent. Cambridge University Press.

Hazlewood, C. H. (1965) *Lady Audley's Secret*. In George Rowel (ed.), *Nineteenth Century Plays*. Oxford University Press.

Ionesco, Eugène (1970) *Exit the King*. Trans. D. Watson. In *Plays*, Vol. 5. London: Calder & Boyars.

—— (1958) *L'Avenir est dans les Œufs*. In *Théâtre*, Vol. II. Paris: Gallimard.

—— (1959) *Rhinoceros*. Trans. D. Watson. In *Plays*, Vol. 4. London: Calder and Boyars.

Jarry, Alfred (1962) *Ubu Roi*. Librairie Générale Française (Livre de Poche).

Jerrold, Douglas (1965) *Black-Ey'd Susan*. In George Rowel (ed.), *Nineteenth Century Plays*. Oxford University Press.

Lea, K. M. (1962) *The Three Cuckolds*. In *Italian Popular Comedy* (Appendix G). New York : Russell & Russell; 582–4.

Lorca, see García Lorca.

Maître Pierre Pathelin, see Anonymous.

Menander (1987) *Old Cantankerous*. Trans. N. Miller. In *Plays and Fragments*. London: Penguin.

—— (1987) *The Arbitration*. Trans. N. Miller. In *Plays and Fragments*. London: Penguin.

Molière (c. 2001) *Don Juan*. Trans. R. Wilbur. San Diego: Harcourt. French: (n.d.) *Don Juam*. Paris: Classiques Larousse. French: Dom Juan. In *Œuvres Complètes*, Vol. II. Paris: Garnier-Flammarion.

—— (1965) *George Dandin*. In *Œuvres Complètes*, Vol. III. Paris: Garnier-Flammarion.

—— (1965) *L'École des Femmes* (*The School for Wives*). In *Œuvres Complètes*, Vol. II. Paris: Garnier-Flammarion.

—— (1965) *Les Fourberies de Scapin* (*The Trickeries of Scapin*). In *Œuvres Complètes*, Vol. IV. Paris: Garnier-Flammarion.

—— (1962) *The Miser*. Trans. J. Wood. In *The Miser* and Other Plays. Harmondsworth, Middlesex: Penguin. French: *L'Avare*. In *Œuvres Complètes*, Vol. III. Paris: Garnier-Flammarion.

—— (1957) *Tartuffe*. Trans. M. Bishop. In *Eight Plays by Molière*. New York: The Modern Library. French: *Le Tartuffe*. In *Œuvres Complètes*, Vol. II. Paris: Garnier-Flammarion.

—— (1965) *L'Amour Médecin*. In *Œuvres Complètes*, Vol. II. Paris: Garnier-Flammarion.

—— (1965) *Amphitryon*. In *Œuvres Complètes*, Vol. III. Paris: Garnier-Flammarion.

—— (1965) *Le Malade Imaginaire*. In *Œuvres Complètes*, Vol. IV. Paris: Garnier-Flammarion.

Pinter, Harold (1976) *A Slight Ache*. In *Plays*, Vol. I. London: Methuen.

—— (1976) *The Birthday Party*. In *Plays*, Vol. I. London: Methuen.

Pirandello, Luigi (1985) *Six Characters in Search of an Author*. Trans. J. Linstrum. London: Methuen.

Plautus (1972) *The Brothers Menaechmus*. Trans. E. F. Watling. In *The Pot of Gold and Other Plays*. Harmondsworth, Middlesex: Penguin.

—— (1972) *The Pot*. Trans. E. F. Watling. In *The Pot of Gold and Other Plays*. Harmondsworth, Middlesex: Penguin.

—— (1972) *The Swaggering Soldier*. Trans. E. F. Watling. In *The Pot of Gold and Other Plays*. Harmondsworth, Middlesex: Penguin.

—— (2001) *Amphitryon*.Trans. W. de Melo. In *Plautus*, Vol. I. Harvard University Press, Loeb Classical Library.

Racine, Jean (1961) Phèdre (*Phaedra*). Trans. R. Lowell. In E. Bentley (ed.), *The Classic Theatre*, Vol. IV. Garden City, New York: Doubleday. French: (n.d.) *Phèdre*. Paris: Classiques Larousse.

Sartre, Jean-Paul (1947) *Huis Clos [No Exit]*. Paris: Gallimard.

Scribe, Eugène (1995) *A Glass of Water*. Trans. Robert Cornthwaite. USA: Smith & Krauss.

Shakespeare, William (1982) *Hamlet*. Ed. H. Jenkins. London: Methuen.

—— (1985) *King Lear*. Ed. K. Muir. London: Methuen.

—— (1973) *Macbeth*. Ed. K. Muir. London: Methuen.

—— (1984) *Othello*. Ed. N. Sanders. Cambridge University Press.

—— (1980) *Romeo and Juliet*. Ed. B. Gibbons. London: Methuen.

—— (1975) *Twelfth Night*. Eds. J. M. Lothian & T. W. Craik. London: Methuen.

—— 1984) *A Midsummer Night's Dream*. Cambridge University Press.

Shaw, George Bernard (1963) *Pygmalion*. Harmondsworth, Middlesex: Penguin.

Sophocles (1968) *Oedipus the King*. Trans. D. Grene. In D. Grene and R. Lattimore (eds.), *Greek Tragedies*, Vol. 1. The University of Chicago Press.

—— (1968) *Antigone*. Trans. W. Wyckoff. In D. Grene and R. Lattimore (eds.), *Greek Tragedies*, Vol. 1. The University of Chicago Press.

—— (1968) *Philoctetes*. Trans. D. Grene. In D. Grene and R. Lattimore (eds.), *Greek Tragedies*, Vol. 3. The University of Chicago Press.

Strindberg, August (1960) *Miss Julia*. Trans. P. Watts. Harmondsworth, Middlesex: Penguin.

Synge, John M. (1960) *The Playboy of the Western World*. New York: Vintage Books.

Terence (1976) *The Brothers*. Trans. B. Radice. In *The Comedies*. Harmondsworth, Middlesex: Penguin.

Vega Carpio, Lope de; see Lope de Vega Carpio.

Weiss, Peter (1991) *Marat/Sade*. English version: G. Skelton. London, New York: Marion Boyars.

Wilde, Oscar (1962) *The Importance of Being Earnest*. In *The Genius of the Later English Theater*. New York and Toronto: Mentor.

Analyzed and Cited Works of Art

Amram, David & Papp, Joseph (1986) *Twelfth Night* (opera). New York: Summer Musical Theater.

Ashby, Hal (1979) *Being there* (film). US. Based on Jerzy Kosinski's novel *Being There*.

Benigni, Roberto (1997) *Life is Beautiful* (film). Italy.

Brook, Peter (1966) *Marat/Sade* (film). England. Based on Peter Weiss play.

Brooks, Mel (1974) *Blazing Saddles* (film). US.

Chaplin, Charlie (1936) *Modern Times* (film). US.

Deverell, Walter Howel (c. 1850) *Twelfth Night* (painting).

Deverell, Walter Howel (n.d.) *Twelfth Night* (reproductions).

Eifman, Boris (n.d.) *Twelfth Night* (ballet). Academy of Ballet, Saint Petersburg.

Fosse, Bob (1974) Lenny (film). US.

Grandage, Michael (2008) *Twelfth Night* (theatre) London: Wyndham Theatre.

Horejs, Vit (2009) *Twelfth Night* (Marionette). The Czech–American Marionette Theater, under the auspices of La Mama.

Lindsay-Hogg, Michael (2001) *Waiting for Godot* (TV). UK. Based on Samuel Beckett's play.

Nunn, Trevor (1996) *Twelfth Night* (film). England.

Marshall, Garry (1990) *Pretty Woman* (film). US.

Marshall, Garry (1999) *Runaway Bride* (film). US.

Muat, Maria (1992) *Twelfth Night* (animation). YouTube.

O'Connor, Pat (1998) *Dancing at Lughnasa* (film). Ireland, etc.. Based on Brian Friel's play.

Radio 3 (2006) *Twelfth Night* (audio cassette). BBC.

Robbins, Brian (2007) Norbit (film). US.

Saks, Gene (1969) *Cactus Flower* (film). US.

Welles, Orson (1941) *Citizen Kane* (film). US.

Zarate, Oscar (n.d.) *Twelfth Night* (strip-cartoon). Can of Worms.

Zinnemann, Fred (1952) *High Noon* (film). US.

Index

Note: Bold number indicates a definition or explanation of the term.

Index

Index

Index